MARY

Reflection of the Trinity and First-Fruits of Creation

Rosa Lombardi, MPF

Preface by Jean Galot

Translated by Matthew J. O'Connell

NEW CITY PRESS
Hyde Park, NY

Published in the United States by New City Press
202 Cardinal Rd., Hyde Park, NY 12538
www.newcitypress.com
©2008 Rosa Lombardi

Cover design by Leandro De Leon

Library of Congress Cataloging-in-Publication Data:

Lombardi, Rosa.
    Mary : reflection of the Trinity and first-fruits of creation / by Rosa
Lombardi ; translated by Matthew J. O'Connell.
       p. cm.
    Includes bibliographical references.
    ISBN 978-1-56548-292-0 (pbk. : alk. paper) 1. Mary, Blessed
Virgin, Saint. 2. Trinity. I. Title.
    BT603.L6613 2008
    232.91--dc22   2008018178

Printed in the United States of America

MARY

May the Virgin Maria
always accompany and
guide you in the walks
of your life.

With much Love
Sister Rosa Lombardi
M. P. F.

To the Virgin-Mother
who by her "Yes,"
so immersed in infinity,
embraced all of us and involved us
in God's ineffable mystery of salvation:
that she may always be better known,
loved, and praised ...
and every creature may experience
her vibrant and light-filled presence.

To the dear and revered
memory of my father,
a lover of life and beauty

Contents

Preface

Mary's beauty can be a source of authentic enthusiasm. In Rosa Lombardi's *Mary: Reflection of the Trinity and First-Fruits of Creation* the enthusiasm is not superficial but solidly based and rooted in mariological teaching, and it makes constant reference to Scripture, tradition, the documents of the magisterium, and the reflections of contemporary writers.

The work does not simply assert that Mary is an "enchanting creature, the most beautiful flower that ever bloomed in the garden of humanity, who sprang from God's creative mind, from the very heart of the Trinity." It also shows us how and why this masterpiece came into being through God's marvelous plan.

More specifically: Mary's relationships with God are explained in a trinitarian perspective as can be seen from the division of the chapters: Mary in the plan of God, in the mystery of the Trinity, in relation to the Father, in relation to the Son, and in relation to the Holy Spirit, followed by supplementary and concluding remarks. The author's concern to develop fully this trinitarian perspective makes clear her intention of giving Mary her true place in the work of salvation, a very important place that cannot be reduced to a marginal or completely secondary role. Given this intention, we can properly evaluate the statement: "Mary is not the center, but she is central in Christianity."

The person of Mary is not the center and cannot be made the center of the doctrine on salvation. Christ always remains the center as the source of all the divine life given to the human race. But the Son of God entered the human world as child of Mary and can no longer be separated from his Mother, who has been recognized as being the Mother of God. In virtue of this motherhood Mary belongs to the center that is her Son.

More particularly, this place at the center is seen in Mary's cooperation in redemption, a cooperation that has drawn a great deal of attention to her on the part of theologians. The issue here is not simply the use of the title "co-redemptrix" but the fundamental problem of the nature and extent of Mary's contribution to the redemptive work of Christ. This contribution began with the divine motherhood itself, the education given to the Son by the Mother, and, more specifically with the preformation in Mary of basic attitudes of Jesus himself; these include service, docility to the Father's will, and receptivity to the Spirit. Then there was her cooperation in the mission of salvation, which climaxed in her self-sacrifice at the cross.

This journey of the Mother of the Savior never ceases to elicit our admiration.

We thank the author for bringing out the wonders of grace and trinitarian life that were revealed in Mary.

Jean Galot

Abbreviations

CCC	*Catechism of the Catholic Church.* Liguori, MO: Liguori Publications, 1984
CELAM	Latin-American Episcopal Conference
CMP	Corpus Marianum Patristicum, ed. S. Alvarez Campos. 8 vols.; Burgos: Adelcoa, 1970–85
CSCO	Corpus Scriptorum Christianorum Orientalium
CSEL	Corpus Scriptorum Ecclesiasticorum Latinorum
DB	Dictionnaire de la Bible
DEC	*Decrees of the Ecumenical Councils.* Edited by Norman P. Tanner, S.J. 2 vols. Washington, D.C.: Georgetown University Press/London: Sheed & Ward, 1990
DME	*Documenta Magisterii Ecclesiastici*
DV	*Dei Verbum* (Vatican Council II)
GCS	Die Griechischen Schriftsteller der Ersten Drei Jahrhunderte
GS	*Gaudium et Spes* (Vatican Council II)
IM	*Incarnationis Mysterium*
LG	*Lumen Gentium* (Vatican Council II)
LM	*Lodi alla Madonna nel primo millennio delle Chiese d'Oriente e d'Occidente.* Edited by C. Berselli and G. Gharib. 3rd ed.; Rome: Ed. Paoline, 1981
MC	*Marialis Cultus* (Paul VI)
Mdig	*Mulieris Dignitatem* (John Paul II)
NDM	*Nuovo Dizionario di Mariologia.* Edited by S. De Fiores and S. Meo
OT	*Optatam totius* (Vatican Council II)
PG	Patrologia Graeca
PL	Patrologia Latina
PO	Patrologia Orientalis
RM	*Redemptoris Mater* (John Paul II)
SC	Sources chretiennes (Paris, 1942ff.)
TMPM	*Testi Mariani del Primo Millennio*
TMSM	*Testi Mariani del Secondo Millennio*
True Devotion	*Treatise on the True Devotion to the Blessed Virgin Mary*

Biblical Citations are from the *New American Bible*.

Translation of Vatican II documents is from *Vatican Council II: The Conciliar and Post-Conciliar Documents*, edited by Austin Flannery, O.P. Collegeville, MN: The Liturgical Press, 1975.

Introduction

Love moves me to speak of her who is beautiful
but the lofty language required is beyond me.
What shall I do? I shall openly cry out
that I have not been nor am fit to praise her,
but then I shall lovingly apply myself
to telling the mystery of her who is on high.
Love alone does not fall short in speaking of her,
because her nobility is lovable and enriches
those who heed her. With wonder I speak of Mary,
but I am fearful, because this daughter of earth
has ascended to the heights.[1]

Thus speaks James of Sarug, and I make his sentiments my own. Mary, the Mother of Jesus, is the "chaste container of the infinite Nature" (Theoto-Karion, 26, Ode 1), or she is that chariot of fire that carried the fire hidden and veiled beneath the ashes of her humanity (St. Catherine of Siena). She is the "door through which heaven will come down to earth" (Paul VI), "the marvel of marvels ... wholly with God" (St. John Damascene). In her the rays of the divinity are reflected, as through a crystal prism; her life is woven entirely of silence and wonder.

"Who can narrate her mystery? Who will have the courage to proclaim her greatness? Who will ever be able to set forth her splendor? Who will ever be able to find words for her extraordinary beauty? She has made human nature beautiful; she has risen above the angelic hosts.... She has far surpassed every other creature, because her purity has shone

---

1. James of Sarug, *Homily on Mary, the Blessed Virgin and Mother of God*, verses 85–92, in *TMPM* IV, 145.

more brightly than that of any creature, so that she received within herself the Creator of all the other creatures … and gave him his flesh" (Photius). "She carried him in her womb, she gave him birth, and, alone among creatures, became Mother of God." Therefore, "no one has ever been robed in splendid light as she has.… No one has ever shone with heavenly light as she has; no one has ever reached such a lofty height as hers.… No one else has drawn so close to God and been so enriched with God's gifts; no one else has ever shared so fully in God's grace.… She transcends all the things regarded as great by human beings; she transcends all the gifts which God in his goodness has abundantly bestowed and poured out on humanity. She is richer than all others because she possesses him who is All: she possesses God who dwells in her."[2]

The reflection of the Son's divine greatness descended into the Virgin Mother. "Everything called great is inferior to her; the Creator alone is greater than this heavenly creature,"[3] who came forth from the hands of God to enchant heaven and earth.

Athanasius of Alexandria cries out in astonishment: "To what in all of creation shall I compare you, O Virgin? Your glory surpasses everything created. Indeed, can anything compare with you in nobility, O Mother of God the Word?"[4]

"What can we envisage that is more divine or greater than you, O Mother of God? To draw near to you is like drawing near to holy ground; it is like drawing near to heaven."[5]

How can we define in time your mystery that is familiar with eternity? No one can reveal it entirely or ever worthily

2. Sophronius of Jerusalem, *Homily on the Annunciation* (PG 87), in *TMPM* II, 141 and 145.
3. St. Peter Damian, cited by Stefano Maria Manelli, *La devozione alla Madonna. Vita mariana alla scuola dei Santi* (Frigento [AV], 1975) 85.
4. Coptic homily on "The Virgin Mary, Mother of God and Dwelling of God," in *LM*, 29.
5. Severus of Antioch, *Homily* 67 (PO 8), in *TMPM* I, 648.

proclaim the perfection and glory that emanate from your being. "Whatever mortals can say of her can never do justice to the loftiness of her merits" (St. Peter Damian).

With good reason, then, Turoldo begins his hymns to Mary with these words:

How can we sing to you, O Mother,
without troubling your holiness,
without violating your silence?[6]

With this awareness I enter joyfully, but also with trembling, into the world of Mary, "this boundless ocean of gifts and merits,"[7] this divine world that contains incomprehensible treasures. It is a mystery so great, sublime, and holy, that it can never be wholly penetrated and enough can never be said of it. As a centuries-old devout antiphon says: *De Maria numquam satis* ("Enough can never be said of Mary").[8]

This last is very true: enough cannot be said or sung or written of the Mother of Jesus. We can indeed say that in the Virgin of Nazareth, a creature located between God and humanity, the threads of the divine and the human are intermingled and become blurred in an interplay of lights and shadows, of the intangible and the tangible, of the comprehensible and the incomprehensible. Together they paint a many-colored picture of unique variety and richness. "The divinity itself dwelt in her unveiled, and in her it put on the robe of our flesh" (St. Germanus of Constantinople).

The desire to know Mary is, then, a desire to plunge into the very heart of the mystery and to retrace the course of the hidden, gushing flood that broke into her life and turned her into an exceptional, indeed incomparable creature.

---

6. *Laudario all Vergine*, in *NDM*, ed. Stefano de Fiores and Salvatore Meo (Cinisello Balsamo [Milan]: Ed. Paoline, 1988) 1248.
7. Photius, in *TMPM* II, 825.
8. The phrase is St. Bernard's (*Sermon on the Nativity of Mary*, PL 185:437D). It expresses both faith and popular piety.

"She is the living icon of the Invisible, the reflection of the eternal Light, the image of infinite Goodness. In her the greatness and power of God shine forth" (from the Liturgy).

As an icon gives us a vision of things unseen, so the Virgin Mother presents herself to the eyes of believers as a pure and spotless space for God's presence, as a place for the Eternal in time, as a dwelling in which the Inaccessible One makes himself accessible to all by means of the human nature which he took from her. "Behind the shadows of her mortal flesh the omnipotent God has hidden the eternal wellsprings of life and of the true light that enlightens every human being."[9] In the unity of her person, on which the full life of the triune God placed its lasting seal, she points to the infinite mystery and at the same time reflects it.[10]

---

9. Guerric of Igny, *Sermon* 1 on the *Assumption of the Blessed Virgin Mary* (PL 185:189).

10. See Bruno Forte, *Maria, la donna icona del mistero* (Alba [Cuneo]: Ed. Paoline, 1989) 161 and 154.

Chapter One
Mary in the Plan of God

A. At the Heart of the Plan

You made us for yourself, O Lord, and our
heart is restless until it rests in you
(St. Augustine, *Confessions*)

If in the final analysis the human person is thought to be
made for God this is all the more true of her who was to
become the Mother of God.

The hymn of praise that opens St. Paul's letter to the
Ephesians proclaims the great "Thank You" of humanity to
God for having carried out the plan which he conceived
from eternity: the Incarnation of the Word for the salvation
and "divinization" of human beings. "Blessed be the God
and Father of our Lord Jesus, who has blessed us in Christ
with every spiritual blessing in the heavens, as he chose us in
him, before the foundation of the world, to be holy and without blemish before him" (Eph 1:3–4).

On the backdrop of this plan is written, like a watermark,
the history of humanity, of every human being who is called
to make God present and visible, as Mary did and does.

The salvation effected by the Word has for its fruit the
transformation of humanity from the state of anonymity in
which sin placed it to the state of "children" loved by
God. Using the language of the Bible, the New Testament
describes this change as a "blessing"; the word applies in a
special and indeed unique way to Mary, whom Elizabeth
greeted as "blessed among women" (see *RM* 8). "Thanks
to her the Father's blessing had radiated upon humanity"
(liturgy).

Forechosen as she was from all eternity to be "the Mother of him to whom the Father has entrusted the work of salvation" (*RM* 7), the Virgin of Nazareth became the prototype of divine election in the history of humanity at the moment when God burst into her life with his plan. She is the supreme embodiment of this magnificent enterprise in which God wills that "in love" we be "holy and without blemish before him." In her the people of God see the exemplar of the virginal "innocence" to which believers are called by an unmerited gift of the Lord.

The plan of salvation, which Paul would call "the mystery hidden from ages past in God" (Eph 3:9), was born in the heart of God. Its source is the love within the Trinity, and it unfolds in the work of creation, in the entire history of salvation after the "fall," and in the mission of the Son and that of the Spirit, which is continued in the mission of the Church. The plan is eternal and universal: it embraces all times, all things, and all human beings, but "it reserves a special place for the 'woman' " (*RM* 7), the one who was uniquely blessed by the Father "in Christ with every spiritual blessing in the heavens."

Paul describes the activation of the plan in the most important mariological text of the New Testament, a text in which the simplicity of the reference to the Mother of the Lord proves to conceal a truly substantial content. Here is the passage: "When the fullness of time had come, God sent his Son, born of a woman, born under the law, to ransom those under the law, so that we might receive adoption" (Gal 4:4–5).

This event, which embraces as a seed the Son's entire work of salvation and is completed by his return to the Father in the paschal mystery, is the central fact in the history of the world. Mary is the only human being directly associated with this event that occurred in the fullness of time. Due to the fact that our salvation is the work of Christ Jesus who was "born of a woman," this woman plays a decisively important part in the history of salvation because the inscrutable will of God so disposed it so. In Paul's phrase "born of a woman," the Mother of God is shown to be closely linked to the salvation of humanity and of all creation. She can be said to be "at the center of this salvific event" (*MD* 3).

A. Serra remarks that Galatians 4:4 contains the seed of a Marian teaching that would later be developed by the other New Testament writings. He goes on to say how priceless Paul's testimony is, for, restrained though it is, it asserts that the person of Mary plays an essential part in God's plan of salvation (see *NDM*, 233).

If the entire Old Testament gravitates around Christ as the center of salvation history and of its ultimate goal, this movement also embraces the Mother of Christ since she shares with him in the "fullness of time." She gave birth to this fullness, so that nothing else can claim to fill time, for the Eternal is already in time due to her (see *RM*1).

Together with Christ, Mary is both the key person in humanity's history and the omega point toward which history is moving.[1]

Christ is clearly the pivotal figure in God's plan: in him God speaks his definitive word and accomplishes his most astounding gesture: he hides himself within our human history. Yet without the Virgin Mother we would not have Christ, for it was she "who gave us the author of life" (collect for First Vespers of January 1, in the pre-Vatican breviary).

---

1. Mariano Magrassi, *Maria nel mistero della Chiesa* (Bologna, 1974), in *Liturgia*, no. 226.

B. God Thought
Mary from Eternity
(Mary: The Wonderful Dream of the Trinity)

As the goal or, better, as the "person" who was chosen to fulfill the eternal decree of God, Mary is present with Christ in the eternal divine counsel. She is "the fixed goal of the eternal counsel," as the divine poet Dante says (*Paradiso* XXXIII, 3).

St. John speaks of the Lamb slain from eternity (see Rev 5). In this same eternity we must locate Mary as well, since she was destined "from eternity" to be the Mother and dear collaborator of the Lamb. "In the mystery of Christ she is present even 'before the creation of the world,' as the one whom the Father 'has chosen' as Mother of his Son in the Incarnation. And, what is more, together with the Father, the Son has chosen her, entrusting her eternally to the Spirit of holiness" (*RM* 8).

This is her "origin" in the eternal thought of God, that is, in the eternal Word. This is also her origin on earth. Because of this origin she is absorbed in an ineffable way into the very eternity of God. That is, before she was created, before she came into being, she was the object of predilection on the part of the adorable Trinity.

Mary is the creature willed by God before any other creature: "She was not yet born, yet for millennia God had been planning her in his mind, along with all the privileges with which he intended to adorn her."[2] From all eternity the Son gazed on her with a special, unbounded delight. It can be said that "God looked upon her with love," as an artist does his masterpiece.[3]

---

2. St. Bernard in PL 183:84.
3. Msgr. Francesco Franzi in the collective work, *Maria Santissima e lo Spirito Santo* (Rome: Ed. Centro Volontari della Sofferenza, 1976) 120.

Only God's language can worthily put the ineffable mystery of Mary into words for us:

> From the mouth of the Most High I came forth,
>   and mistlike covered the earth....
> Before all ages, in the beginning, he created me,
> and through all ages I shall not cease to be.
>
> (Sir 24:3, 9)

> The Lord begot me, the first-born of his ways,
>   the forerunner of his prodigies of long ago;
> From of old I was poured forth,
>   at the first, before the earth.
> When there were no depths I was brought forth,
>   when there were no fountains or springs of
> water; before the mountains were settled into
> place, before the hills, I was brought forth....
> When he established the heavens I was there....
> When he fixed fast the foundations of the earth;
> When he set for the sea its limit ... ;
> Then I was beside him as his craftsman,
>   and I was his delight day by day,
> Playing before him all the while ...
>   and I found delight in the sons of men.
>
> (Prov 8:22–31)

These lovely passages of Scripture deal with divine Wisdom, which is poetically personified as the archetype of created things. The liturgy boldly applies this theme to Mary regarded as the point of departure of the great plan of salvation.

The goal here is to rebuild the lost paradise, and indeed Mary is the first member of this new world, for in her we see the first manifestation of "the wonders of God" which the Holy Spirit will accomplish in Christ and his Church.

Mary is thus seen as a thought firmly fixed in the mind of God. When he was about to create, when nothing existed as yet, she was there as the divine craftsman. "Although she was a creature of this world, she shared in the most radical and important self-manifestation of God in history" (Pikaza).

In God there is, of course, no before and after, no temporal succession as far as he is concerned; instead, everything is present to him from all eternity. "But if among his works some exceptional marvel was always to be radiantly before his eyes, some one element in the divine mind in which he took pleasure and delight, then after Christ, the incarnate Word, this was certainly Mary, Christ's Mother."[4]

Such is the thought that shines through in the following verses:

> In the eternal nursery
> of possible beings,
> you, Mary, were the most longed-for dream
> of the divine Creator;
> he willed you
> and you emerged,
> as the jewel of creation,
> out the deep abysses
> of his thought, as a unique work
> already perfect and complete.[5]

C. The Presence of Mary
in Sacred Scripture

The Fathers forcefully and persuasively claimed that the Scriptures form a single book (H. de Lubac). Therefore a theme, an isolated assertion, a verse do not disclose their full riches until they have been seen in the setting of all the sacred books. St. Bonaventure argued that the whole of Scripture can be likened to a lyre, of which no one string by itself creates a harmony but does so with the others: "The same thing is true of Scripture: one passage depends on

---

4. Andrea Agnoletti, *Maria Sacramento di Dio* (Rome: Ed. Pro Sanctitate, 1973) 12.

5. Sr. Renata Tariciotti, M.P.F., *Natività di Maria* (manuscript; Rome, June 18, 2000).

another; indeed, one passage is connected with countless others" (In *Hexaemeron* 19, 7).

The same rule applies to biblical Mariology, which is the true ally of Marian devotion. If we look simply at numbers, we must agree that the passages speaking of Mary are not many. But the quantitative "little" is compatible with a qualitative "much." God not only foresaw and willed Mary from eternity, but over the centuries he gave humanity an advance knowledge of her image and mission (even if this knowledge was figurative and veiled). The Father did this in the sacred Scriptures in which he set down the plan he had conceived for our salvation.

In fact, the scriptural sources, which are the "soul of all theology" (*OT* 16), especially as they are read and understood "in the light of further and full revelation" (*LG* 5), offer us a very extensive and many-sided picture of Mary. They are an indispensable path to be followed by those desirous of entering deeply into the ineffable mystery of the Virgin of Nazareth, for they enable us to know what God himself decided to make known, in concrete ways, about the Mother of Christ.

1. Symbols, Prophecies, Prefigurations in the Old Testament Time of Preparation

The symbolic Mariology of the Bible is full of analogies, types and antitypes, and evocative allusions to future realities. It can therefore be said that biblical testimony about Mary resembles an icon inasmuch as it is both narrative and symbolic.

The unique event that was Christ's coming and redemptive work was appropriately foretold and prepared for by means of countless symbols, figures, prophecies, and signs of every kind. The same must be said of Mary of Nazareth, in whom "scattered symbolisms are brought together in a bundle" (A. Serra).

The Old Testament, and everything in it about the religious history of humanity, prefigured the Virgin as well as Christ, for Mother and Son were so closely bound together that they had also to be closely linked in prophecies.

2. *Prefigured from the Beginning*

a) Symbols of Mary

The holy Fathers saw many Old Testament symbols as prefiguring the magnificent and exceptional triumph of the Virgin, her spotless innocence and remarkable holiness, her ineffable fullness of grace and virtue, and her lofty privileges.

Here we shall look at only some of these symbols and numinous details that, as history shows, had a major impact on the religious consciousness.

The first symbol of Mary is the *earthly paradise*, that place of pleasure in which human beings lived in perfect peace and harmony with God and in which the tree of life was planted, and wonderful flowers and fruits grew (see Gen 2:8–15).

The Virgin Mary would be the new earthly paradise, the "paradise of never-fading chastity" (Basil of Seleucia), in which the original innocence and holiness would be restored and the true "tree of life" (Gen 2:9) would appear and flower. This tree is Jesus, who would "provide everyone with the generous fruit of immortality" (Germanus of Constantinople) and "produce the fruits of salvation for all" (Basil of Seleucia).

In this new garden of delights "there are ... riches, beauties, rarities and inexplicable sweetnesses, which Jesus Christ, the New Adam, has left there; it was in this paradise that He took His complacence for nine months, worked His wonders and displayed His riches with the magnificence of a God."[6]

Some other Marian symbols:

The *Ark of Noah*, which alone was saved in the catastrophic universal flood and carried the human race to safety (Gen 6:13ff.). While the storm of original sin raged, Mary alone was preserved from it, and through her God brought salvation to the entire human race. The announcement made to Mary on the day of the Annunciation that she was favored (Lk 1:28) recalls the description of the flood: "Noah found favor with the Lord" (Gen 6:8). "This passage shows that the favor shown to Mary was given for the formation of a new universe that would be saved from the devastation caused by sin" (J. Galot).

The *dove from the ark*, which foretells the end of the flood by returning with an olive branch in its beak (Gen 8:10ff.), prefigures Mary who breaks the chains of sin and points to the end of divine punishment and the return of peace among human beings.

Jacob saw a *ladder* reaching to the heavens, with the angels of God going up and down on it (Gen 28:12). Mary was to be this ladder let down by the eternal God, by means of which he would bring mortals up to heaven.

There is also the *temple of Solomon* which God consecrated and in which he placed his name (1 Kings 9:3; 2 Chr 7:16ff.). Patristic and liturgical texts celebrate Mary as one who became in a preeminent way a temple consecrated to God, "a temple which God prepared in an ineffable way for his Son" (liturgical collect). She fulfilled all the prefigurations associated with the temple, in particular, *the closed gate facing eastward* (symbol of her virginity) and

---

6. Louis-Marie Grignion de Montfort, *Treatise on the True Devotion to the Blessed Virgin Mary*, trans. Frederick William Faber (rev. ed.; Bay Shore, N.Y.: Montfort Fathers, 1941), no. 261, p. 201.

the Holy of Holies, whose treasures were symbols of her holiness and her closeness to God. As Toniolo says in his notes on *The Akathistos Hymn*, just as the temple had its treasury, so Mary is the inexhaustible treasure house from which everyone draws life.

Mary is the new temple of the messianic age: a living, primordial temple, built not by hands (as the temple of Jerusalem was) but by God himself through his Spirit, who is its architect and builder. Henceforth God's dwelling on earth will no longer be built of stones but of faith in Christ, active charity, dedication, and hope.

The *bush on Horeb* that burned without being consumed (Ex 3:2ff.) represents the marvelous virginity of Mary. She, like a bush permeated by God, burned interiorly with the fire of the Holy Spirit through whose action she conceived, virginally, the Son of God. "As the bush burned on the mountain but was not consumed, so the Virgin gave birth to the light but suffered no corruption" (Gregory of Nyssa); "It was as a virgin that she gave birth, and a virgin she remained" (John Damascene).

Gideon's fleece that remained dry though everything around was soaked, and remained soaked when everything around was dry: this image calls to mind the Immaculate Conception and Mary's fullness of grace.

The *little cloud that forecast the coming of rain* after the great drought in the time of the prophet Elijah (1 Kgs 18:44–45): Mary, as the *dawn* of redemption that preceded the light of salvation, foretold by her appearance in the world the imminent "showering down" of Christ and the messianic blessings.

The *golden urn* that contained the manna (Ex 16:33): the Virgin was to be the *casket* of the Word, the living *table* that provides the bread from heaven which Christ was to bring: the true manna, the true bread from heaven (see Jn 6:3–51).

"If Paul could be called a *chosen vessel* (Acts 9:15) because he brought the revered name of Jesus Christ to every part of the world and preached it there, how much more would the Mother of God be such a vessel, for she did not contain manna after the fashion of the golden urn but instead contained in her womb the heavenly bread that is distributed to the faithful as food and source of strength!" (Basil of Seleucia).

The *ark of the covenant* was built of expensive and lasting materials and covered with gold both inside and out; in it God manifested himself to his people, and they received his commands there (see Ex 25:10–22).

The Fathers, theologians, and preachers of the Church have seen in this ark an image of the pure and incorruptible body of the Virgin Mother and a prefigurative sign of salvation that brings to mind Mary, more than anyone else, for she was adorned interiorly and exteriorly with the splendid gifts of the Holy Spirit. Everything about the ark bids one think of her, not only the special materials of which it was built but also its form, its characteristics, and the gifts placed within it. The Virgin was overshadowed by the Spirit in order that she might be the true ark of the covenant, the holy ark that is the true dwelling of the Most High, the ark of a new age, in whose bosom she carried God.

The ancient ark contained the tablets of the law, which was the basis of the first covenant; Mary, the new ark, was pregnant with the very heir of the covenant, the "living tablet" of the law of love, the one who establishes and sums up in his own person the covenant between God and his people. The former ark guarded the law, the new ark the legislator; the former contained the written word of God, the new contained the living Word of the Father, the Word incarnate, Jesus Christ, in whom the Father speaks to us and listens to us.

The *mountain of God*: a fertile mountain, a mountain of abundance, a luxurious and rich mountain, on which it pleased God to dwell (see Ps 68:16ff.).

Among the symbols of Mary that foretell her lofty dignity as Mother, *Jerusalem* calls for special mention. For the psalmist sings of this city as the preferred dwelling place of God and the mother of peoples and as the holy city of which glorious things are said (see Ps 87). Another is the *column of fire* that pointed out the paths to be taken by the people as they wandered about in the wilderness (Ex 13:21).

But Marian symbolism reaches its most elevated form in the celebration of the Virgin Mother as *wisdom*. She is the dwelling of incarnate wisdom, "the most pure womb in which Wisdom built for itself a dwelling that would receive into time the creator and Lord of the ages" (Preface for Marian feasts). To her therefore the liturgy applies the most beautiful texts on wisdom, placing on her lips such sublime passages as these:

> I am the mother of pure love, of fear, of
>   knowledge and holy hope.
> In me are all the graces of the way and the
>   truth, in me all hope of life and virtue.
> I bud forth delights like the vine,
>   my blossoms become fruit fair and rich.
> Come to me, all you that yearn for me,
>   and be filled with my fruits;
> You will remember me as sweeter than honey,
>   better to have than the honeycomb.
> He who eats of me will hunger still,
>   he who drinks of me will thirst for more.
> He who obeys me will not be put to shame,
>   he who serves me will never fail.
>   (Sir 24:17–21)

The memory of my name will endure through all ages.

b) Prefigurations of Mary

It pleased God, during the time of the earlier covenant, to describe in broad outline the marvelous elements of Mary's personality, prefiguring them now in one individual, now in another. He thus gave a glimpse of them to a world whose hope and glory the Virgin would later become.

Among these prefigurations the most important and obvious was *Eve*, the first woman. Since her childbearing produced only death, the first Eve could not become what her name meant: "mother of all the living" (Gen 3:20). In contrast, Mary completely fulfilled the mystery she embodied (see *LG* 56): she would be the true mother of all the living.

In addition to Eve, all the famous women of the Old Testament who kept alive the hope of Israel, as well as some poetic personifications of women, prefigured in some way the Virgin of Nazareth. She is the most splendid of them all.

Like *Queen Esther*, Mary would not hesitate to risk death in order to save her people (see Esth 5).

Like *Sarah*, Abraham's wife, Mary would be blessed by God and made fertile beyond belief.

Mary would be pure and kind like *Rebekah*, beautiful and favored like *Rachel*.

She would be a *prophetess* and sing of God's wonders, as *Miriam*, Moses' sister, did (Ex 15:20–21) and, even more, as *Hannah*, mother of Samuel, did (1 Sam 2:1–10; see the Magnificat).

She would be strong and courageous as *Judith* was. Therefore, with much greater right than the heroine of Israel, all peoples would sing of Mary: "Blessed are you ... above all the women on earth....Your deed of hope will never be forgotten by those who tell of the might of God....You are the glory of Jerusalem, the surpassing joy of Israel; you are the splendid boast of our people" (Jud 13:18–19; 15:9).

Among the feminine poetic personifications that speak of
Mary allegorically and in lyrical language, one especially is
inspired and has mystical dimensions, namely, the *spouse in
the Song of Songs*. The description of an unblemished relationship that is wholly permeated by love, freedom, and a
mutual delight in the harmony of the surrounding natural
world symbolizes Mary's ineffable spousal union with God.
No one has a greater right than Mary to speak thus to God,
the beloved of her heart:

> Let my beloved come to his garden
> and eat its choice fruits....
> For stern as death is love.
>
> (Song 4:16B; 8:6)

In turn, the Lord, the Spouse of the soul that thirsts for
him, can say more appropriately to Mary than to anyone
else:

> O my dove in the clefts of the rock ... ,
> Let me see you
>   and hear your voice,
> For your voice is sweet,
>   and you are lovely....
> How much more delightful is your love than
>   wine, and the fragrance of your ointments
>   than all spices! ...
> Ah, you are beautiful, my beloved,
>   ah, you are beautiful ...!
>   and there is no blemish in you....
> You have ravished my heart ...
>   with one glance of your eyes.
>
> (Song 2:14; 4:10; 1:15; 4:7, 9)

Mary was prefigured not only by courageous devout
women but also, from several points of view, by *Abraham*,
of whom she is the most perfect fulfillment.

Abraham through his faith and obedience became the
father of all believers (see Rom 4) and bearer of divine bless-

ings to all of humanity (see Gen 13:3b). So, too, Mary, having become Mother of the Messiah and Lord by her faith and obedience, would henceforth be at the service of God and of his plan for the whole human race; she would also be the bringer of God's definitive blessing, given in Christ for all human beings. We may say that just as Israel, the former people of God, had its origin in Abraham's act of faith, so the new Israel (the Church of Christ) had its beginning with her who "having entered deeply into the history of salvation ... unites in her person and re-echoes the most important doctrines of the faith" (*LG* 65).

If, with the Apostle, we can say that Abraham "believed, hoping against hope" (Rom 4:18), all the more can we say the same of Mary. For her faith was severely tested, a testing that reached its climax on Calvary, where we see her prostrated by suffering under the cross of her Son.

Moreover, if Isaac prefigures the sacrificed Christ, then Abraham who leads his son to sacrifice (Gen 22:3–10) prefigures God the Father in heaven and Mary, the Mother, on earth.

c) Prophecies of Mary

The Old Testament contains not only symbols and prefigurations but also true prophecies about Mary that are part of the divine plan of salvation as it looks to the future.

The first prophecy is the one in the *Protevangelium* (first proclamation of salvation). It has to do with the *Woman*, the irreconcilable enemy of the serpent, who is closely united with her Son in his victorious struggle against the forces of evil, here symbolized by the snares of the serpent (see Gen 3:15). This poetic portrayal hides within it the first prophecy about Mary immaculate, Mother of the redeemer.

Especially important, too, is the great messianic promise given by the prophet Isaiah: "The virgin shall be with child, and bear a son, and shall name him Immanuel" ("God with us"; Isa 7:14). Mark the evangelist will see in the virginal childbearing of Mary an accurate fulfillment of this prophecy (see Mk 1:22–23).

We may also call to mind the well-known prediction of the prophet Micah, who speaks of the exceptional (virginal) childbearing of an extraordinary woman (Mary). Her son will strengthen his brothers and sisters by the power of the Lord, "in the majestic name of the Lord, his God ... and his greatness shall reach to the ends of the earth" (Mic 5:2–3).

The figure of Mary emerges with crystal clarity not only in these and other prophecies that can be singled out in Sacred Scripture, but also in the exquisite language of the prophet Isaiah's canticle-monologue with its lofty poetry and deep spirituality:

> I rejoice heartily in the Lord,
>   in my God is the joy of my soul;
> For he has clothed me with a robe of salvation,
>   and wrapped me in a mantle of justice,
> Like a bridegroom adorned with a diadem,
>   like a bride bedecked with her jewels.
>   (Isa 61:10)

Such is the hidden dynamic way in which the Holy Spirit, using very few and simple words but with the magisterial power proper to God, described "in luminous form the supreme individual among the children of men,"[7] a "personage outlined by the Old Testament" (A. Bea), who opens the door to the "fullness of time" and with Christ shines brightly in the New Testament story.

---

7. Agostino Merk, "La figura di Maria nel Nuovo Testamento," in *Mariologia* I (Turin: Marietti, 1952) 80.

Not even the biblical writers themselves suspected the great and lofty reality conveyed by their words. And yet, using the resources of human language, God was preparing his people to understand Mary.

3. Mary in the New Testament

On the threshold of the New Testament the Virgin of Nazareth makes her appearance in salvation history as an ideal embodiment of the chosen people of God and as mother of Messiah-Christ. Then, hand in hand with Christ, the "sun of justice" (see Mal 3:20), she advances into the world of the new covenant; she follows its course as servant and disciple of her Lord while growing constantly in faith.

Mary's person is presented and given its paschal depth on various levels, from the beginning on to the rich symbolism of John's gospel and the Apocalypse. We see her unique vocation and mission, which are marked at every point by a profound relationship with her Son, with the Trinity, with Israel, and with the Church. Whereas she is present and yet hidden in the divine plan of the Old Testament, her appearance on the stage of history in the New Testament reveals her full individuality and mission.

Here the evangelists bring out in various ways the fulfillment of the prophecies about her: the virginal birth of Jesus (Mt 1:22–23); the great works God has done in her as he had promised the patriarchs (Lk 1:55); the entrusting of the Mother and the disciple to one another as something that had to be done (Jn 19:26–28). Mary "arises before us in all her exquisite and radiant majesty, thus giving joy to Christians and consolation to those who can call themselves children of so great a Mother."[8]

---

8. Agostino Merk, "La figura di Maria nel Vecchio Testamento," in *Mariologia* I (Turin: Marietti, 1952) 38–39.

We have to admit that the New Testament witness to Mary, the Mother of the Lord, is quite restrained, but it is also exceptionally rich in meaning and filled with resonances. P. Nigido very appropriately remarks that "in the gospel there are few references [to Mary] ... but these few contain everything. Can anything not be contained in the simple reality that is the Mother of God?"[9]

4. *Mary: A Prophetic Life*

The Second Vatican Council emphasized a now well-known idea of revelation as taking form in both actions and words, these two being closely interconnected (see *DV* 1–2). As St. Gregory the Great used to say, God instructs us sometimes through words, sometimes through deeds. This principle expresses a very important aspect of the Bible, namely, that it contains not only words but also deeds and symbolic actions, and even lives that are prophetic and therefore are of interest for what they do and are and not only for what they say.

It is in this perspective that we must rightly see the true person of Mary as it is set forth for us in the sacred writings: Mary is a word of God not only in what she says or in what is said of her in Sacred Scripture but also, and above all, in what she does and is. In her own way, she is a "visible word" or "word in act," to use St. Augustine's definition of a sacramental sign. Her every behavior, as we know it from the gospel, is a lesson in silent love; thus her restraint during the public life of Jesus and her simple presence under the cross are "signs," and how full of meaning they are! They tell us of Mary's ability to hold fast to her assigned place and to accept even supreme sorrow.

---

9. Cited by Stefano de Fiores, *Maria madre di Gesù. Sintesi storico salvifico* (Bologna: Ed. Dehoniane, 1992) 189.

Beginning in the first centuries, Christians who were inspired to continue the heroic deeds of the martyrs found in Mary the model of a no less radical but silent witness to an unceasing love and discipleship. In fact, Mary seems to disappear, as it were, into a reverent silence: an active, adoring silence; a silence filled with contemplation and adoration of the Word, which in her becomes "Life"; a silence that is worth more than all our "good words" and turns the Virgin of Nazareth into a kind of "lived exegesis" of the gospel. It is a silence that makes of her the "book of God and the Word," as the Fathers put it, "in which, even without sound and without writing, God and the Word are read every day."[10]

Of Mary alone can it be said, in a real and not merely figurative sense, that she was "pregnant with the Word." Through her God speaks to the Church and each of us.

D. God's Ways in Mary

In God's plan the entire economy of salvation seems to be concentrated on Mary. Her particular destiny has a primordial historical importance, because it is a pre-eminent part of the history of salvation. In her the main paths of the old and new covenants meet; in her is fulfilled the covenant between earth and heaven, which is Jesus, her Son.

She reflects in her individual person the work which the Holy Spirit accomplishes over time in the entire community of the redeemed.

> In her modest person Mary concentrates the entire history of salvation and of the manifold relationships of which that history is woven. So true is this that one might see her as a summary of the scriptural message and say that she is the icon of the entire Christian

---

10. Andrew of Crete, "Encomium IV on the Birth of the Most Holy Mother of God," in PG 97:861–81; Fazzo, 93–110.

mystery, the "abridged statement" of what the trinitarian God does for humanity and, at the same time, of what God enables creatures to offer him by their free response.[11]

From this point of view, the history of salvation and Mary shed light on each other. As the well-known French exegete A. Feuillet has written, "Whoever wants to thoroughly understand Marian doctrine from the viewpoint of the Bible cannot do so apart from a more extensive exploration of the history of salvation. Conversely, whoever wants a deeper understanding of the history of salvation must necessarily deal with the Mother of the redeemer, for she is connected by unbreakable bonds with the very center of salvation history."[12]

11. Bruno Forte, *Maria, la donna icona del mistero* (Alba [Cuneo]: Ed. Paoline, 1989) 103.
12. A. Feuillet, "L'heure de la femme et l'heure de la Mère de Jésus," *Biblica* 47 (1966) 572.

Chapter Two
Mary in the Mystery
of the Trinity

A. Introduction

Mary the Most Theocentric of Creatures

Hail, divine and most worthy
palace of the most august Trinity.

(Nicetas Paphlagon)

The Father is with you and makes his own Son
yours. The Son is with you and, in order to
accomplish the wonderful mystery in you, he
    unveils in a marvelous way the secret of your
womb and yet preserves intact the seal of your
    virginity.
The Holy Spirit is with you and, together with
    the Father and the Son, sanctifies your womb.

(St. Bernard)

In these wonderful expressions of interior inspiration we sense immediately how very special and indeed unique is the communion of the Virgin Mary with the three divine Persons.

As a person and as a presence she emerges, radiant, out of the mystery of the Word to whom she gave birth: the only-begotten Son, consubstantial with the Father in his divinity, consubstantial with us in his humanity.

By reason of her close connection with the life and destiny of Christ she became, in an extraordinary way, a participant in the trinitarian mystery. The Father's love, the

Son's grace, and the splendors of the Holy Spirit embraced her from the first moment of her existence. As a result, the light radiating from the entire Most Holy Trinity shines forth in her, as does the unity of the Trinity, and serves as a sign, so to speak, of the same yet different way in which the Virgin is present to the three divine persons. Her presence to each Person is different because she has different relationships respectively with the Father, with the Son, and with the Holy Spirit. Yet this presence is one because the embracing divine love of the Father, the Son, and the Holy Spirit is one, as is the purpose of her life: the glorification of the supreme Trinity and the divinization of humanity.

As Mother of the Word incarnate, she herself was born out of the very heart of the Trinity and is therefore united by unbreakable bonds to the three divine persons. Her existence is purely relational, being an unparalleled relationship of love with the tripersonal God. Just as the "event" that is Mary cannot be understood except in the perspective of salvation history, so too it cannot be understood apart from a clear connection with the One and Triune God.

In the mystery of the Church everything is trinitarian: its origin, its purpose, its life; everything comes from the Trinity and everything is directed to it. With greater reason the same can be said of Mary, the most outstanding member of the Church. The work of the three divine persons is accomplished in her in an exemplary way, the same work that must be accomplished in the Church until the Lord's return.

In the divine plan the Virgin is what she has always been in the liturgy and in Catholic thought: the most theocentric and christocentric of creatures, who in her humility has been caught up in the whirlwind of the trinitarian life. God loved her so much that he made himself his own creature in Christ. It was precisely the mystery of the Incarnation that brought Mary into the fullness of the trinitarian life; true enough, it is due to the redemptive Incarnation that Mary's life became entirely centered in Christ, but Christ in turn led her to the Trinity. For there is in fact a real connection, even if one mysterious to us, between the Word who takes flesh and the other divine Persons.

The very special relationships of the Virgin with the Trinity began when the angel told her that she was to become Mother of the Son of the Most High and that this was to come about through the power of the Holy Spirit.

Here, then, we see the beloved daughter of the Father, the bride of the Holy Spirit, and the Mother of the Word. Thus Mary establishes the closest possible relationship with the entire Trinity, a radical bond that henceforth unites her permanently with the three divine persons and not only with Christ.

These relationships were not only permanent (they were not restricted to the period during which Mary was pregnant with the incarnate Word but extended to her entire life). They were also exceptional (they gave Mary a place not occupied by anyone else before or after her) and made of Mary the pre-eminent temple of the Most Holy Trinity.

Because the divine nature of Christ, in whom "dwells the whole fullness of the deity" (Col 2:9), reposed in Mary, she carried within herself the unity of the Father, the Son, and the Holy Spirit.[1] Mary is great because she has been associated, as no one else has, with the mystery of the God of mercies. She received Christ and, with him and through him, the fullest possible creaturely participation in the "eternal mystery," that is, in the inner life of the Father, the Son, and the Holy Spirit.

This trinitarian life or uncreated grace, which was concentrated as it were in the Incarnation of the Word, was united

---

1. Jean Galot, Maria, *la donna nell'opera di salvezza* (Rome: Gregorian University Press, 1984) 304.

with Mary in a unique way: not only spiritually and morally but personally, that is, with her entire being. The whole personal existence of Mary was informed and given a new ontological status by the uncreated grace that is the three divine Persons. This "ontology" became full, total, and integral when she was "dynamized" by the created grace of Christ Jesus.

The action of the tripersonal God can be said to produce in Mary's life a relationship of likeness; that is, what she becomes through grace makes her like the Trinity, with a likeness that, as we said, penetrates to the ontological level. By her threefold state as Virgin, Mother, and Spouse, Mary mirrors the very mystery of the relations within God.

> As a virgin she carries in her virginal faith the imprint of the eternal attitude of the Son before the Father, the eternal attitude of the Beloved before him who is the eternal origin of love. She thus appears to us as the image of him who in eternity is purely receptive and simply allows himself to be loved: the Only Begotten ... the Word that comes forth out of silence, the Beloved who shows us that not only giving but also receiving is divine. Thus amid the infinite divide between creator and creature but also in the closeness and conformity established by grace, the Virgin is the created object of the divine pleasure, the creature who accepts God's initiative with complete receptivity and endless gratitude, the beloved who in everything obeys the will of the Eternal One.
>
> As Mother of the Word incarnate, Mary is connected with the Father by his unmerited gift, with him who is the source of lifegiving love. She is therefore the maternal image of him who constantly gives, who has always been the first to love, and is pure wellspring, pure giving....

As spouse in whom the eternal God unites with himself the history and fulfillment of his amazingly unparalleled gift, Mary is linked to the communion between
Father and Son and between them and the world. In
that sense she is an image of the Holy Spirit by her
everlasting spousal character; she is the link with infinite love and embodies the permanent openness of the
mystery of God to human history.[2]

The Virgin Mary, humble servant of the Almighty, thus
mirrors the very mystery of the divine relations. By conceiving and giving birth to the Son of God in his hypostatic union
with a human nature, Mary enters, in a sense, into the circle of
life of the divine family. As far as is possible for a human
creature, she shares in the vitality, dignity, honor, and holiness of that family, to the point of becoming a "kinswoman of
God," a "complement of the Trinity," and the "wholly deified
one," to use the language of the holy doctors of the Church.[3]

Due, once again, to the hypostatic union of the Word
(human nature and divine nature united in one person in
Christ) Mary truly enters into the divine sphere, more so than
she does through grace and the beatific vision. This is because
the union of the creature with God through grace and the
beatific vision always remains on the accidental level. In contrast, the hypostatic union effected in the womb of Mary is a
substantial union, since the assumed nature really participates
in the personal existence of the Word. In this sense, the entire
Trinity enters into Mary so that "the fullness of the divinity
that had previously dwelt in her spiritually, as in many saints,
now [after the Incarnation] begins to dwell in her even corpo-
really, something that never happens in any other saint"
(St. Bernard, *Sermons on Missus est*, 4,3).

---

2. Bruno Forte, *Maria, la donna icona del mistero* (Alba [Cuneo]: Ed. Paoline, 1989) 161.

3. See Andrea Agnoletti, *Maria Sacramento di Dio* (Rome: Ed. Pro Sanctitate, 1973) 67.

The idea that Mary has an utterly special and unparalleled
relationship with the Father and the Holy Spirit, who are
inseparable from the Son, is not a new one. It appears
throughout the history of mariological thought, from Gregory of Nyssa (331–400), who views the Virgin in the light of
the Trinity, down to studies made in our own time.

In the medieval period, St. Francis of Assisi sets Mary in
the context of the Trinity in one of the few prayers of his that
have come down to us: "Holy Virgin Mary, among all the
women of the world there is none like you; you are the
daughter and the handmaid of the most high King and Father
of heaven; you are the mother of our most holy Lord Jesus
Christ; you are the spouse of the Holy Spirit."[4]

During the same period St. Thomas Aquinas provided an
unusual description of the Virgin as "the noble dinner table
of the entire Trinity" (*Nobile triclinium totius Trinitatis*).[5]
This rather bold poetic image, so profound and meaningful, describes Mary as the exquisite table around which the
Father, the Son, and the Holy Spirit express their fellow-
ship. It brings out clearly the very close bonds uniting
Mary with the One and Triune God. Because of the presence within her of God incarnate, Mary is seen as the
means, necessary yet given with utter freedom, by which
the Father and the Son, together with the Holy Spirit, can
meet.

These ideas emerge with special clarity in the *Treatise on
the True Devotion to the Blessed Virgin Mary* with its
refined trinitarian atmosphere. Here Montfort calls Mary the
sanctuary and resting place of the Trinity, a magnificent

---

4. Antiphon for all the hours of the *Office of the Passion*, trans. in Marion A. Habig,
   O.F.M. (ed.), *St. Francis of Assisi: Writings and Early Biographies* (Chicago:
   Franciscan Herald Press, 1973) 141.
5. *Opuscula theologica* 6: *In Salutationem Angelicam, Vulgo "Ave Maria," Expositio.*

divine world in which God exists in a more divinely sublime way than he does anywhere else in the universe (see no. 5).

Using other language, Mary is also called "the place of satisfaction for the Trinity" (St. Mary Magdalene de'Pazzi) and "the paradise of God" (St. Germanus of Constantinople).

In our own time, with its new theological and exegetical approaches, the placing of Mary in a trinitarian context is regarded as something fundamental that should provide a very original structure for the whole of Mariology.

B. The Virgin Mary Is Associated with the Most Astounding Work of the Trinity: The Incarnation

> O Mary, you draw heaven down, and behold ...
> the Three come to you,
> and all of heaven opens up and stoops to you:
> and in this diaphanous, eternal moment
> your chaste womb itself becomes heaven.[6]

These splendid and profoundly inspired expressions summarize the lifegiving dynamism at work in the history of salvation, which is dominated by a surprising decision of God: the Incarnation of the Son. This thrilling mystery transcends all the language and logic of reason and "is beyond the capacity of our weak mortal intelligence to think of or understand ... how the wisdom of God can have entered into a woman's womb and been born as a little child and uttered noise like those of crying children."[7] Though he is the Wholly Other, God became a man; "the Infinite allowed himself to be contained within a woman's womb."[8]

---

6. Elizabeth of the Trinity, cited in Fausto Casa (ed.), *Meditazioni Mariane. Pagine scelte dagli autori di tutti i tempi* (Padua: Ed. Messagero, 1979) 290.

7. Origen, *On First Principles* II, 6, 2, trans. G. W. Butterworth (London: SPCK, 1936; New York: Harper & Row, 1966) 108.

8. This idea occurs often in the writings of not a few Fathers and Doctors of the Church.

Here, then, "God's salvific giving of himself and his life, in some way to all creation but directly to man, reaches one of its high points in the mystery of the Incarnation" (*RM* 9). Henceforth the entire Christian mystery will take place under the sign of the God-man.

1. The Trinity, Author of the Incarnation

> If I look within you, Mary, I see that the hand of the Holy Spirit has inscribed the Trinity in you. It wrote there the Wisdom of the Father, that is, the Word. It wrote there the Power, because it was powerful enough to accomplish this great mystery, and it wrote there the mercy of the Holy Spirit himself, since only through divine grace and mercy this great mystery was ordained and accomplished.
>
> (St. Catherine of Siena)

As the divine Persons are inseparable in their substance, so too they are inseparable in their operations or activities. Everything that God does in creatures or on their behalf (his creative activity and his providence over the whole created order) is a work common to all three persons of the Trinity.

The entire mystery of the Incarnation is to be seen in light of these fundamental principles of our faith. The Incarnation is thus the work of the Father, who entrusts his own Son to the Virgin, and of the Son, who gives himself to her in order to assume, in her womb, flesh and blood that are taken into the unity of his own Person, and, finally, of the Holy Spirit, who forms this body in Mary's virginal womb.

Although the Son alone is born of the Virgin, Mary becomes a mother because she is overshadowed by the power of the whole Trinity. When faced with this abyss of inexhaustible and unfathomable love that envelopes and overwhelms all creatures, human beings can only bend their knees in adoration and praise:

Praised be you, O holy Trinity, for this divine decision and holy plan that makes the Son of man to be the Son of God and makes a virgin become the Mother of God! What a sublime plan, worthy of the Most High! What an unfathomable plan, worthy of the Father's majesty, the Son's wisdom, and the Holy Spirit's love! ... It is a plan inspired by love; in it you raise up the Virgin Mary to be your cooperator in the carrying out of this supreme work. And as you united human nature to one of the divine Persons, so too you willed to associate a human being with one of your divine works.

When I contemplate this work, O holy Trinity, and see this Virgin in your company, I look upon her and venerate her as one second only to you. I gaze on her and honor her as the creature most set apart, the holiest, and the one most worthy of your greatness and love.... Therefore, O holy Trinity, you made her solely for yourself.

You made of her a world and a paradise apart: a world of sublime things and a paradise of delights for the New Man who was to come into the world.

You made of her a new heaven and a new earth, as it were: an earth that yields only the Man-God and a heaven that contains him alone and acts only for him.

You made her to be, as it were, another universe within the universe.[9]

2. Mary, the Womb That Welcomes the Trinity

> Hail! for thou bearest him who beareth all....
> Hail! thou womb of God's incarnation.
>
> (The Akathistos Hymn, stanza 1)

In its fundamental content the Annunciation at Nazareth represents the culminating and definitive point in the self-

---

9. Pierre de Bérulle, *Les mystères de Marie* (Paris: Bernard Grasset, 1961) 199–200.

revelation of God to humanity (see *MDig* 3). Its narrative structure "for the first time reveals with utter clarity the Trinity of God" (Hans Urs von Balthasar); it reveals "the inscrutable unity of the Trinity" (*MDig* 3).

If it be true that the economic Trinity is also the immanent Trinity, in the sense that our only way of knowing the Trinity is from the history of salvation, then we must acknowledge that Mary in her poverty and receptivity becomes the place in which the trinitarian history of God — the plan of the Father, the sending of the Spirit, and the mission of the Son — pitches its tent within the history of humanity. The Annunciation thus reveals the Trinity as the adorable womb that receives the holy Virgin, while at the same time it shows Mary to be the womb of God.[10] It shows her to be as it were the emblem of the ability to receive the unforeseeable, the Wholly Other, even while fully actuating her feminine identity in the most deeply creative sense of this term, which expresses fruitful acceptance, receptivity, and the willingness to "become the womb" of him who "is a womb."

According to St. Bernard, in the mystery of the Incarnation not only does God enclose himself in the bosom of Mary but he also encloses Mary within the bosom of the Trinity. God, who is a devouring fire, has wrapped his mother in his light and divine warmth.[11]

We may compare the scene of the Annunciation to a flash of light that breaks up and scatters the darkness. In this light the goal of our life is shown to us and history acquires a meaning. With moving simplicity Luke the evangelist tells us of this central moment in which God's plan and humanity's expectations come together. In this

---

10. See Bruno Forte, *Trinità come storia. Saggio sul Dio cristiano* (Cinisello Balsamo [Milan]: Ed Paoline, 1985) 44 and 160.

11. See his ninth sermon on the Assumption, in *Marianum* 54 (1992) 136.

decisive moment "the Eternal One chooses the welcoming, rich silence of life in a woman's womb as the setting in which to make his Word resound in the flesh of the world."[12]

Mary was thought, willed, and loved by God from all eternity; over the centuries she had been proclaimed and foreshadowed in the Scriptures; she had been created and, as time passed, she had been prepared for her mission in a divinely munificent style. Now, as the only purely human agent in the Incarnation, she is asked to receive, on behalf of all of us, the revelation of the gift of infinite love, of love in the form of a person; she thereby becomes the sign and instrument of God's action in favor of humanity as a whole.

That love which is God's very being, the existence of the Trinity "yesterday, today, and forever" (see Heb 13:8), is focused on humanity. It desires to give human beings an unmerited share in God's life, his nature, even the divinity itself. But, see, on the path taken by this generous outpouring there stands the one who is "full of grace"! In her a creaturely heart and the history of a human being become the first dwelling of Emmanuel.[13] Here we see an utterly new and surprising action of God as he makes a direct appeal to the humble girl of Nazareth and waits for her conscious, free, and responsible answer. God is a disturbing God who eludes being made the captive of our desires and our prisons. His imagination is inexhaustible; his surprises never cease to astonish believers.

From the moment of the Annunciation on, the mind of the Virgin Mother was confronted with the radical "newness" of God's self-revelation and made aware of the mystery: "She is the first of those 'little ones' of whom Jesus will say one day: 'Father ... you have hidden these things from the

---

12. Forte, *Maria, la donna* ..., 172 and 175.
13. *Acta Ioannis Pauli II, in basilica liberiana habita*, December 8, 1988.

wise and learned and revealed them to babes' (Mt 11–27)"
(*RM* 17).

After having so often promised and proclaimed Christ in
the Scriptures, God at last acts, now that the hour has come
for initiating the fullness of time.

> In their changeless and yet life-giving eternity the three
> Persons are attentive to this turning point in their eter-
> nally conceived work, for everything depends on this
> moment. Billions of individuals have a stake in what is
> to happen in a hardly noticed instant. The Father is
> about to manifest his power through a new creation.
> The Son is about to undergo a birth in time…. The
> Spirit is about to make fruitful and to embrace in love,
> thus completing the action of the Father and the pres-
> ence of the Son.[14]

God was coming to satisfy the restless human heart by
offering it a savior.

In this unique moment Mary's heart is a door for the
world, as the Church has sung of her for centuries on the
feast of the Annunciation: "You are the royal door for the
heavenly King" (hymn for Lauds in the old breviary).

> Her appearance on earth, like a star that precedes the
> dawn, as well as the delicate work God had done
> in her during the years of her childhood were the
> immediate preparation; the message given to Zecha-
> riah (Lk 1:5–15) and the recent virginal marriage to the
> Virgin and Joseph constituted the final touches in the
> plan to be carried out. Everything was ready now for
> the marriage of the Son of God to humanity: the bridal
> chamber, the house, the garden fragrant with flowers

---

14. Jean Guitton, *La Vierge Marie* (Paris: Aubier, 1949) 42.

and surrounded by a hedge — in short, the little paradise on earth.[15]

The zero hour has come, and the good news is in the air. Look, the angel Gabriel is sent by God to a town in Galilee called Nazareth in order to bring about there the most extraordinary act of presence and revelation: the Incarnation (see Lk 1:26–38). Through his angelic messenger God himself visits the Virgin and tells her something never heard before; he shares with her, a creature, his lowly servant, the mystery of his eternal plan: "Behold, you will conceive in your womb and bear a son, and you shall name him Jesus. He will be great and will be called Son of the Most High ... and of his kingdom there will be no end" (Lk 1:31–33).

Mary listens to the angel's mysterious words, and with her all of creation and the whole of humanity listen, for in Mary the entire world receives the proclamation of salvation and places its trust in her. The entire universe is involved in the announcement of the good news, in this announcement of the true, the supreme gift: Emmanuel (= God who gives himself to us).

Mary's answer is anxiously awaited by heaven and earth; God had made the Incarnation of the Word and the redemption of the world depend on her. "It may be said that just as heaven and earth await Mary's answer, so even the hidden Word anxiously waits for it in order that he may immediately make the Father's eternal plan a reality."[16]

On this point a great lover of Mary speaks forcefully:

> The whole world prostrates itself at your feet and prays and waits; it waits for the words that will bring consolation to the afflicted, freedom to prisoners, pardon to the condemned, salvation to all.... O Virgin, answer soon!

---

15. Agnoletti, *Maria Sacramento di Dio*, 59.
16. *Acta Ioannis Pauli PP. II*, in *Marianum* 46 (1984) 375.

O Lady, speak the words that earth and the underworld and even heaven await! Even the King and Lord of all human beings, having been so drawn by your holiness, desires no less ardently your positive answer, for he has determined, depending on that answer, to save the world.... If you, then, let him hear your voice, he will let you see our salvation.[17]

Mary's decision, her response to the unforeseeable new action of God, which has no precedent in the history of the chosen people, demanded everything of her: the depths of her person, the whole of her being, her entire life. The angel's words had confronted her with the inscrutable divine mystery and brought her into the orbit, as it were, of that mystery. She was called upon to conceive him in whom "dwells the whole fullness of the deity bodily" (Col 2:9). After a startled moment of ineffable, painful, deeply felt, and heroic effort, the Virgin recognized by the light of faith the authenticity of the divine call, and she answered quickly and unhesitatingly: "Behold, I am the handmaid of the Lord. May it be done to me according to your word" (Lk 1:38). "And the angel left her; he received her faith-inspired words and went away."[18] Thus was accomplished the most venerable mystery of Christianity, the greatest wonder in history.

At the Virgin's "Yes" the heavens opened, and in a mystery of unparalleled depth God, the Word, became flesh in her. The Son of God became also the Son of Mary. The Virgin's womb opened, and the Word of life "descended into the most perfect of created beings: Mary Immaculate."[19] He

---

17. St. Bernard, *Sermo IV in Laudem virginis Matris*, in PL 183:83.
18. Antipater of Bostra, *Homily on the Mother of God* 11, in *TMPM* I, 617.
19. Cited in Ernesto M. Piacentini, O.F.M Conv. (ed.), *Maria nel pensiero di s. Massimiliano Kolbe* (Vatican City: Ed. Vaticana, 1982) 55.

who had formed the womb descended into the womb.[20] "The Lord of majesty, he whom the whole world cannot contain, became a human being and enclosed himself in Mary's virginal womb. Here the One who is inaccessible, incomprehensible, invisible, and unimaginable ... willed to become understandable, visible, and imaginable to all."[21] "A divine condescension,/ not a change of place, occurred,/ but the childbearing of a God-filled virgin" (*The Akathistos Hymn*, stanza 15).

Such is the celebrated design of grace that we know as the Incarnation (Paul VI), a sublime design in which heaven came down to earth and sank roots there. Eternity entered time, the created was united with the uncreated; "earthly realities were united with heavenly realities" (Geoffrey of Admont). "The earth buds forth the Savior and has a foretaste of God's tomorrow, which is given and promised to it" (liturgy). A human creature is raised up to a dignity almost divine, and history becomes the history of salvation.

From her womb and her heart Mary offers the Child to a weary, wounded, and tired world. This Child is the desire of all the nations, the peacemaker and renewer of humanity. The human race is composed of sinners but henceforth it contains the Son of God, in whose Person God and humanity are forever united. What fulfillment could be greater than this?

Teilhard de Chardin wrote that "the world will belong to those able to give it the greatest hope. But the greatest and even the only hope is Jesus the Savior, and Mary Most Holy is the one who gave and still gives him. She lent her voice to all those who awaited and await the Redeemer, and now she places the adorable fruit of her virginal womb, him who is the source of resurrection and life, in the arms of this

---

20. See Pseudo-Augustine, *Sermo* 126 (PL 39).
21. St. Bernard, in *Marianum* 54 (1992) 134 and 166.

worn-out world as she would one day place him in the arms of aged Simeon." In her the entire human race gives birth to God.

"In a moment that will never pass away but remain in force for all eternity, Mary's words to the angel were the words of the human race, and her Yes was the Amen of all creation to the Yes of God."[22] In the white flower that was the Virgin, human words became receptive of the Holy Spirit and thus of the entire Trinity.

As the redemption wrought by Christ took place in time but transcends all times, so too Mary's free consent, given in the full power of the Holy Spirit, was uttered in a brief instant but its power and efficacy reaches to all times. It runs through the history of the people of Israel and echoes through the coming centuries; it will continue undiminished through all eternity as a typological response, that is, the perfect example of the response of faith that the self-revealing God expects of every human being.

> What more beautiful, more humble or more prudent answer could men and angels together have devised in all their wisdom if they had thought about the matter for a million years? It was the answer that made all heaven rejoice and brought an immense sea of graces and blessings into the world! Scarcely had it fallen from her lips when the only-begotten Son of God was drawn from the bosom of the Eternal Father to become man in her most pure womb! ... O powerful *Fiat*! ... O efficacious *Fiat*! ... With a *Fiat* God created light, heaven, earth; but with Mary's *Fiat*, God became man, like

---

22. Karl Rahner, cited in R. Cantalamessa, *Maria uno specchio per la Chiesa* (Milan: Ed. Ancora, 1990) 45.

us,[23] in order that human beings might live the divine life "than which nothing is more precious to us here on earth, nothing more agreeable to us mortals."[24]

Similar sentiments, springing from an enthusiastic faith, occur often in the vast ocean of patristic texts. With their lofty and profound spirituality they pass over into joy or into feelings of veneration and deeply felt wonder before the fascinating, suprahuman mystery of a God who becomes flesh. Through the door opened by Mary's *fiat* this God descends into the vale of our history in order to redeem it. Andrew of Crete puts his finger on the reality:

> Today [feast of the Annunciation] we celebrate the union of God with humanity, the reshaping of our image, our elevation and ascent to heaven.... Therefore let everything that is exult today, and let nature rejoice! For the heavens have opened, and the earth receives, invisibly, the king of the universe....
>
> Today the Father of glory, having come out of compassion for the human race, looks benevolently on human nature that in Adam had fallen into ruin.
>
> Today the bestower of mercy unveils the depths of his supremely kind heart and pours out mercy on nature that it may cover the earth like flooding water....
>
> Today brings the announcement of joy, gladness for all creation ... the revelation of God's love for human beings, a festive jubilation over universal salvation.... From this source human nature receives the foretaste of joy and the beginning of divinization.... What mind,

---

23. St. Alphonsus Maria de Liguori, *The Glories of Mary* (2 vols.; Baltimore: Helicon Press, 1962–63) 2:46.
24. Sophronius of Jerusalem, *Homily on the Annunciation*, in PG 87.

what tongue could comprehend all this? Words cannot expound it nor can the ear receive it.[25]

Today is the holy day "on which earth celebrates its marriage with heaven, the flesh is reconciled with the Spirit, and human beings play in the presence of the great God."[26] "This is the day that inaugurates our salvation; from it freedom shines forth for us; from it springs our adoption as children of God."[27]

All this is a summary of the joyous message brought to Mary or rather to human nature: the message of reconciliation with the Father of lights and the beginning of the joy of salvation for the whole of reality. "Now the earth exults as it receives in its arms the God of heaven through Mary Most Pure. Now the angels rejoice, as do lovers of what is good and lovers of humankind, for already they contemplate our salvation. Now, together with the angels, humanity is gladdened, for it has received, through Mary, true joy and the wellspring of grace."[28]

C. Mary Chosen by the Trinity for the Sake of the Covenant

Hail, Summary and Recapitulation of
the Old Covenant!
                                                    (Nicetas Paphlagon)

1. Introduction

Beginning in the Old Testament, God's relations with his people were based on a covenant, the distinctive aspect of

25. Andrew of Crete, *Homily on the Annunciation of the Most Holy Mother of God*, in *TMPM* II, 413–15.
26. Leonardo Boff, *Il volto materno di Dio. Saggio interdisciplinare sul femminile e le sue forme religiose* (Brescia: Queriniana, 1987) 129.
27. Sophronius of Jerusalem, *Homily on the Annunciation*, in *TMPM* II, 162.
28. Nicetas Paphlagon, *Homily on the Annunciation of the Most Holy Mother of God*, in *TMPM* II, 884.

which was that it was bilateral and involved reciprocal commitments on the part of both God and human beings. God asks for the consent and cooperation of those in whose favor he wishes to act. He is not content simply to manifest his sovereign power but, even while maintaining his transcendence and while being the sole energizer and master of the covenant, he wants his relations with human beings to be based on mutual agreement. God's every action in human history is done with respect for the free will of men and women. God loves to offer himself to human beings, but he never forces his way into their lives.

That is precisely what happens at the Annunciation: the angel proposes to Mary the plan of motherhood, but asks for her express consent. As we know, Mary does not disappoint the One who asks for her cooperation but shows herself to be completely open to the angel's message and ready to believe the impossible. With complete freedom, in response to God's predilection for her she says "Yes" to the new covenant.

Before consenting, the Virgin of Nazareth brings up the obstacle when she asks "How can this be, since I have no relations with a man?" (Luke 1:34). She thus shows that her consent is given with complete clarity and full freedom. In a spirit quite different from that of Zechariah, she does not discuss the carrying out of the plan or ask for an explanation that will enable her to understand the plan; she asks only for an explanation that will enable her to do God's will. She says, literally, "How can this be?" That is, Mary believes *that this will be*, but asks *how she is to act*, what she must do, since she has no relations with a man.

2. Mary's Yes: Entryway into the New Covenant

> Behold, I am the handmaid of the Lord.
> May it be done to me according to your word.
>
> (Lk 1:38)

The words are few and simple but they are prophetic
and more than sacramental, for they place Mary at the
very origin of the new covenant and redemption. From
her consent springs the new covenant signified by the
Incarnation of the Son of God. The intradivine Trinity
becomes the economic Trinity, and an inviolable relationship is definitively established between God and his
people. With the message to Mary the dawn of the new
covenant breaks. As happened to Israel at Sinai (Ex
19–24), "heaven" comes down once more to converse
with earth and asks this earth to enter into an indissoluble
embrace with it.

Nazareth, then, is a repetition of Sinai. But what a difference! No more thunder and lightning and flames on a
scorching mountain. Instead, a God who silently passes
into the womb of a young girl from among us. Moreover,
this covenant is eternal and irrevocable and even more
wonderful than that made with the Israelites. It brings to
pass everything that the Old Testament covenants had
only prefigured. "Precisely because this covenant is to be
fulfilled 'in flesh and blood' [of Christ the Redeemer], its
beginning is in the Mother. Thanks solely to her and to her
virginal and maternal 'fiat,' the 'Son of the Most High'
can say to the Father: 'A body you have prepared for me.
Lo, I have come to do your will, O God' " (*MDig*19).

Mary is the Virgin-Mother who accepts the mystery
into herself and reveals it to the world. She offers herself
as the site of a marriage in which the covenant with the
Eternal One is established forever. In this context the
Fathers of the Church once again provide splendid and
appropriate images which they express in lapidary forms.
"The womb of Mary is the bridal chamber in which the
marriage of God with humanity took place, the loom on

which the tunic of the union was woven, the workplace in which the union of God with humanity was effected."[29]

In the Virgin Mother two worlds touch: that of God and that of humanity; that of gift and that of acceptance, that of an unprogrammable and marvelous coming and that of an exodus, laden with all the human weariness with life.[30]

3. A Nuptial "Yes"

Mary, the Virgin Mother, responds to God's plans with the readiness of a detached heart and with a complete gift of herself. In so doing, she embodies the authentic Israel by reliving its choice and its mission of begetting and welcoming the Messiah.

Despite the history of infidelity of God's people, his gracious face bends down to her and turns her into the summation and personification of the ancient Zion-Jerusalem, but one now redeemed, renewed, and to be described as "my delight" (Isa 62:4). What takes place in Mary makes concretely real all that the faith and hope of Israel had meant by the image of a nuptial covenant: "The Lord delights in you, and makes your land his spouse. As a young man marries a virgin, your builder shall marry you; and as a bridegroom rejoices in his bride, so shall your God rejoice in you" (Isa 62: 4–5). "I will espouse you to me forever: I will espouse you in right and in justice, in love and in mercy; I will espouse you in fidelity, and you shall know the Lord" (Hos 2:21–22).

Mary possesses the quality of a faithful spouse who is capable of making this ideal matrimonial union fully real. She will be *par excellence* the beloved spouse of the Spouse. The beauty of her act of faith consists in the fact that it expresses the nuptial "Yes" of bride to bridegroom, beloved to beloved.

---

29. See St.Basil, *Homily on the Holy Generation of Christ* 3 (PG 31:1464), and Proclus of Constantinople, Homily 1 on the Mother of God 1 (PG 65:681).
30. See Forte, *Maria, la donna icona*, 262.

When Mary says to the angel "I have no relations with a man," she is asserting herself as the one who will fulfill the promise: "You shall know the Lord." Behind her virginal intention not to "know" a man lies the intention of knowing God: it is with God that Mary desires to have her closest relationships.[31] Her virginal motherhood tells us, on the one hand, of the absence of a man; but, on the other, it tells us of the exceptional nearness, the utter closeness, of Mary to God, an intimacy "that exceeds all the expectations of the human spirit" (*MDig* 3).

Theodore of Studios assures us that, truly, no one was ever as close to God as was the Blessed Virgin Mary, no one was more pure, no one more beyond reproach.[32] Mary is a virgin because she belongs entirely and radically to God. In fact, "the deeper meaning of virginity is not that a woman withdraws into herself in order to preserve herself but that she opens herself in a more direct and complete way to God. It is a search for the closest possible contact with the Lord. We must recognize its positive value, which is a spousal relationship with a personal God."[33]

"You shall know the Lord"

Knowledge of the Lord, a term that summarizes authentic religion (see Isaiah and Hosea cited above), is one of the main subjects of Jeremiah's preaching (see 2:8; 22:15–16; 24:7; 31:34).

In the Bible the verb "to know" is a concrete one, signifying "to experience, to savor." Knowledge of the Lord is accompanied by *hesed* (a deep, tender, inward love, like that of a mother) and is therefore not to be regarded as a simple intellectual knowledge. The Lord God "makes him-

---

31. See Jean Galot, *Maria: itinerario spirituale della donna nuova* (Rome: Gregorian University Press, 1990) 57.
32. *Homily on the Nativity of Mary* 4, 7.
33. Galot, *Maria, la donna,* 139.

self known" to human beings, binding them to himself through a covenant and showing his love (*hesed*) for them through his blessings. Similarly, human beings "know God" by means of an attitude that implies fidelity to his covenant, acknowledgment of his blessings, and love (see Job 21:14; Prov 3:25; Isa 11:2; 58:2).

When the verb "to know" is seen in this light, we can understand how it is packed with a truly profound meaning. It is an activity belonging less to the cognitive faculties of the mind than to the realm of very deep interpersonal knowledge. This last implies a strong experience of vital intimacy or, better, an intense relationship of love between an "I" and a "Thou," such as is typical of a spousal relationship.

In this light it must be said that no one truly "knew" the Lord more than Mary, to whom the divinity gave itself in a unique and unrepeatable way. No one experienced more than she did the *hesed* of God, his profound, entrancing, and yet unsettling love. To no one more than to her can St. Bernard's words be applied: "The title 'spouse' belongs to the soul that loves."[34]

Mary, a creature formed by the Holy Spirit, loved God with every fiber of her being and made him the sole beginning and sole end of her existence. As Mother of the Son of God, her life was given to God alone. In fact, we can see in the lowly accumulation of the events of her everyday life only a continuous manifestation of fidelity, consecration, and tenderness, and an exclusive love of the Lord.

4. Representative of Humanity

Mary's act of faith was not only personal but also corporative. That is, her personal activity was activity on behalf of humanity, in keeping with the universal law at work in the history of salvation. In the language of Semitic cultures,

---

34. *Sermon 7 on the Song of Songs* 2 (PL 183:807).

"corporative personality" means that the individual, while remaining an individual, is functionally identified with the community. We must bear in mind that after the *fiat* uttered by this young girl of Nazareth, the evangelist ends his narrative by saying that the angel departed from her, as though in order to bring Mary's acceptance back to God, just as Moses brought back to Yahweh the response of the people (Ex 19:8b, 9b).

At this fundamental turning point in the history of salvation, we see how the purest religious spirit of the *anawim* (the poor who depend on the Lord, who have no resources and no wealth except God himself) is concentrated in Mary. The pyramid of election narrows as it moves up from plurality to oneness. No longer is it the assembly of the chosen people that is asked about the covenant (see, e.g., Ex 19:8; 24:3, 7; Jer 42:20; Josh 24:21–24; Ezra 10:12; Neh 5:12; 1 Mac 13:9), but an individual person, a daughter of that people. This individual is the Virgin of Nazareth, in whose womb God has decided to clothe himself in our flesh as the first sign of the new covenant (see Luke 22:20). The response of faith that had been typical of the people of Israel in response to the covenant with the Lord is now placed on the lips of this Virgin, a true "daughter of Zion."

In the divine intention, the messianic people was expanded to include humanity as such, both male and female, with the result that Mary must be regarded as the representative of the entire race. It is in its name that she is asked to say "Yes."

According to St. Thomas, at the Annunciation God awaited from Mary a consent to be given in the name and place of human nature itself.[35] Such a universal representation is readily explained by the principle at work in the covenant, the benefits of which are to be extended to all human beings; and the whole of humanity is committed by the cove-

---

35. *Summa of Theology* III, q, 13, a. 1.

nant to collaborate in God's work. It is this commitment in the name of all human beings that Mary is called upon to make in response to the divine initiative. Her consent at the Annunciation must be regarded as one that commits the entire human race. Only if others make Mary's decision their own can it be salutary for them.[36]

As all the saving actions of God are recapitulated in Jesus Christ, the Word of the Father, so Mary's response sums up all the assents of faith made by God's people and all its members. That which Israel failed to bring to fulfillment because of its unbelief and disobedience, Mary did fulfill. Through her faith and obedience to the God of the covenant, the Church and the entire human race are introduced into the depths of the mystery of the tripersonal God.

From the very beginning of his message the angel Gabriel shows that he means to address Mary as the representative of the people of God that has been ceaselessly formed throughout the entire history of salvation. In fact, his salutation, "Rejoice" (Greek: *chaire*), which is improperly translated into Latin as *Ave* ("Hail"), calls to mind the messianic prophecies of salvation that had been addressed to the "Daughter of Zion." They, too, had been introduced by "rejoice," a word expressing the intense jubilation which the community of the chosen people were to experience through the intervention of Yahweh, who was coming to save them.

> Rejoice heartily, O daughter Zion,
>   shout for joy, O daughter Jerusalem! …
> Sing and rejoice, O daughter Zion!
>   See, I am coming to dwell among you.
>   (Zech 9:9; 2:14)

> Shout for joy, O daughter Zion!
>   sing joyfully, O Israel! …
> The Lord your God is in your midst,
>   a mighty savior:

---

36. See Galot, *Maria, la donna*, 44 and 399.

> He will rejoice over you with gladness,
>   and renew you in his love,
> He will sing joyfully because of you,
>   as one sings at festivals.
>
> (Zeph 3:14–15, 17)

In the eager outpouring of these Old Testament words we hear the entire vocabulary of overflowing joy — from the gladness of liberation to messianic exultation — with which the prophets proclaim the Messiah-King who was to come among his people. The Virgin Mary would actually give him lodging; her maternal womb would be his new dwelling. The Child she conceived was the awaited King-Messiah who would bring about the extraordinary presence of the Lord so extolled by the prophets. This presence was willed by God to be a presence first and foremost with Mary, in order then to become a presence with the entire human community. The Lord was with the Virgin Mary because he willed to be also with each of us, even if his presence with Mary was extraordinary in manner and degree.

The Mother of Jesus was urged therefore to exult and rejoice, as the Daughter of Zion had earlier been: "Rejoice … the Lord is with you" (Lk 1:28). Obviously, the reason for the joy is the same: "The Lord is with you." In both instances there is question of the visitation of the Messiah, which God had long been promising but which occurs only now to Mary of Nazareth.

Luke's intention was to depict the Virgin Mother as the "Daughter of Zion." In his view she represents Jerusalem and the entire chosen people. In her person, in which the faith of ancient Israel comes to a point and the movement of faith in Christ begins, the entire people of the promise — the old (Israel) and the new (the Church) — is present in its optimal expression. The angel's greeting to Mary, therefore, is not the simple greeting of the Greek world, "hail (*Ave*)," as the Vulgate and the ancient Syriac version chose to translate *chaire*. This word, the imperative form of the verb, points rather to the joy accompanying the good news (see the *Ecumenical Translation of the Bible*). It announces an involvement in the mystery of the messianic and divine motherhood, and Mary must reply with complete awareness and collaboration.

As far back as 1939, S. Lyonnet published an article proposing that the *chaire* of the angel to Mary be interpreted not as an ordinary, commonplace greeting "hail (*Ave*)," but as a call to joy and exultation.[37] The day of the Annunciation is thus the day par excellence of joyous announcement, the day on which everything is enveloped in the joy of heaven. For a gospel of joy does begin with Mary: the announcement that God has become a human being. It is an unending announcement of indescribable rejoicing that is addressed to all of humankind down the centuries. "To Mary first was announced a joy that would later be proclaimed to all the people" (John Paul II).

This amazing, overwhelming truth of our faith is a theme that runs so fragrantly and with ever-fresh inspiration through the writings of the Fathers as they pour out their joy:

> Rejoice, O full of grace; show a joyful face!
> For from you will be born the Joy of all,
> the one who will end the ancient curse
> by annihilating the power of death
> and giving to all the hope of resurrection.[38]
> It is fitting that joy be yours and no one else's,
> for you are full of grace because the Lord is
>   with you.[39]

---

37. See A. Serra, "Aspetti mariologici della pneumatologia di Lc. 1, 35a," in *Maria e lo Spirito Santo* (Rome: Marianum, 1984) 135.

38. Basil of Seleucia, *Homily on the Mother of God* (PG 85), in *TMPM* I, 598.

39. Germanus of Constantinople, in *TMPM* II, 383.

> What a greeting, so full of sweetness and joy,
> the angel utters![40]

Surely, no joy, no delight can ever be found that is not far surpassed by the announcement to the Blessed Virgin and Mother of joy! What is there more sublime than this joy, O Virgin Mother? The miraculous event revealed in you outdistances everything else; everything else is inferior to the favor bestowed on you; everything else, no matter how excellent, takes second place.... The joy in which you share comes not only to human beings but even to the powers on high....

> Rejoice, O Mother of supernatural joy!
> Rejoice, O nourisher of heaven's joy!
> Rejoice, O mystical dwelling, of ineffable joy!
> Rejoice, O most blessed fountain of inexhaust-
> ible joy! Rejoice, O treasure of eternal joy, who
> gave birth to God! Rejoice, spectacle most
>   marvelous of all![41]

5. New Aspects of the New Covenant

In the framework here used in interpreting the Annunciation certain elements stand out that characterize the new covenant entered into with the Virgin of Nazareth. The first to be mentioned is that this is *a covenant with a woman.*

In the perspective given by the Bible no one could imagine that the new covenant would be struck with a woman. In fact, in all the covenant stories told in the Old Testament it is clear that in making his covenants with humanity God turned only to men (that is, males; for example, Noah, Abraham, Moses). This might suggest that only males could suitably represent the people to the creator.

Against this background, a covenant with a woman is a completely new element of the Good News. It is a sign that in

---

40. Eleutherius, *Sermon on the Nativity of the Lord*, in *LM,* 83.
41. Sophronius of Jerusalem, *Homily on the Annunciation* (PG 87), in *LM,* 141–42.

Christ Jesus "there is not male and female" (Gal 3:28). In her the reciprocal opposition between man and woman (a heritage from original sin) is essentially overcome: as the Apostle goes on to say, now "you are all one in Christ Jesus" (Gal 3:28) under the banner of the divine teacher.

By taking a woman as a free partner in his covenant and granting her a decisive influence on the destiny of the entire human race, God effects a genuine emancipation of all women, one that not only sets them free but elevates the female personality to the level of collaborator with him. From this point of view, the Annunciation proves to be a unique moment in the world history of women, being the most notable instance of their emancipation.

A further point for our attention is the way chosen to bring about the new covenant: it consists in the *coming of the Holy Spirit* or, in other words, in the coming of the "new Spirit" that produces a new covenant (see Ezek 11:19–20; 36:27–28). In the past, during the first stages of salvation history, God gave a share of his spirit to chosen individuals: commanders of military undertakings, the king of Israel, and educators of his people, especially the prophets. Now, at the dawn of a new period, the Holy Spirit is sent to Mary for an entirely special reason.

In the Jewish tradition the Messiah had been thought of as an ideal king upon whom the Spirit of God would descend. But never had anything been said of a coming of the Spirit on the mother of the Messiah. This coming would bring about something great and, humanly speaking, impossible: a *virginal motherhood,* "a sign of the newness of the Kingdom, which comes to overturn the laws of the created world" (Max Thurian). The divine action, aimed at the conception of the child while completely respecting the virginity of its mother, is another great novelty of the new covenant, since never before in the Bible had there been a child conceived by a virgin.

In the history of the people of Israel God had previously limited himself to causing a woman hitherto barren to become fruitful, but always as a result of conjugal intercourse. He had never acted to replace a husband in making a woman conceive; the human couple retained their role. See, for example, the births of Isaac (Gen 17:14), Samson (Judg 13:2–5), Samuel (1 Sam 1:20), and John the Baptist (Luke 1:5–25). In these circumstances, the birth of a son was simply foretold; the prediction was an announcement of good news that satisfied the intense desire to have a son and for this reason could not but bring joy to a barren woman. Such announcements obviously did not require asking the consent of those benefiting from them.

Mary's case is completely different. There is no question here of ending a painful state of barrenness, but rather of giving a son to a virgin who wants to preserve her virginity. Her *consent* is explicitly requested. We may add that in accepting her virginal motherhood, Mary shows a *much bolder faith* than any found in earlier Judaism. She had, as it were, to cut herself off from the past in order to accept the utter newness of the divine plan. Her faith has no external support; we might say that the past disappears and is replaced by an entirely new kind of faith, one that is freed from "established" Judaism and is deprived of all sensible support. Mary's whole security comes from the word of God; her only strength derives from his fidelity. The future is full of mystery for her; it requires a constant response of faith. On the other hand, she could not foresee what the mystery of the Annunciation implied.

The complete newness of the new covenant attests that the story of the Annunciation was not invented using the model of previous announcements of motherhood. No previous instance of virginal motherhood has been found in the Jewish tradition or even in pagan myths; therefore no act of human invention can be supposed. No human inventiveness would have been sufficient; only a divine inventiveness can explain a plan for a virginal maternity that includes a request for the mother's consent.

D. The Eruption of Grace

> O woman full and overflowing with grace,
>   plenty flows from you
>   to make all creatures green again.[42]

In the Bible the word "grace" means "gift," and in particular a completely free gift, given without respect to merit, "a special gift, which according to the New Testament has its source precisely in the Trinitarian life of God himself" (*RM* 8). In virtue of this gift human beings share in the inner life of God, who confides his own mystery to them and at the same time gives them the ability to bear witness to it and to fill their being, their life, their thoughts, their wills, and their hearts with it.

The special privilege granted to the Christian community is to be filled with grace in "the beloved," that is, in Jesus (see Eph 1:6), who himself possesses the fullness of grace and is its source. "A smallest degree" of this sanctifying grace "is worth more than all the natural realities in heaven and earth";[43] created beauties pale before its brilliance.

In the realm of those who receive this grace Mary's unique vocation gives her precedence over the rest of the human race, for she is given this privilege in anticipation of her vocation and she receives the first fruits of full, indeed superabundant, grace. That which thus occurs in her is a prelude to what is given to the whole of humanity. As the waters

---

42. St. Anselm, *Prayer* no. 7, in Sister Benedicta Ward, S.L.G., *The Prayers and Meditations of St. Anselm with the Proslogion* (New York: Penguin Books, 1973) 120.
43. St. Thomas, cited by Giuseppe Taliercio, *Maria la Donna Nuova. Una riflessione antropologica* (Turin: Ed. Paoline, 1986) 47.

fill the sea, so grace fills the soul of Mary. Who is closer to Christ than his Mother and who, consequently, shares more fully in the grace of Christ than she does? And what is the favor which Moses and the patriarchs and prophets found in the eyes of God, as compared with Mary. In her case grace is the deepest core of her being, the root of her existence; it is that which makes her what she is.

The Virgin is the creature so wrapped in and shaped by God's favor that he was present in her not only by his power and his providence but also in person, with a physical presence. God gave Mary not only his favor but his very self in the person of his own Son: "The Lord is with you!" Was there anyone God was more "with" than with Mary? Indeed, in the Mother of God grace reached a perfection that will never be equalled. "She was placed on the highest level of grace and merit, so that she surpassed all creatures except for the Word incarnate."[44]

Philosophy teaches that the closer things are to their cause, the more they feel its effects. As we know, the Blessed Virgin was the person closest to Christ due to the human nature which he acquired from her. It follows that she ought to have received from Christ a fullness of grace greater than that of all other human beings. "There are no words to express the glory and extraordinary power of the outpouring of God's grace that descended on this creature" (Paul VI). Her entire being proclaims that at the beginning of all relations between God and creatures there is grace, as the place and the soil in which creatures can encounter their creator.

A new and unique human being

In laying out the interior features of the Madonna, God could not but reveal himself and his plan of grace. From the account of the Annunciation, which may be regarded

---

44. G. M. Roschini, *Il Tuttosanto e la Tuttasanta. Relazioni tra Maria SS. e lo Spirito Santo* (Rome: Marianum, 1976–77) II, 145.

as a *summa* of what revelation says about the Virgin of Nazareth, we learn that "by God's command" (*LG* 56) the
angel greeted Mary with surprising words: "full of grace
(*kecharitomene*)." That is, in greeting Mary the divine messenger does not call her by her own name but gives her a new
one: *kecharitomene*. He does not say "Rejoice, O Mary," but
"Rejoice, O Full of Grace." We might dare claim that this is
her proper name.

As a matter of fact, she is the only creature in whom God's
grace could display itself with its full effectiveness from the
first moment of her existence in her mother's womb. Everything in her, down to the very roots of her being, was controlled and guided by grace. Her true name, then, is this
grace that filled her soul.

"Full of grace": truly surprising words, full of mystery,
that echoed in the silence of the lowly house of Nazareth,
two thousand years ago. And yet they marked the beginning
of God's mightiest works in the history of humanity and the
world.

It is necessary to emphasize, among other points, that the
use of the verb *kecharitomene*, which the evangelist applies
to Mary, is exceptional. It occurs only one other time in the
New Testament (not surprisingly, in Ephesians 1:16), Since
it appears so rarely, we ought to assume that Luke is giving it
its full semantic value, that is, as signifying an abundance
that verges on fullness. In fact, the translation "full of
grace" captures the meaning of the Greek perfect participle
kecharitomene (= a person provided with or filled with
grace), which signifies a reality that is complete and flaw-
less. Like all Greek denominate verbs ending in *oo*, the verb
charito, from which *kecharitomene* is derived, signifies of
itself a specific abundance of, a large amount, a fullness.

What the evangelist intends to convey, then, in using the
word *kecharitomene* is that the gift of grace given to Mary
was complete and total. This is enough to justify concluding

that the greeting "full of grace" addressed to the Virgin of Nazareth had a scope so vast and filled with meaning as to include in it, as in a seed, her entire life. It expressed an attribute attached to Mary's person because, as Luke's gospel makes clear, it was equivalent to a proper name. But the purpose of a name, as we know, is to distinguish one individual from another, to make the individual known. That which distinguishes Mary from all other creatures is that she received an exceptional grace and possessed grace in a supreme way.

"Full of grace" is indeed a new name, but one that is also a ministerial name inasmuch as it is directed toward a mission. For it is a divinely assigned name that contains an entire plan of life; it is a title that describes the vocation and function of the Virgin of Nazareth, and is therefore a unique name, since her holiness is unique, as is her mission and her virginal motherhood.

More than a greeting by the angel, the words "full of grace" are a revelation of Mary's plenitude of grace and a summation of what God accomplished in her in order to prepare her to be the Mother of Christ.

The grace, then, that permeated the hidden recesses of her being, creates the deepest identity of the Virgin Mother; it is that which defines her entire person and is the complete explanation of her greatness and beauty. Yes, Mary is Mary because she is full of grace; to say that she is full of grace is to say everything about her.

E. Mary: Sign of the Sovereign Initiative of God and His Unmerited Love

The supreme "law" that governs the entire history of salvation is the statement: "God is love."

(C. Vagaggini)

The account of the Annunciation, with the expression "full of grace" as its capstone, proclaims a fundamental truth: that at the origin of all relationships between God and creatures is a completely unmerited gift, namely, the sovereignly free choice of God or, in other words, everything that the Bible includes in the term "grace."

Mary, as we have seen, receives the revelation of an unheard of plan that breaks into history from on high: she would, by the power of the Holy Spirit, give birth to the Son of God. What an unexpected idea, utterly unique and unrepeatable! We truly find ourselves here in the realm of the entirely unmerited love of God, who always manifests himself in the history of salvation as the One who "freely justifies" all "by his grace through the redemption in Christ Jesus" (Rom 3:24). The grace of God is thus the ultimate explanation of all the greatness of Mary and of the entire Church.

The Virgin Mary, who from the very outset had always been favored by God, is a tangible sign manifesting the two essential attributes of divine love: its unmeritedness and its predilection for the poor. She could say with Paul: "By the grace of God I am what I am" (1 Cor 15:10). Bruno Forte says:

> God chooses a Virgin in order to manifest himself, a Mother in order to communicate himself, a Spouse in order to enter into a covenant with humanity. He chose what seemed weak and obscure in the world's eyes, because this most clearly reflected the intensity of his love for the weak and the little people of the world....
>
> The divine plan of salvation, which is carried out by means of Mary, is in its entirety linked to the mystery of the tripersonal God, for in this plan God reveals himself as utterly free giver, as eternal source of love, and as displaying the initiative of One who loves, not because he needs to or is compelled to love, but solely for the pure diffusive joy of loving.[45]

---

45. Forte, *Maria, la donna icona*, 172 and 204.

The new beginning of the world, the eruption of what we cannot deduce or think up, is something that we cannot bring into existence but can only be given by the pure unbounded freedom of him who has loved us: by God, who as Luther put it so well: "He does not love us because we are good and beautiful, but he makes us good and beautiful because he loves us."[46] The divine image manifested in the account of the Annunciation and in the miracle of the Incarnation is precisely that of the God whose outgoing love of his creature is unmerited, the Lord of heaven and earth who in his kindness stoops to his maidservant and, in her, to all of waiting humanity, the Father of mercies who emerges from silence to speak his Word into time and link it with an unimportant moment, a place, a flesh (see Lk 1:26ff.).[47]

In keeping with this divine logic, Mary of Nazareth, who was chosen for the most sublime task, was born in silence. The world did not speak of her, even Israel did not think of her, although she was Israel's finest flower, the most beautiful in all the earth. But if the world did not think of her, heaven saw and venerated her.

But why was Mary of Nazareth in particular chosen to be the Mother of God? At this point, every human explanation fails; the answer is hidden in the secret plan of the Eternal One. Our minds are disconcerted by the choices of an infinitely free God and surrender to adoration and praise.

In human enterprises and those that are idolatrous, the greater the result sought and the greater the impression to be created, the greater must be the display, the show, and the expense.[48] God, however, does not choose worldly grandeur, power, wisdom, or logic and common sense, which he seems to disregard, nor does he turn to more famous and clever

---

46. Cited ibid., 207.
47. See ibid., 172.
48. Tertullian, *On Baptism* 2, 1f. (CCL 1, 277).

individuals. In order to accomplish "great things" he turns
lovingly to a poor, simple girl with a very common name and
no social standing, who belongs to the lower classes and to
people who are humble and without influence. She lives in
Nazareth, a village that is scorned and unimportant, as we
can see from Nathanael's spontaneous reaction: "Can anything good come from Nazareth?" (Jn 1:46). In her village,
Mary did not stand out in any way. To her relatives and
fellow-townspeople she was perhaps simply "Mary," an
unpretentious girl, polite, but in no way exceptional.

The fact, too, that she was a woman certainly did not give
her any standing, for women were widely accepted as inferior in the ancient world. Furthermore, Mary's virginity,
which she accepted as a way of life, elicited only incompre-
hension and scorn in a culture in which motherhood counted
for a great deal (the psalms sing the praises of motherhood:
114:9; 127:3; 128:3; and the point is dramatically brought
out in the lament of Hannah, who was barren, and of the
daughter of Jephtah: 1 Sam 1:9–18; Judg 11:29–40). Then,
too, after the Annunciation Mary must have found herself
completely isolated. To whom could she explain what had
taken place in her? Who would believe her when she said
that the child she was carrying was the work of the Holy
Spirit? Such a thing had never happened before and would
never happen again.

In short, this girl of Nazareth, as described for us in the
gospels, has no claim to the outstanding role assigned to her.
It is the Father who chooses her in order to carry out, with
her, his definitive act of salvation, the greatest wonder that
human history could gaze upon. In her lowly state the
Virgin Mary shows God's preferences in a concrete way and
reveals to us his disconcerting way of acting. It is an action
that aims to free human beings from self-sufficiency and
pride, which render them unsuited for collaboration with
him. Mary, in contrast, is the "handmaid of the Lord"

(Lk 1:38); she is therefore able to collaborate with him and make the transition from obscurity to a salvific mission. It is precisely in conditions of poverty and dejection that her love-inspired "Yes" springs forth and causes hope to flower once again in human history.

Tertullian wrote that "there is nothing that so upsets the human mind as the simplicity of God's actions as compared with the magnificent effects he obtains by means of them.... How narrow-minded human disbelief is that denies God his own attributes of simplicity and power!"[49]

Tertullian is admittedly referring here to the grandeur of baptism's effects and the simplicity of the means and external signs used, which consist of a little water and a few words. But we must admit that the same contrast is to be seen in Mary and the Savior's entrance into the world. Mary is the living example of the divine disproportion between what is visible outwardly and what takes place interiorly. "In her, magnificent grace and a marvelous vocation coexist with the uttermost simplicity and realism. When speaking of her we must always keep in mind the two characteristics of God's distinctive way of acting, which are, as we have seen, simplicity and magnificence."[50]

Too often, even we believers forget that God always chooses lowly, everyday things in making himself and his grace present. We forget that divine wisdom loves paradoxes and delights in astounding short-sighted human wisdom.

"Everything is grace," said Philo, speaking of the world as God's gift. Everything is grace in Mary, too. She is the most perfect expression of omnipotence and the complete sufficiency of grace, the supreme revelation of the possibilities grace offers to humanity, and the most transparent reflection of God's distinctive style.

---

49. Ibid.
50. Cantalamessa, *Maria, uno specchio per la Chiesa*, 43–44.

Chapter Three
Mary in Relation to the Father

A. God the Father, Mary, and the Double Generation of the Son

When the fullness of time had come,
God sent his Son, born of a woman.

(Gal 4:4)

Despite its terseness this well-known passage of Paul provides the earliest biblical basis for understanding the relationship between God the Father and Mary. We can grasp this relationship only indirectly through careful reflection on the two births of Christ: his eternal generation from the Father and his temporal birth from Mary.

Mary is the Virgin Mother, that is, the woman who gave birth on earth to the very Son of the Father (see *MC* 19). This revealed truth was already mentioned in the Nicene-Constantinopolitan Creed of 381 and solemnly defined at Chalcedon in 451, during the pontificate of St. Leo the Great. Here is the definition: "One and the same Son, our Lord Jesus Christ ... begotten before the age from the Father as regards his divinity, and in the last days the same for us and for our salvation from Mary, the virgin God-bearer, as regards his humanity" (*DEC* I, 86).

The Word, who existed from all eternity in the bosom of the Father would become, within time, the Son of Mary. Thus, just as the one Christ is consubstantial with the Father in his divinity, so too he is consubstantial with his Mother in his humanity; consequently, through her and in her, he is consubstantial with us. It is always the same one Son, common to God and to the Virgin: the only Son of the Father in heaven and the only Son of his Mother on earth. He proceeds both from God the Father and from Mary.

As Son, he is like both, because he has been born of both. From the Father he receives his divine nature and from his Mother his human nature.[1] This Son who is truly hers because he was truly born from her according to the flesh is identically the only Son of the Father who was begotten before the ages. Therefore, in addressing Jesus Mary can join the Father in the eternal ecstatic cry: "You are my Son; this day I have begotten you" (Ps 2:7; Heb 1:5). She is the only one in the universe who can say to Jesus what the heavenly Father says to him.

The Virginal Motherhood: Marvel of Divine Omnipotence and Sign of the Father's Paternity

> The garrulous rhetors
> became as dumb as fishes
> before thee, O mother of God.
> We see them toiling in vain to say
> how, remaining a virgin, thou couldst beget.
>
> (*The Akathistos Hymn*, stanza 17)

In addition to Luke's passage on the Annunciation, an interesting stylistic peculiarity in 1:16b of Matthew's gospel also sheds a bright light on the mystery of Mary's virginal motherhood as well as on the truth which the latter implies: Jesus has God alone as his Father.[2] In their different ways the two evangelists intend to bring out a particular theological truth, namely, that the Lord chose a virgin for his birth among us in order to show that the Son of God truly comes from the Father from the very moment of his conception and

---

1. See Isaac of Antioch, *Poems on the Incarnation of the Lord* 1, in *TMPM* IV, 218.
2. On this point see A. Serra in *NDM*, 240–41.

that salvation is not the result of any human work. While expressing the extraordinary character of birth from a Virgin Mother (extraordinary because of the absence of a human male agent), the event also attests to God the Father's direct and exclusive paternity of this child. What, then, must Mary's dignity be if she shares with God alone this eternal generation of the Son made man?[3]

We must indeed say that the virginal conception with its aspect as "revelatory sign" of the paternity of God the Father is a marvel of divine omnipotence, a sublime suprahuman event that takes place "in the silence of God" (as St. Ignatius of Antioch beautifully put it). It belongs to the order of mystery, one to which only Mary and Joseph could attest; it could not be verified by any other human being. It is a matter for each individual's faith and has its gospel foundation in the conviction, accepted by Mary, that "nothing will be impossible for God" (Lk 1:37; compare with the Magnificat in Lk 1:46–55).

In this connection, St. Augustine, a great doctor of the Church, eloquently reminds us:

> It was not difficult for God, who formed the entire creation out of nothing, to form the body of a dove without the intervention of other doves, just as it was not difficult for him to form a real body in Mary's womb without the intervention of a male. The reason is that corporeal creatures obey the command and will of the Lord, whether to form a human being in the womb of a virgin or to form a dove here in the world.[4]

---

3. See St. Bernard, *Sermon* 2, 2, in Marianum 54 (1992) 165.
4. St. Augustine, *The Christian Combat* 22, 24 (CSEL 41: 124; PL 40:303).

B. The Highest Possible Relationship of a Child with the Father

As not a few Christian thinkers, exegetes, and outstanding theologians have recognized, the relationship of Mary with the Father is primarily and essentially that of a child. The Father bestowed his paternal love in great abundance on Mary. As the well-known theologian Jean Galot observes, she is daughter of the Father in an eminent way precisely because of the paternal love he poured out on her and because he filled her with extraordinary graces in view of her motherhood. This filial relationship with the Father (Galot continues) was a permanent element in the life of Mary. It cannot be interpreted as the relationship of a spouse,[5] as some have maintained.[6]

After the Incarnation the loving gaze which the Father directs to his Son from all eternity, embraces also the Mother at Nazareth.[7] In virtue of the descent of the Word into her she in turn becomes for ever the "special possession" (Ex 19:5) of the Father, a creature whom he grasps and possesses, a creature whom he makes his own in the most radical sense of the phrase. In a commentary on the mariological thought of St. Bernard, E. Iablczynsky rightly remarks, among other things: "How great must the love of God for the Mother of his Son be if in order to redeem the human race he places the

---

5. See Jean Galot, *Maria: itinerario spirituale della donna nuova* (Rome: Gregorian University Press, 1990) 62.

6. In ecclesial tradition the title "Spouse of the Father" has often been given to Mary. The basis for the attribution can be the analogy between the fatherhood of God and the motherhood of Mary in the incarnation of Jesus Christ (the Father as husband gives his Son to Mary after asking her consent). Or the basis may be the fact that the Father links himself to Mary by the bond of predilection, love, fidelity, and grace. In other words, Mary is a creature so immersed in the mystery of God and so closely united to the Father that she can be called his "spouse." This elegant literary term implies her virginal self-giving to the divinity in order to become his living instrument in the saving mystery that embraces all of us. See the extensive documentation in A. Amato, "Dio Padre," *NDM*, 478–79.

7. See Ignazio M. Calabuig in *Marianum* 58 (1996) 10.

entire price of it in Mary! If she received the Word from the very heart of the Father? It is not surprising, then, to hear St. Bernard saying that Mary is God's treasure. Wherever she is, there God's heart is. His eyes are fixed on her."[8]

The filial experience of the Father reaches its highest point in Mary once she has become the Mother of the incarnate Son. For once she is a mother, her relationship with the Father takes on a deeper intimacy. At the same time, however, it was as a privileged daughter, the most favored and most beloved daughter of the Father, that Mary became the Mother of Jesus and acquired a maternal "face" that made her the supreme reflection of the Father's face.[9]

Due to her unparalleled motherhood she was united in an unparalleled way to the Son of the eternal Father.

> Her unmediated contact with God-made-man and her close union with Christ (not only through grace but also because of the human nature he had assumed from her) placed her in a state of complete openness to the Father. The result was a paradoxical situation: in the Son, Jesus Christ, Mary was not only a daughter of the Father but also the mother of the Son. Therefore the fatherhood of God in her was also experienced as motherhood of the Son.

Hers were the sweet feelings of a daughter for her God and the tender feelings of a mother for her Jesus, the Son of the Father. Because of this profound and marvelous interweaving of ineffable life and love, "just as the Son was entirely from the Father and turned to the Father, so Mary was entirely from the Father and turned to the Father" (*NDM*, 482).

---

8. "Assunzione e mediazione di grazia in s. Bernardo," *Marianum* 54 (1992) 165.

9. See Galot, *Maria: itinerario spirituale*, 62.

The vocation of all Christians is to be children of God in the Son and to live with the freedom of their filial state, but Mary was the first to have this experience. More than any other human being she carries within herself the mysteries of those divine destinies that enfold humanity in the beloved Son of God: for humanity is meant to share the grace and holiness of the children of God. She therefore goes before all of us in the great procession of those who possess faith, hope, and charity (see *LG* 53).

Prior to any other creature and in a higher way than any other, Mary, as Mother of Christ, obtained divine adoption, and as "the attentive Virgin" who listens to the Father (*MC* 17), she allowed herself to be formed and "used" (in the true and proper sense of the term) by the Spirit of the Lord. To her, therefore, the words of Paul the Apostle apply in a special way: "He [God] destined us for adoption to himself through Jesus Christ" (Eph 1:5); "Those who are led by the Spirit of God are children of God.... You received a spirit of adoption, through which we cry *Abba*, 'Father!' " (Rom 8:14–15).

It was not by accident that the Apostolic Exhortation *Marialis Cultus* highlighted the paradigmatic role which Mary's filial attitude toward the Father has for the Church and for all Christians, for she has given back to human beings their true identity as children of God.

The Spirituality of the Magnificat: The Most Meaningful and Profound Revelation of Experience of the Father

If it be true that Christ is the human face of God, it is also true that Mary plays an active part in revealing the merciful face of the Father. The face, that is, of the Father who gives his beloved son to the world, who is concerned about the liberation of the poor and the oppressed, and who defends their rights against their abusers.

The Magnificat is evidence of this claim, for it is a remembrance and reflection about the "being" and "action" of God, a joyous and compendious celebration of the entire history of salvation, and a religious song that springs from a heart full of vibrant gratitude and from a mind able to recognize the great signs given by God throughout history and in her own life. It is a poem filled with exultation, praise, and love, and with an almost ecstatic adoration of the "holiness," justice, and wisdom of God and of his providence in guiding the course of history. It is a prayerful exegesis of God's great deeds in the history of salvation, an exegesis born of a vision inspired by faith and of a profound experience of God the Savior.

As herself the subject of God's saving action and blessing, Mary praises God her Savior for using her to fulfill his promises. She sings of the God who has "remembered his mercy" (Lk 1:54). The people of Israel has experienced this mercy, which henceforth will spread its blessings throughout the world like an inexorable torrent, "from age to age" (Lk 1:50). She sings of the "great things" the "Mighty One" has done for her and, through her, for every human being.

Even if the language of the Magnificat is affected and marked by the post-Easter experience of the first witnesses to the faith, the text with all its freshness and energy seems to be truly Mary's song or, better, the "mirror of Mary's soul" (John Paul II). Before being a song of exultant joy, the Magnificat expresses what for Mary is the reality of her life. We need only think of the short but pregnant sentence: "He has looked upon his handmaid's lowliness," a sentence which Luke could hardly have included if it had not had some reference to the historical experience of the humble handmaid of the Lord. Because she had embraced God's will in an exemplary way (Lk 1:38a) and had persevered in faith (v. 45), she could claim that God's strategy had not changed. God — the same yesterday, today, and forever (v. 50) — is the helping God who looks with kindness on the lowly, the poor, and those least considered by the world, "those who fear him." He is the God who comes to the aid of those who recognize their need of his salvation (vv. 52b, 53a) and seek him with a sincere heart, while confounding those who remain the prisoners of their own false sense of security (vv. 51, 52a, 53b).

As a hymn of praise and as a reflection of experience, Mary's song is the only one that could have given God the praise which his glory deserved. It wells up from a heart accustomed to praising the Lord's goodness and mercy. Its subject, with its rich maternal overtones, is essentially the subject of love.

Pope John Paul II pulls together all the threads when he writes: "In the sublime words" spoken by Mary on the threshold of Elizabeth's house "Mary's personal experience, the ecstasy of her heart shines forth. In them shines a ray of the mystery of God, the glory of his ineffable holiness, the eternal love which, as an irrevocable gift, enters into human history" (*RM* 36).

The Magnificat, "Mary's prayer par excellence" (*MC* 18) and a most precious pearl in the Church's liturgy, can rightly be called "Mary's hymn to the Father." More particularly, it is a hymn to the fatherhood of God in relation to the new Israel according to the spirit, a "hymn that introduces the new gospel of Christ and is a prelude to the Sermon on the Mount" (John Paul II).

As she magnifies and glorifies her Lord with these outpourings of her soul, Mary shows herself as the first believer of the new creation. In a joy proper to the "time of times," she welcomes the great gift of God's goodness. She does so with a humble acknowledgment of her emptiness and with a ceaseless hymn of praise to him who is the source of her blessedness and the very origin of the mystery being accomplished in her. In all of time, no creature can be the singer of a thanksgiving to God that is as joyous and overflowing as hers.

A. Serra has written very appropriately: "The Magnificat, a gift which the Spirit has bestowed on the Church through Mary — a gift to be accepted, made part of life, and passed on — is both an outstanding model of prayer and an exceptional text to feed our meditation and our life of faith."[10] Cantalamessa, for his part, says we have the right to use the Magnificat in order to understand the soul and history of Mary, just as we use Isaiah 53 in order to understand the passion of Christ; even more so, since the Bible itself attributes the words to Mary. One of the psalmists says: "Glorify the Lord with me, let us together extol his name" (Ps 34:4). Mary says the same to us. There is perhaps no greater joy we can give her than to raise up from earth her song of praise and gratitude to God for the great things he has done in her for the benefit of us all.[11]

C. The Maternal Face of the Father

1. Introduction

> "You have brought together in yourself
> three sweet and cherished names:
> mother, daughter, and spouse."
>
> (Petrarch)

The mystery of Mary as icon of the Trinity would not be adequately explored if we did not highlight and reflect on the aspect of it that is most basic and dearest to our hearts: her motherhood. This is the foundation of Mary's dignity and greatness, and one of the most wonderful and brightest facets of this incomparable prism of created grace.

---

10. A. Serra, "Dimensioni mariane del mistero pasquale," *Marianum* 58 (1996) 34.
11. Cantalamessa, *Maria uno specchio per la Chiesa*, 245 and 252.

While the image of the Son whom she receives shines forth in Mary the Virgin, her motherhood is the image of the Father who generates and who gives and gives himself in an eternally active love. "God is also a mother," as John Paul I solemnly asserted from the balcony of St. Peter's Basilica.[12] Excellent catechist that he was, this pope knew how to make careful and accurate use of the biblical category that views God as a mother. Relevant here is the penetrating insight of the great German theologian Moltmann, who in his essay on "the motherly Father," interprets the Father as a maternal Father who by himself begets and gives birth to his Son.[13]

God is evidently neither male nor female. He transcends the sexes and their male or female attributes, and yet these categories have their foundation in him. It is from him, as participations in his most perfect being, that the qualities or perfections characteristic of man and of woman come. Moreover when he reveals himself he uses these categories, which then become sacraments of his presence and activity. It is therefore not odd that he should appear with male and female traits: those of a mother, on the one hand, and those of a spouse and Father, on the other. He can reveal himself as a Father and as a Mother, although he transcends both categories, because he dwells in inaccessible light.

In fact, this God has decided to let himself be mediated by a mother as an image and vivid revelation of his own fatherhood. This idea is being taught by an ever increasing number of modern exegetes and theologians, as well as by the Church's magisterium. Thus Jean Galot remarks that through the presence of a mother the Father determined to manifest in a more concrete and moving way his own divine

---

12. *L'Osservatore Romano*, September 21, 1978, p. 5.
13. Jürgen Moltmann, "The Motherly Father; is Trinitarian Patripassionism Replacing Theological Patriarchalism?" *Concilium*, no. 143 (March, 1981) 51–56.

love, which is both paternal and maternal.[14] Evdokimov, for his part explains that Mary's charismatic presence in our day depends on the free plan of God, who manifests himself in a "feminine and maternal" way in order to unify the world in Christ through the irresistible appeal of his Mother.[15]

If we look at the matter closely, we see that the new covenant seeks to oblige Mary to a motherhood that unites her in the closest possible way to the fruitfulness of God. For, in establishing a covenant in which he seeks the maternal cooperation of Mary, the Eternal Father willed to associate a human motherhood with his own divine fatherhood, and this in the gift of his Son and in the formation of his adoptive children.

The connection has been noted by, among others, Grignion de Montfort, who observes that "God the Father communicated to Mary His fruitfulness, inasmuch as a mere creature was capable of it, in order that He might give her the power to produce His Son, and all the members of His Mystical Body" (*True Devotion*, no. 17). Along the same lines Gibieuf has written: "Since God had planned from all eternity to go forth from himself on the path of love in order to form a family that would be born of himself, he needed, first and foremost, to choose a spouse and helpmate who would be like himself. And he thought of Mary, and made of her a helpmate like himself."[16]

This gift of fruitfulness from on high so deeply marked Mary that her very being was purely "a maternal being," on which was imprinted the mark of the source of the eternal generation, namely, the Father. The fact that the eternal Generator within the Trinity acted in Mary in order, in the fullness of time, to generate with her his only-begotten Son,

---

14. See his *Maria, la donna*, 377.
15. Paul Evdokimov, *La donna e...*, 155.
16. *Mémoires,* November 19, 1651; *Solitudes* IV, 389.

means that he formed the depths of her being in the image of his own fruitfulness as Generator. As a result, the Father made himself a "maternal being" who is inseparably connected with the entire history, both temporal and eternal, of the holy Virgin.[17]

*Mary, Expression of the Tender
Maternal Love of God the Father*

At the point, then, at which humanity's need and God's benevolence met, there stands the attractive and important person of the Virgin Mary. Indeed, such deep roots does she have in the human heart and in the cultural manifestations of the Christian people that she can be regarded as the providential way for discovering the "maternal" face of God, as well as for experiencing the "sweet" yoke which the following of Christ entails.

To those able to hear the song that arises from the depths of the soul, every woman is to be seen as a message from the Eternal One, a microcosm, as it were, in which the riches of God are adjusted to our limited vision and made readable.[18] In fact, woman is by her nature a specific and an original way in which God reveals his face. She expresses in a unique manner the tender maternal love of God for humanity.

If this be true of every woman, much more is it true of Mary, the "blessed among women" and the "woman" par excellence. In her, womanliness is elevated, in a completely unique manner, to the rank of a sign and concrete expression of the maternal face of God and of his tender love for creatures. In her the mercy of God acquires a face, a concrete form that helps demonstrate to Christians the fervor of

---

17. See Forte, *Maria, la donna icona*, 207–209; Grignion de Montfort, *True Devotion*, no. 17; L. Boff, *Il volto materno di Dio*, 155; J. M. Alonso, Trinità, in *NDM*, 1411–15; and others.
18. G. Biffi, *La Bella, la Bestia e il Cavaliere* (Milan, 1984) 132–33.

God's paternal love. In a heart that is human Mary manifests the power of God's infinite love. Hers is the "talent" of a mother that adorns the exercise of God's merciful love with an unlimited tenderness. A stupendous mystery this, and one closely connected with the mystery of the Incarnation. This connection has not been missed by the Christian faith-based tradition, which has given voice to it both in praise and in astonished invocation ("Mother of mercy, our life, our sweetness, and our hope"); in iconography (recall only the twelfth-century icon of the Mother of God, from the Province of Vladimir, known as the "Mother of Tender Love," and, in general the type of icons known as *eleousa*, "the tender *or* merciful"); and in poetry:

> In you is mercy, in you compassion,
> in you munificence, in you is combined
> whatever is good in creatures.[19]

As the *Puebla Final Document*, issued by the Conference of Latin American Bishops, reminded us: "From the very beginning … Mary has constituted the great sign of the nearness of the Father … endowed with a maternal, compassionate aspect…. A sacramental presence of the maternal features of God."[20]

The Virgin Mother gives us a glimpse of the transcendent femaleness within the trinitarian mystery, an aspect which the biblical tradition associates especially with God the Father. His female attribute of deeply felt love such as a mother has becomes clear in the beautiful divine soliloquy reported by Jeremiah: "Is Ephraim not my favored son, the child in whom I delight? … My heart [= *rahem, rahamim* = maternal womb, deeply felt love] stirs for him, I must show

---

19. Dante, *Paradiso* XXXIII, 19–21.
20. John Eagleson and Philip Scharper (eds.), *Puebla and Beyond: Documentation and Commentary*, trans. John Drury (Maryknoll, NY: Orbis Books, 1970), nos. 282 and 291 (pp. 16162).

him mercy" (31:20). And in the well-known passage of
Isaiah (49:15) in which God assures us that his love is
marked by a tenderness greater than that of any mother:
"Can a mother forget her infant, be without tenderness for
the child of her womb? Even should she forget, I will never
forget you."

This moving image of God as a mother was part of the
purest Hebrew tradition, but Mary was able to reinterpret it
in light of her own unique experience and consequently to
let it shine forth in every aspect of her life.

To realize this truth, we need only contemplate the
freshness of the evangelical account. Here Mary's motherhood finds expression in a radiant, selfless outpouring of a
love that is active and deeply felt and is translated into a
maternal kindness, care, tenderness, and foresight toward
the incarnate God.

In sum, it is translated into her own openness to God, her
readiness to say "Yes," even though she knows that this
assent and readiness will lead her on the path of a dark destiny in which she is not delivered from the cross. We see in
her the completely selfless love of which, at the human
level, only maternal love in its purest form is capable, the
kind of unconditional selflessness that is able to give, and
to give the self, prudently and humbly, day after day. In the
deepest sense Mary of Nazareth actuated her existence as
maternal icon of God's fatherhood, so that all her maternal
attitudes and attentiveness were transformed by love and
permeated by the love which God bestowed upon the
world through the Incarnation. So absorbed was she in this
outpouring of divine love that all the love with which God
fills souls to the brim bears the mark of her divine maternity and the nuances of her maternal love.

When we say that the Mother of God is the icon or maternal image of the divine fatherhood, we are not saying simply

that we contemplate in her the face of God's tender love. Rather we also recognize that her maternal existence, bearing as it does the image of the divine fatherhood, has a permanent and universal value and meaning.

2. *The Mother of God Speaks to Us of God*

The divine motherhood is the earliest of the mysteries surrounding the person of Mary and her role in the history of salvation. As such, it has always been for theological study (as well as for the magisterium of the Church, for art, and for popular devotion) a vital and ever-relevant subject of study and of constantly renewed reflection in the light of sacred Scripture, which always supplies us with its very valuable sources of understanding.

The title "Mother of God," the use of which began in the third century, only expresses what follows from the information in the gospels: Mary is the Mother of God because Jesus is a divine being. He is "son" of God in an absolutely special and profound sense that was unknown to the Old Testament and to Judaism. He is the Son of God because his birth was owing to a special act of the divine power of Love, that is, the Holy Spirit. The most important result of the virginal conception of Jesus was that Mary gave birth to the "Holy One." It is this conceptual implication, which is in harmony especially with the theology of the third evangelist, that underlies the great fundamental truth of faith in Jesus: he is the Son of God (see Luke 1:32a).

In him the human nature and the divine nature, hypostatically united, form a single person: the divine Person. According to this true belief, the human nature of Jesus was, from the first instant of his conception, united to the divine Person of the Word and could not exist apart from the Word. It is this oneness of person in Christ Jesus that makes Mary be the mother of the divine Person of the incarnate Son. She was Mother of the whole person and not only of the body or even only of the human nature. As Maximilian Kolbe correctly pointed out: "Mary, then, is truly Mother of God.... A woman is not called a mother nor is she mother of only a part of her son, just as a father is not father of only part of that son; the father and the mother are parents of the entire son. Thus Mary, too, is called and is mother of the entire Jesus, the man-God, and therefore is also Mother of God."[21]

The title "Mother of God," far from doing an injustice to Jesus in any way, helps bring out his twofold identity as true God and true man by emphasizing his real humanity and real divinity. Apart from showing the completeness of the Incarnation, Mary's motherhood guarantees the very truth of the Incarnation. If the Word had appeared unexpectedly among human beings with a human nature fully established and developed, it would have been possible to doubt the reality of his human flesh.

In the final analysis, the title "Mother of God" is a kind of bulwark that resists both the ideologization of Jesus (turning him into an idea or a "personality" rather than a real person) and the separation of his humanity from his divinity, which would imperil our salvation.

a) Conformity of the Divine Motherhood to the Supreme Fatherhood of the Father

> He who was the thought of peace
> in the heart of the Father
> became our Peace
> in the arms of his Mother.
>
> (St. Bernard)

---

21. St. Maximilian M. Kolbe, *Scritti*, Italian trans. by Father Cristoforo Zambelli (Florence: Ed. Città di Vita, 1975–78) III, 690.

Mary received the Spirit of the Father and, following his inspirations, devoted herself to the incarnate Word in a personal and unmatched way and focused on him outwardly with a human sensitivity and a motherly heart. To the Son she had borne she was the representative of the Father in heaven.

God the Father gives the Son and, through him, the Holy Spirit to the human race and, in the same Spirit, receives from the Son the offering of the redemptive sacrifice, in which the sacrifice of all of humanity is present. In like manner, by sharing, out of pure unmerited grace, something of his paternal being in the form of Mary's maternal being, the Father allows her to share in the offering of the Son. In the descending line this sharing by Mary consists in giving Jesus to humanity; in the ascending line it consists in uniting her own intercession and self-offering to the one, perfect sacrifice of Christ.[22]

As Berulle sums up the matter, Mary's motherhood "imitates" the Father's fatherhood. She shares, within time, in the power and fruitfulness of the first Person. In the mystery of the Incarnation she participates in this first Person in his character as Father (*NDM*, 1411). St. John Eudes explains even more clearly and explicitly: "As the eternal Father originates the Son from all eternity within his own bosom and his own adorable heart, as he causes the Son to be born in the heart and bosom of the Virgin, and as he forms and produces the Son in the hearts of the faithful, so too the admirable Mother gives birth to the same Son in her virginal heart, conceives him in her blessed womb, and makes him live on in the hearts of the faithful."[23]

---

22. See Alessio Martinelli, "La Vergine Maria Dimora escatologica di Dio ad opera dello Spirito Santo," in *Maria Santissima e lo Spirito Santo*, 89 and 210.
23. St. John Eudes, *Le Coeur admirable* I, vi, chap. 1.

God has thus made the human sonship of the Word to be an image of his divine sonship.

b) Mother of God:
The Highest Degree of Motherhood

> Your name, O Mary,
> is awe-inspiring to us.
> This name means "Mother of God" to us.
> Hail, Blessed One! Can any name
> among mortals match this one
> or come close to it?[24]
> You bore an honored name,
> O blessed through all ages![25]

Memorable verses, these, that over the centuries have sung the greatness of Mary's name: Mother of God.

Humanity brings its purest offering: the Virgin. God makes of her the "place of his birth," this Mother of all the living, this Eve fulfilled. On the vigil of the Nativity of Jesus the Byzantine Church sings: "The angels offer you the heavens; the earth brings you its gifts; but we human beings offer you a Virgin-Mother," who "is endowed with the high office and dignity of Mother of the Son of God": the highest peak, the throne of God, the summary of all the wonders worked by the Most High. "Because of this gift of sublime grace she far surpasses all creatures, both in heaven and on earth" (*LG* 53).

In this perspective the title "Mother of God" has not only a christological purpose (it protects the mystery of Christ as man-God) but also a mariological one. It emphasizes the pre-eminent place of Mary in the faith consciousness of Christians, since to be the Mother of God in his Incarnation is a mission that belongs to her alone.

---

24. Alessandro Manzoni, *Il nome di Maria*, vv. 19–23.
25. Venantius Fortunatus, *In laudem sanctae Mariae*, in *TMPM* III, 612.

"Mother of God" is a permanent and irreversible title because the Incarnation of the Word in the womb of the Virgin is irreversible. It is also a truth that sheds rays of light on all the other truths about Mary, since the latter are best and most fully understood when considered in relation to that first title. For the divine maternity is the primary principle of all Mariology and the essential foundation of a whole series of supernatural privileges enjoyed by the Blessed Virgin. The latter, while separating her in a sense from sinful humanity, also bring her closer, in a more intimate way, because of her entirely special participation in the economy of salvation.

We ought not to forget that while the title "Mother of God" speaks to us of Mary, it also has for its purpose to bring out the extreme love of the God who has so humbly linked himself to this creature of his. "Mother of God" speaks to us first and foremost of the humility of God and only then of the humility of her who liked to call herself a "handmaid."

God willed to have a mother! This means that he depended radically on someone, that he did not alone form himself and could not independently plan his own being. What a contrast with the god of the philosophers! What a cold shower for human pride! And what a call for humility!

Everything suggests that the marvels involved in being Mother of God were essentially two: the diminishment or self-abasement of God and the elevation of humankind to the level of God. Here is a God who "stripped" and "humbled" himself to the point of making himself a human being like us, and a woman who was so "exalted" as to become nothing less that the mother of God. Here we see the madness of God's love, an abyssal love that fills the soul with trembling and profound astonishment.

In the face of the magnificent, indescribable spectacle of Mary's motherhood, exegesis turns into contemplation and silent adoration. Human reason falls silent; rationality loses the ground beneath its feet and is replaced by ecstasy, the exuberance of the heart, and a vibrant flood of elevated astonishment.

> O abyss of the goodness and love of God for humanity!
> O astonishing miracle,
> not seen since the beginning of time!
> He who is becomes, and the uncreated is created. He
> who created the ages begins to exist
>   in what he created....
> God has shown himself as an infant ... as a baby,
> and yet he is the Lord of glory!
> What an utterly new bonding,
> what an extraordinary union! ...
> He who enriches others becomes a beggar;
> he goes in search of my flesh
>   in order to enrich me with his divinity.
> What an awesome and wonderful mystery!
> Most holy the womb of Mary,
>   wider than the heavens,
> that has given birth to the endless ages!
> O birth laden with salvation,
> for you became the redemption of the world!
> How divine and sublime:
>   he is born of a virgin,
>   yet had first been born of the Father.
> He is carried in the arms of a lowly mother,
>   the first living monstrance of the body of Christ.
> He who supports the entire world and the endless ages
>   is wrapped in swaddling clothes.
> He who holds in his hand the entire immense universe
>   and who is by his essence is beyond reach,
>   lets himself be placed on Mary's knees,
> which are now the throne and first altar
>   of the great and only King,
>   the One who sits above the cherubim!
>   (Medley of passages from the Church Fathers)

Even creation itself shared ecstatically in the unheard of and indescribable event of the birth of God. Lossana: "Then creation marvelled at what it had never seen before ... a child who existed before its mother. Creation wondered and smiled.... Believe that when this Mother gave birth, there was a smile on the face of creation."[26] We might say that the whole of creation, wonderstruck, stopped its movement. In the *Protevangelium of James* Joseph, the husband of Mary, observes the marvel and says:

> I looked up to the vault of heaven, and saw it standing still, and I looked up to the air, and saw the air in amazement, and the birds of heaven remain motionless.... And behold, sheep were being driven and (yet) they did not come forward, but stood still; and the shepherd raised his hand to strike them (with his staff), but his hand remained up.... And then all at once everything went on its course (again).[27]

Along the same line — and this can serve as a conclusion and summary of what we have been discussing — John the Geometer found some especially felicitous, artistically dignified, and formally complete expressions that turn the heart's gaze to the wonders wrought by God:

> There is [in Genesis] a grandiose vision of a heaven that reaches beyond the eye's power to see. How astonishing that the earth should be grounded on nothing and that in obedience to the word of God the light should radiate out over the entire world....Yes, all this is extraordinary, but we are left even more astounded by the fact that God allowed himself to be formed and carried in a womb (in *TMPM* II, 897).

---

26. Cited in *TMPM* I, 599; III, 291.
27. *Protevangelium of James* 18, 2, in *New Testament Apocrypha*, ed. Wilhelm Schneemelcher, English trans. by R. McL. Wilson (2 vols.; Westminster: John Knox Press, 1991–92) I, 433.

"Who can fail to tremble at this thought? Who can fail to be amazed? Who can but break out into thanksgiving?" (Leo IV the Wise).

"In Mary a new and astonishing wonder has appeared, a wonder never seen since the beginning of the world: the childbearing of the Virgin, the newness of the Savior, the infancy of the Creator."[28]

At the center of this mystery and at the heart of this astonishment is the woman who first experienced it: Mary, the "Virgin Mother, daughter of her Son" (Dante, *Paradiso* XXXIII, 1), she who "to the wonderment of nature bore [her] Creator" (*LG* 69, cited in *RM* 51), she who alone cradled in her arms the only Son of almighty God.

Antonino Bello exclaims in inspired words, "You, Mary, are the first creature to have contemplated God's wonders as revealed in our history. You are the first to have contemplated the flesh of God-made-man, and we desire to look through the window of your eyes and enjoy these first fruits with you."[29]

b1. Mary, a Creature Set Between God and Humanity

> Hail, wondrous sight,
> greater than any miracle!
>
> (Sophronius of Jerusalem)

What kind of motherly heart was it that could receive God? In the Virgin of Nazareth, who was chosen to be the Mother of God, "there is a greatness that descends from on high and is not made by human hands. Orthodox theology speaks of 'divine wisdom,' the whisper of God's footsteps, the wind of the Spirit, the imprint of the Eternal

---

28. Chromatius of Aquileia, in *TMPM* III, 277.
29. Antonino Bello, *Maria, donna dei nostri giorni* (Cinisello Balsamo [Milan]: Ed. San Paolo, 1993) 46.

One. How, then, was the mantle of our humanity to be laid on his shoulders?"[30]

"Truly," Agnoletti remarks, "the most surprising and disconcerting aspect of the mystery of the divine mother-hood is the fact that it is an authentic reality, namely, that a poor, simple creature could become the true mother of God.... God will indeed empty, abase and humble himself by taking the state of a servant and becoming like other human beings in everything except sin (Phil 2:7–8; Heb 4:15), but he always remains God."[31] "He lowered himself to become little, but his greatness was never lost" (James of Batna). "How could he, the Son, be received into the tiny receptacle that is a human creature? For this to happen, the creature was exalted and strengthened (almost infinitely!) in order that as a mother she might provide suitable and, in a way, worthy hospitality to God" (Agnoletti).

St. Maximilian Kolbe explains:

> The being of every creature is shaped by the end it is to achieve and the missiom it must carry out. It comes into existence with powers suitable for accomplishing the task entrusted to it ... and throughout its life every-thing is arranged for it to pursue its goal more easily. All this holds also for the Virgin Mary.... God pre-pared her by granting her all those graces and privi-leges and leading her in time to the most complete likeness to the divine perfections of which any pure creature is capable, in order that she might worthily carry out her mission as Mother of God. Everything

---

30. On this set of themes see especially F. Boespflug, *Dio nell'arte* (Casale Monferrato: Marietti, 1986); C. Bo, *Sulle tracce di Dio nascosto* (Milan: Mondadori, 1984) 136.

31. Agnoletti, *Maria Sacramento di Dio*, 65–66.

she is and has is geared to the divine maternity; everything is essentially related to this.[32]

We must say, however, that the expression "Mother of
God" is beyond the ability of the human mind to understand:
"No human tongue is able to describe what Mary really is as
Mother of God."[33] This extraordinary and incomparable gift
elevated her to such a suprahuman state and to such heights
of dignity and holiness as to constitute a mystery of faith that
cannot be grasped by the human mind. "Of herself," says
Kolbe, "Mary is only a creature; but she is a being so exalted
by God that we would have to understand what God is in
order to understand what the Mother of God is."[34]

"Nothing in the world is comparable to Mary, the Mother
of God."[35] After God himself, nothing in heaven or on earth,
among human beings or among the angels, in time or in eternity, can be loftier or more sublime than the mystery of
the divine maternity (Agnoletti). Proclus of Constantinople
exclaims: "O man, survey in thought the whole of creation
and see whether there is anything equal to or greater than the
holy Virgin, the Mother of God. She alone received into her
virginal chamber him whom all of creation praises with fear
and trembling" (in *TMPM* I, 565).

Being the mother, the real mother of Christ, the man-God,
means that Mary — and the human race which she represents and bears within herself — has, in a way, crossed the
"borders of the divinity," as Cajetan used to say. She has
become akin to God in a union that is physical, biological,
and spiritual, and stands at the summit of the hierarchical
ladder of creaturely relationships with God, being inferior

---

32. Cited in E. M. Piacentini, *Maria nel pensiero di san Massimiliano M. Kolbe*, 46–48.
33. Guillaume-Joseph Chaminade, *La conoscenza di Maria. Diamanti di spiritualità*
    (Rome: Ed. Monfortane, 1984), 53.
34. Kolbe, *Scritti* III, 690.
35. Proclus of Constantinople, *Homily 5 on the Mother of God* 2 (PG 65:717).

only to the hypostatic union, with which her motherhood is closely linked.

The divine maternity leads us into a metaphysical abyss, that is, into an order of things that surpasses and transcends every human category and condition and creates in Mary a unique connaturality with God,[36] so that as a creature she is close to us but as Mother of God she is in contact with the divinity. Here we can understand the well-known words of St. Dionysius in which he tells us that in the presence of Mary he had to remind himself that she is a creature, lest he give her honor due to God alone.

"God has so honored Mary in making her the Mother of God that no one can render her any greater praise … ; in calling her the Mother of God one includes all her other dignities; no one can say anything greater of her or to her, even if one had as many tongues as there are blades of grass or stars in the heavens or grains of sand in the sea."[37] As the Mother of God she possesses a dignity that is quasi-infinite, given to her by the infinite good that is God.[38] Never has the dignity of the human person reached so high on the scale of true values as it has in the Virgin Mary.

God can create a greater and more perfect world, but he cannot raise any creature to a dignity higher than that to which he has raised Mary (St. Bonaventure). "Who is nobler than you, holy Mother of God?"[39] "You are more immense than the heavens, for you enclosed within yourself him whom the heavens cannot contain."[40] "Who will not call you blessed? … Who will not praise your immaculate birth, O Virgin?" (St. John Damascene).

---

36. See R. Laurentin, *La Vergine Maria* (Rome: Ed. Paoline, 1973⁴) 260–65.
37. Cantalamessa, *Maria uno specchio per la Chiesa*, 78.
38. St. Thomas Aquinas, *Summa of Theology* I, q. 25, a. 6, ad 4.
39. St. Ambrose of Milan, *De virginibus* 2, 6–7 (PL 16), in *TMPM* III, 163.
40. John Paul II, *Insegnamenti*, in *Marianum* 58 (1996) 513.

b2. In the Virgin Mother of God
Our Human Nobility Had Its Beginning

If the title "Mother of God" is glorifying for Mary, it is equally glorifying for us who have been redeemed by Jesus Christ and have become her children and the brothers and sisters of her divine Son. Astonishing, indeed, and immensely so, is the conception of Christ in the womb of Mary, but we ought to be no less astonished to see him becoming a guest in our hearts (St. Peter Damian). "By becoming a man the divine Person of the Son caused the highest possible development of the human person of Mary," elevating her to an immeasurably sublime state. "In doing so he also announced the development that every human being would derive from the Incarnation."[41]

Mary offered herself for this divine action, thus involving all of us in a wonderful adventure of greatness, joy, grace, and salvation. She appears to our eyes as the most lovable and admirable of all human creatures, "the boast of human nature" (Maximus the Confessor), "the glory of Jerusalem, the joy of Israel, the honor of our people" (Gradual of the Mass for the Immaculate Conception in the pre-Vatican II Sacramentary).

The choice of our sister to be Mother of God, the extraordinary graces and gifts given to her, and then the accomplishment in her of this exceptional event bestow such honor on the human race as to rouse the envy of the angels and every other spirit under God. For in Mary all of humanity has taken on its most complete form and reached its zenith. As Mother of "the fairest among the children of men" (Ps 45:3) she bears within her the thrilling Mystery, the manifest sign of the new dignity of the human race.

---

41. Galot, *Maria, la donna*, 106.

As we follow this line of thought we find the insights of artists who have been able to suggest in brief form the complexity of the whole. Indeed, in the mystical and truly inspired terzinas of the divine poet the approach to the mystery turns into an invocation that is liturgical in its style:

> O Virgin Mother ...
> you are she who so ennobled human nature
> that its maker did not disdain
> to make himself his own creature.[42]

What greater sign could God give of his admiration for his own creatures than to entrust to one of them the task of deeply imprinting her own likeness on the human nature of the Word? Think of the destiny of this body of Christ, which was not only to become the instrument of our salvation in the passion but, after robing itself in the splendor of the resurrection, was also to continue indefinitely its presence in the Church under the eucharistic signs and to give itself as food to all Christians. Then we begin to grasp the immensity of the divine act of trust that caused this body to be born of the Virgin Mary.

All over the universe and through all the centuries until the end of the world this body will bear the deep marks of its maternal origin. But, then, a son "never ceases to be the son of his mother. Therefore, throughout eternity, Jesus will always be the son of his mother, and she will always be his mother" (St. Maximilian M. Kolbe). Montfort adds: "Jesus [is] at present as much as ever the fruit of Mary — as heaven and earth repeat thousands of times a day, 'and blessed is the fruit of thy womb, Jesus' " (*True Devotion*, no. 33).

Pietro Parente, for his part, remarks that "from the moment of the Incarnation and throughout all eternity a human heart beats in the bosom of the Trinity: the heart of Jesus Christ.

---

42. Dante Alighieri, *Paradiso* XXXIII, 1–6.

This heart belongs to Mary, who clothed the Word with her virginal flesh."[43] John Paul II expressed the same idea when he said: "The Body which we eat and the Blood which we drink are the risen Lord's priceless gift to us who are pilgrims, but the sweet-smelling bread still carried within it the savor and perfume of the Virgin Mother. This Body and this Blood preserve their original form derived from Mary."[44] When we receive the eucharistic Jesus, we indeed receive his Body and his Blood, but we should reflect that these are also the body and blood of Mary, formed as they were in her most pure womb.

In virtue of the divine maternity God and man, while infinitely distant from each other, became one flesh in Mary. The Father's sending of his only-begotten Son among the children of men is a "guarantee that nothing truly human can be completely alien to him. The Mother, who provided the human womb of God incarnate, testifies to the solidarity between Creator and creature, to the depth to which the flesh is not foreign to the Spirit, and to the fact that God himself is as it were the adorable, transcendent womb of the entire human adventure" (Bruno Forte).

c) Mother in Every Way

It is clear that Mary's motherhood was not a matter of Christ's body alone, as the Nestorians erroneously taught. Mary is a mother in the true and proper sense, as all mothers are for their children. They do not give their children only bodies, while God bestows souls and personalities; no, they are mothers of concrete persons who exist and develop over time in those bodies. So too the Virgin of Nazareth is a mother in the fullest meaning of the term.

---

43. Pietro Parente, "La teologia della Madre del Buon Consiglio," in *Lo Spirito Santo e Maria Santissima*, 201.
44. Address to a General Audience, December 2, 1983.

To this end we need only look at the content of the gospels, which are always there to enlighten us: "Son, why have you done this to us? Your father and I have been looking for you with great anxiety" (Lk 2:48). The inherent power of these simple words immediately tells us the extent to which the physical aspect of motherhood is closely connected with a psychological and spiritual element. The physical element is joined with a deep interior involvement.

After giving birth to Christ Mary will perform for him all the tasks and duties of authentic motherhood, and will do so for many years until his death. Because she had a mother's thoughts and affections, her motherhood was complete, not only on the human physical level but also on the psychological and affective and the spiritual and moral levels. Important and basic though the biological aspect was, Mary's motherhood embraced more than that. In fact, the Fathers of the Church tended to play down that aspect in favor of the Virgin's "spiritual kinship" with her Son. "She was blessed not only because she had nursed the Son of God but also, and even more, because she nourished herself with the salutary milk of the word of God" (St. John Damascene).

The depth of her life of faith established between her and her Son a relationship even closer than that created by her bodily motherhood. The latter in fact was only an entirely personal privilege. But "if Mary had been only the physical mother of the Lord, we could not speak of her as 'blessed among women.' "[45] Her unique place and pre-eminent dignity spring more from her personal free commitment and her spiritual attitude of deliberate and therefore meritorious fidelity to her divine mission than from her happy role as the mother of the promised Messiah.

St. Augustine, a Father and Doctor of the Church, contributed more than anyone else to developing the connection

---

45. O. Casel, *Il mistero dell'Ecclesia* (Rome: Città Nuova, 1965) 438–40.

between Mary's motherhood according to the flesh and her motherhood according to the spirit, and he explicitly gives priority to the latter.

In commenting on the Synoptic text, "Who is my mother?" (Mt 12:48–49; Mk 3:33–35; Lk 8:21), St. Augustine attributes to the Virgin the supreme degree of that spiritual motherhood that flows from doing the Father's will. He writes: "In doing God's will ... physically Mary is only Christ's mother, but spiritually she is both mother and sister."[46] She "conceived the Son first in her heart and only then in her body." Before seeing Jesus she believed in him: "she was first a believer, then a mother." "Christ is Truth, Christ is flesh: Christ-the-Truth in Mary's mind, Christ-flesh in Mary's womb.... God has already been born in her soul. Therefore she could conceive him in her body."[47]

Unlike her physical motherhood, which is unique and unrepeatable, Mary shares her spiritual motherhood with the entire Church, in which she is and will remain the abiding model of how all souls can conceive Christ, carry him in their hearts, and give birth to him, through faith, in their own lives. In the flesh one woman alone is the Mother of Christ, but through faith all souls give birth to Christ when they accept the word of God. "Every soul that believes conceives ... the Word of God" (St. Ambrose) and thereby "makes himself or herself the sanctuary of the divine indwelling" (John Paul II). According to St. Augustine, "it can be said of every devout soul that it is the mother of Christ in the sense that by doing the will of Father with love, which is the most fruitful of all the virtues, it transmits life to all those on whom it imprints the form of Christ" (in *TMPM* III, 317).

---

46. St. Augustine, *Holy Virginity* 5–6; trans. Ray Kearney in *Marriage and Virginity* (The Works of Saint Augustine: A Translation for the 21ˢᵗ Century I/9; Hyde Park, NY: New City Press, 1999) 70.
47. St. Augustine, *Sermon* 25 (Sermones inediti) 7 (PL 46:938).

Another Father of the Church, this time in the East, echoes these thoughts: "Christ is always born mystically in the soul, taking flesh from those who are saved, and making a virginal mother of the soul that gives birth to him."[48]

3. *Mother of the Human Race*

All of us are God's gift to Mary;
we are his gift to her as a mother.

a) Introduction

"In Christian life everything is illumined by a sweet phrase that touches the heart: Mary, our Mother" (John XXIII). To this Mother, full of tender love, God willed to assign a unique place in the history of salvation. The development of this history in the life of Jesus the Redeemer reveals that Mary's mission did not end with the Incarnation; it was not limited to the birth of Jesus but has a role everywhere in the plan of salvation.

She is associated with the work of the Trinity in spreading and developing the divine life in the world. Here her function is essentially that of a spiritual motherhood that is as universal as the fatherhood of the Father: along with Jesus the whole human race is embraced by her motherhood. Due to the gift of her extraordinary divine motherhood, Mary is "super-full of grace," a grace that flows out abundantly to benefit all (St. Bernard). Mary received this unique wealth of grace only in order that she might share it, as a Mother, with all human beings. Every human creature, each of us, lives out his or her own life under the influence of the sweet and precious maternal love which the Love within the Trinity produced in her through a special outpouring of grace.

---

48. St. Maximus the Confessor, *Commentary on the Our Father* (PG 90:889).

This expansion of Mary's maternal role is not unjustified; as we shall show further on, the Bible itself contains the seed of its development.

b) A Mother on Everyman's Journey

> There is no life without a mother.
> Even the supernatural life has a mother:
> the mother of divine grace,
> the common refuge of all Christians.

In the order of nature human beings, who are social beings, are not and can never be alone. They are born, grow, and live in a society, that is, first and foremost, the family, which cannot come into being without a mother. The things a mother represents and does in and for the family cannot be completely described or listed, because many of these things, perhaps the majority of them, remain invisible and ineffable. It is certain, however, that her role is always essential and irreplaceable.

The feeling for a mother is one of the deepest and unsuppressible of the human heart. What would become of us, poor and weak as we are, if during our years of helplessness and need there were not someone to care for us and love us? If we did not carry in our being the certainty that we were valued by someone? Recourse to a mother is one of life's instincts: it is the first cry of the infant in the cradle and the last appeal of a stricken person in a hospital.

Theology teaches that grace does not destroy nature but completes it. Therefore, in his providential plan of salvation God has decreed that human beings cannot be alone in the supernatural order but are rather placed in the communal setting of a great family. This is the family of those redeemed by Christ and invigorated by the powerful movement of the divine Spirit and the radiant presence of a Mother: Mary. She is both a silent, unobtrusive presence and a presence that, more than that of any other mother, is active, creative, and truly concerned about the well-being of all her children. She is a mysterious but undeniable presence, interior to all Christians but also real, alive, and personal; a presence that is gentle and makes no one uneasy but instead opens the hearts of all to life, hope, and joy.

On this point Pope Paul VI wrote: "As in every family home, so too in his family, the Church, God has placed a woman, who in a hidden manner and in the spirit of service watches over it and with kindness protects it on its journey ... until it arrives at the glorious day of the Lord" (see *MC*, Introduction). "She has a motherly heart for us and, while dealing with the needs of each, is concerned about the entire human race" (Pius IX).

"Just as in the natural and corporeal generation of children there are a father and a mother, so too in the supernatural and spiritual generation there are a Father, Who is God, and a Mother, who is Mary" (*True Devotion*, no. 30). God willed that the supernatural life should not be less human than natural life, far from it, and that the human beings he was adopting in his own Son should not be half-orphans. Therefore he created the Madonna.[49] She is the mother of mothers, whose love "cannot be equaled by the sum total of the affection, kindness, and compassion of the mothers of the world" (Chiara Lubich).

The spiritual or supernatural motherhood of Mary completes the Incarnation in the economy of grace, for here the Incarnation displays its full reality as human beings receive the Mother of God as their own mother. Seeing this priceless gift the human heart can only overflow with joy and cry out in amazement: "Blessed assurance, safe refuge, the mother of God is our mother" (St. Anselm, *Prayer 3 to*

---

49. See Emile Mersch, *The Theology of the Mystical Body*, trans. Cyril Vollert (St. Louis: B. Herder, 1951).

St. Mary, Ward, 122). She is the most loving mother of us all! (Pius IX).

It is indeed a wonderful thing to be able to say that our mother is the Mother of Jesus, that the Mother of Jesus is our mother and that Jesus and we are children of the same mother. There is no element of Marian doctrine that is more widespread and universal in the Catholic Church, none more deeply appreciated or dearer to the heart of every believer. Vatican II laid a heavy emphasis on this truth; the experts agree in recognizing that one statement runs like a refrain through Chapter VIII of the *Constitution on the Church*. That statement is: Mary is our Mother. On a good fifteen occasions the conciliar document explains Mary's maternal role in relation to the human race.

Paul VI reminds us that in fact every period of the Church's history has benefited and will continue to benefit from the maternal presence of the Mother of God. The reason? She will always be indissolubly connected with the mystery of the Mystical Body, of whose head it has been written: Jesus Christ, the same yesterday and today and for all the centuries (*Signum Magnum*, no. 23).

If human motherhood never ceases as long as we are in this world, then much more will the spiritual motherhood of the Virgin Mother never be interrupted or reach its end but will continue without ceasing: "By her maternal charity, she cares for the brethren of her Son, who still journey on earth surrounded by dangers and difficulties, until they are led into their blessed home" (*LG* 62).

Gospel Pointers to the Spiritual Motherhood of Mary

The gospel sources tell us that the Mother of Jesus was attentive to the needs of others. For example, she visited Elizabeth who, being advanced in years, needed her help (see Lk 1:39–56); she sought a miracle for those who had no wine at the wedding feast of Cana (see John 2:1–11). In short, she seemed moved by a typically maternal kindness and concern for all men and women; John Paul II speaks of her "solicitude for human beings, her coming to them in the wide variety of their wants and needs" (*RM* 21). There is nothing to which her boundless maternal love is indifferent.

See her at the wedding in Cana, where the most attractive aspect of her maternal love comes out: the anticipation or understanding of need, even in the absence of words. According to the account by John the Evangelist, "on the third day there was a wedding in Cana in Galilee, and the mother of Jesus was there. Jesus and his disciples were also invited to the wedding. When the wine ran short, the mother of Jesus said to him, 'They have no wine' " (Jn 2:1–3). Mary is thus lovingly attentive, which is the first mark of a mother. Isn't it a fact that a mother grasps a child's need without the child saying anything? Outgoing love is able to see unspoken needs. The medieval writers had a fine saying: *Ubi amor, ibi oculus* (Where there is love, there is insight). Exactly! Where there is love, the eye anticipates the tongue. Those who genuinely love realize what the other needs and do not wait for the other to speak; they see with the heart.

This sensitive receptivity, this delicate kindness is the sign of a true mother, who not only helps those who ask for it but is able to anticipate needs with generosity. This outlook shines out in Mary and in the words full of solicitude which she utters at Cana: "They have no wine." Such a characteristic of the Mother of Jesus could not escape the notice of great geniuses. One of them has described it poetically:

> Not only does your kindness
> aid those who ask, but often
> you generously anticipate the plea.

That is what Dante has St. Bernard say in his Prayer to the Virgin (*Paradiso* XXXIII, 16–18), which draws upon the pure wellsprings of the word of God and the great Marian

Doctors. Mary is a mother because she loves and penetrates to places which the eyes of a non-lover can never reach. She "is very close to the faithful who petition her, and even to those who do not know they are her children" (*MC* 56).

"The description of the Cana event outlines what is actually manifested as a new kind of motherhood according to the spirit and not just according to the flesh" (*RM* 21). As at Cana, so too in every age, the noble Mother of God "places herself between her Son and mankind in the reality of their wants, needs and sufferings. She puts herself 'in the middle,' that is to say, she acts as a mediatrix, not as an outsider, but in her position as Mother. She knows that as such she can point out to her Son the needs of mankind" (ibid.).

It is important here to note that the devotion and concern of Mary for this poor couple, who had been unable to buy enough wine for the wedding feast, is a concern which especially recalls the providence of the Father. Of the latter Jesus will later say, with reference to material needs: "Your heavenly Father knows that you need them all" (Mt 6:32).

Mary's motherhood is not some kind of metaphysical motherhood but a motherhood in the true and proper sense. "She is more our mother — each and all of us — than our own mothers are; she loves us more than they do, so much so that we must say: she loves us more than can be said or thought."[50] Her heart "is the crown, the summary, and the perfection of all the works of the Most Holy Trinity that are to be found in the purely created world. For her heart contains within itself in an eminent degree everything that is great and rare in all pure creatures" (St. John Eudes). Like a crystal her heart reflects God.

God the creator has produced the wonder of wonders that is the hearts of mothers. If he is thus able to place in the hearts of ordinary mothers real marvels of deep, tender love

---

50. John the Geometer, *Homily on the Dormition*, in *TMPM* II, 967.

that is stubborn and we might even say irrational, a love ready for every sacrifice and every renunciation, what will he not place in the heart of this Mother par excellence? In fact, her love for the only-begotten Son and for us, her adoptive children, ought to be in a way equal to that of the Father.[51]

We can indeed say that where Mary acts as a mother, heaven becomes closer and the world more lovable. At every happy or sad stage of our journey, in every situation, and on whatever road her child is traveling, the power of Mary's maternal love is present. It gives assurance for the morrow and crosses the thresholds of human weakness, the power of evil, and death.

In pre-Christian religions the cult of mother goddesses showed insight into the archetypal depths of fecundity, of the capacity for limitless dedication, and of the enormous power of hope, all of these represented by the life-giving woman. But all these values are really recapitulated, renewed, and brought to their completion in Mary, Mother of God and of the human race. For she bears within her, fully formed, the imprint and power of God.

I think there could be no better conclusion to this first part of our reflections on Mary's spiritual motherhood than to turn to one of the countless prayers addressed to her over the centuries by her faithful devotees. Let us pause for a moment with this poet who, in church, after having adored Jesus in the Eucharist, rapturously greets the Virgin Mother in the silence of his heart:

> I have nothing to offer you, nothing to ask....
> I come only to gaze upon you, Mother,
> to gaze upon your face
> and let my heart sing in its own language ...

---

51. Emile Mersch, in *Meditazioni Mariane*, 176–77.

and weep for happiness,
knowing that I am your son,
and that you are here …
simply because you exist, Mother.…
Thank you!

(Paul Claudel)

c) How and When a Mother?

c1. *Mother of Divine Grace*

What shall we say, then, brothers?
Isn't Mary our mother?
Certainly, brothers! She is truly our mother.
Through her, in fact, we were born
not into the world but into God.

(Aelred of Rievaulx)

In explaining Mary's motherhood of grace or spiritual motherhood we must refer directly to the person of the Father, who communicates to Mary not only a fruitfulness directed to the motherhood of his own divine Son, but also a real fruitfulness in the realm of grace and in relation to all of the redeemed. This is her spiritual motherhood, which is a sharing in the active generation of God's adoptive children. In adopting human beings as his children in Christ, the Father asks for the maternal co-operation of the Virgin, so that Mary plays a maternal role in the entire work of the distribution of grace.

The mission which Mary assumed and carries out for her children is suggested by the very title "Mother of God." In fact, as the Mother of God Mary shares in the event in which God makes his maximal self-communication to humankind. She is called upon to cooperate with the Father in bringing Christ to the human race and revealing him to it. She becomes thereby, in a sense, the first missionary: the one who by bringing Christ into the world gives him to all: "For over two thousand years the Church has been the cradle in which Mary places Jesus so that all peoples may worship and contemplate him" (*IM* 11).

As a matter of fact, many are the Fathers who, on the basis of what Scripture says about Mary's maternal role, have seen in the Mother of Christ the mother also of the work of our salvation. As we glean in the rich and extensive fields they have left us, we find valuable statements on this point: "In bringing Jesus Christ, our Savior and our life, into the world, Mary gave birth to us all for our salvation and life" (St. William). "In giving birth to Life she has also given birth to the living, that is, to Christians."[52] "She is the mother of the Life by which all human beings live; in giving birth to this Life, she also, in a sense, gave rebirth to all who would live by that Life. Only one was brought to birth, but all of us were reborn in God, there in the pure womb of Mary" (Guerric of Igny). "By the very fact that she brought forth Life for us, she brought forth all of us into Life" (William of Newburgh).

St. Anselm explains even more fully the object of Mary's spiritual motherhood by defining it as embracing the entire work of salvation: "You are the mother of justification and the justified, mother of reconciliation and the reconciled, the mother of salvation and the saved: the mother of 'things recreated,' the mother of the restoration of all things" (*Prayer* 52, 7–8; PL 158:956AB, 957A).

Analogous in meaning is the title "Mother of Grace," the use of which Geoffrey of St. Victor justifies by basing it not only on Mary's intercessory power, which can obtain every grace for us from the Father, but, above all, on the fact that Christ can be said to be "grace" in his very person. But from whom does Christ, this Grace in person, come but from Mary, who "gives birth to him in every soul" (St. Ephraem), in every heart that is reborn in God? If Paul, a servant and

---

52. Cited by A. Amato in *Maria e lo Spirito Santo*, 52.

apostle of Christ, can tell the faithful "I became your father in Christ Jesus through the gospel" (1 Cor 4:15), how much more can Mary, the Mother of Christ, say that she is their mother! She is mother wherever Christ is Redeemer; she is present and active throughout the entire extent of the mystery of salvation. "Wherever the humanity of Christ is the wellspring of salvation, there Mary is as the one who gave him his flesh, there is the person of the Virgin and her activity as mother. Where Christ is present in his mystery and makes himself present with his saving activity, there too Mary is present in communion with the Trinity and with the Church."[53]

The whole life of the Blessed Virgin is summed up in her ministry of motherhood by which she gives her Son to souls. Even in glory she will continue to be the giver of her Son. If we can be "founded" on the apostles because they first transmitted the word of life to us, much more can we be said to be "founded" on Mary and "birthed" by her, since she transmitted the very author of the word and this not to one or other Church, as each of the apostles did, but to the entire world (Raniero Cantalamessa). It is this prerogative that makes Mary our mother in the order of grace: mother of the children of God, "mother of all those who are divinized by grace, because she obtains this divinization for them" (Theophanes of Nicea). Very important in this context is the assertion of St. John Damascene: "The holy Virgin is called Theotokos [Mother of God] not only because of the nature of the Word but also because of the divinization of the human race" (*The Orthodox Faith* 3, 12; PG 94).

It is encouraging to find that agreement on these truths extends even to the initiators of the Reformation, who grant Mary the title and prerogative of Mother, not only of Christ

---

53. Jesús Castellano Cervera, "La presenza di Maria nel mistero del culto. Natura e significato," *Marianum* 58 (1996) 395.

but of us and our salvation. In a sermon during the Mass of the Nativity Luther said: "This is the overflowing consolation given us by God in his goodness, that if human beings believe, they can boast of so precious a blessing, namely, that Mary is their true mother, Christ their brother, and God their Father.... If you believe, you are then truly in the womb of the Virgin Mary and her dear children."

In its present exercise Mary's motherhood in the order of grace is not limited to intercession or motherly concern. It is an activity that has for its aim the two characteristic elements of motherhood: the generation and education of Christians. For this reason it fully merits the name "motherhood."

c2. Special Aspects and Characteristics of the Motherhood of Grace

I) Overview

The operation of Mary's motherhood of human beings can be looked at in its two important phases: its origin and its actualization in several stages over time. For the sake of a clearer and more complete understanding it is appropriate first to give an overview and then to dwell on particular details.

We may begin by saying, first of all, that the establishment of the motherhood of grace had its origin in the divine plan for saving the human race through Christ, born of a woman (Gal 4:4), in keeping with the eternal love of the Father, who after creating human beings in his own image willed to unite them to himself as his children. The very abundant ecclesial tradition speaks often of the motherhood of Mary, linking it to the fatherhood of God and the call of human beings to become children of God.

The plan of salvation became a reality in the Incarnation; thus it began in time with Mary's acceptance of the proposal God made to her through the angel. With her

"Yes" to motherhood Mary acquiesced in the Father's plan and became from that moment on the mother of all the redeemed. Thus the "Yes" at the Annunciation, while leading directly to the conception of the Redeemer, led indirectly to the rebirth of each of us. This spiritual motherhood became operative in Mary through her active cooperation with Christ for the salvation of humanity. On the cross, that is, at the very heart of the mystery of redemption (*RM* 19), Jesus entrusted to Mary the Christians of every age, that she might be their mother.

All this being said, it remains to emphasize the motherhood of Mary in relation to her individual sons and daughters. It becomes a reality for each of them at the moment of their baptism, in their growth throughout life, and in their glorification in heaven. Mary's motherhood thus lasts through time and reaches into eternity. F. Jürgensmeir had good reason for writing that "the spiritual motherhood of Mary was to be permanently active as long as the Church exists on earth. Otherwise it would be difficult not to find in God's work a lack of logic and a breakdown of harmony."[54]

II) Analysis

IIa) *The Mother of the Head Is Also Mother of the Members*

In the New Testament we find very important data confirming the doctrine of Mary's spiritual motherhood as embracing all human beings, even while remaining based on her physical motherhood, which places her in a unique and exclusive relationship with Christ. As a matter of fact, the principal foundation of Mary's motherhood in the order of grace is her divine motherhood. For, just as the Virgin gave birth to the Head (Christ Jesus) of the new human race, so

---

54. F. Jürgensmeir, *Il Corpo mistico di Cristo come principio dell'ascetica* (Brescia: Morcelliana, 1954) 361ff.

too she continues down the centuries to give birth to the Body (the Church) and its new members. It is her concrete motherhood that gives rise to her spiritual motherhood in relation to all the redeemed.

Psalm 87, which the liturgy applies to the Madonna, says (vv. 4–6): "[They shall say] of Palestine, Tyre, Ethiopia: 'This man was born there [i.e., Zion].' And of Zion they shall say: 'One and all were born in her'.... They shall note, when the peoples are enrolled: 'This man was born there.' " It is true: all of us have been born there! It is also to be said of Mary, the new Zion: "One and all were born in her." Of me, you, and every person, even those who do not yet know it, it is written in God's book: "This man was born there." Have we not been "born anew ... through the living and abiding word of God" (1 Pet 1:23)? Have we not been "born ... of God" (Jn 1:13) and "born [again] of water and Spirit" (Jn 3:5)? This is completely true, but it does not deny that in a different, subordinate, and instrumental sense we have also been born of the faith and suffering of Mary (Raniero Cantalamessa).

Together with St. Pius X the ordinary magisterium of the Church appeals to a quite specific principle: "Is not Mary the Mother of Christ? Therefore she is our Mother too" (*NDM* 836). As Mother of Christ, she must also be the Mother of Christians, mother of both the head and the members, because head and body form a single Christ. For this reason St. Leo the Great could write: "The begetting of Christ is the origin of the Christian people, and the birthday of the head is also the birthday of the body" (*Sermon* 26; PL 54:2123). All we who are united to Christ and are members of his body (see Eph 5:20) have come forth from the womb of Mary like a body united to its head. Montfort argues that

> if Jesus Christ, the Head of men is born in her, the pre-destinate, who are the members of that Head, ought

also to be born in her, by a necessary consequence. One
and the same mother does not bring forth into the world
the head without the members, or the members without
the head; for this would be a monster of nature. So in
like manner, in the order of grace, the Head and the
members are born of one and the same Mother; and if a
member of the Mystical Body of Christ — that is to
say, one of the predestinate — was born of any other
mother than Mary, who has produced the Head, he
would not be one of the predestinate, not a member of
Jesus Christ, but simply a monster in the order of grace
(*True Devotion*, no. 32).

The inseparability of the head from his mystical body
means that since the head was formed by the Spirit of God in
the womb of Mary, so too the mystical body of Christ must
be formed by the Spirit in Mary. The Fathers of the Church
explain their faith in this matter in especially felicitous language. "In giving birth to the firstborn [Christ] of the Christian family, the Virgin gave birth also to all the other brothers
and sisters of the firstborn" (Rupert of Deutz). "In giving
birth to the natural Son of God she gave birth also to the
adoptive children of God" (Guerric of Igny). "In giving birth
to the grain of wheat [Christ] she also gave birth to the
mass of wheat that has sprung from it" (St. Ambrose; Ray-
mond Giordano). "At the moment in which she became
Mother of the Creator, she also truly became the Queen, the
mother of all creatures" (St. John Damascene).

We all became children of Mary in her Son and with her
Son, our brother: "The same virginal Mother, who had the
resplendent privilege of bearing the only Son of God the
Father, embraces that same only Son in all his members and
does not disdain to accept the name of Mother of all those in
whom she sees her Christ already formed or to be formed"
(Guerric of Igny). Her heart was not formed with Christ

alone in view but was created also for his Mystical Body: "She embraces in a single love both Christ and us, his members" (Dom C. Marmion).

What has been said makes it clear that Christians did not begin to belong to Mary only from the moment in which the Savior on his cross solemnly entrusted them to his loving Mother. It is true that the price of our redemption was paid to divine justice on Calvary. It was there that the work of regeneration was completed, there that Jesus merited for us the grace of adoption and glorification, and there, strictly speaking, that Mary gave birth to us into the life of faith. Nevertheless it was not at that point that she began to be our Mother.

Rather we must go back to Mary's "Yes" and to the Incarnation, that is, to the moment when the Virgin, accepting Jesus, also conceived and accepted all of us into her womb. It was there that Mary began to be our mother, there that she began to carry all of us in her womb, for in carrying the Savior she was also carrying all whose lives were contained in that of the Savior. In conceiving the Head Mary also "conceived," that is, accepted along with him, at least objectively, us who are his members.[55] This amounts to saying that the Virgin Mary's "Yes" was, in a way, a "Yes" spoken to us as well.

Like her physical motherhood, Mary's spiritual motherhood had and still has two phases: conception and birth. Neither of these is sufficient by itself. Mary experienced both phases: she conceived us spiritually and gave birth to us spiritually. If God loved us first (1 Jn 4:10), so did the Virgin Mary love us first, when by her "Yes" she bestowed her motherhood on us.

---

55. These ideas are forcefully set down in the writings of the Fathers and have been confirmed in authoritative statements of the Church's magisterium. Testimonies can be easily multiplied; it will be enough to mention, in addition to St. Anselm, Saints Albert the Great, Bonaventure, and Alphonsus Liguori, and in our time John Paul II.

IIb) Mary Is Our Mother Inasmuch as She Cooperated in the Restoration of Our Supernatural Life

Mary of Nazareth, a total offering,
without reservation, a life spent
that the redemptive love of Son might
embrace the human race and all things.[56]
Not without a painful birth did she call us all
and give us a new birth into eternal life
in her Son and with her Son.[57]

Everything that is expressed in these powerful, luminous, and penetrating lines may be regarded as the nucleus of the truth we are explaining, for they contain in concentrated form the truth that is the second foundation of Mary's supernatural motherhood. This truth is Mary's association with her Son in the work of human salvation. We need to reference to the fact that the person of Mary, especially in the theological plot of the fourth gospel, is always seen in a profoundly christological context. The latter supplies, from beginning to end, the framework of Christ's messianic activities; for the fourth evangelist the Mother of Jesus is part of "the hour of the Son."

In the event at Cana, which "like a symphonic prelude anticipates the major themes of the fourth gospel" (A. Serra), Mary provides the impulse for the "signs" given by the Son of God, who thereby elicits the inchoative faith of the disciples in him as Messiah (Jn 2:11). Later, on Calvary, at the foot of the cross, she signals "the fulfillment of the Scriptures" (Jn 19:28). John, we see, interprets Mary's actions not as anecdotal material but as an essential part of the history of salvation.

---

56. Paolo Pifano, *Tra teologia e letteratura. Inquietudine e ricerca del sacro negli scrittori contemporanei* (Cinisello Balsamo [Milan]: Ed. Paoline, 1990) 220.
57. *Mariale*, q. 29, III, in Galot, *Maria, la donna*, 367.

Under the guidance of the Holy Spirit the Virgin devoted herself unreservedly to the mystery of human redemption; her participation in the historical unfolding of the mystery of Christ was close, active, and foreseen in the divine plan of salvation. As a result, the gospel events in which she played a part were saving actions done by Christ in union with his Mother (see *LG* 55–58; 61).

> She conceived, brought forth, and nourished Christ, she presented him to the Father in the temple, shared her sufferings as he died on the cross. Thus, in a wholly singular way she cooperated by her obedience, faith, hope and burning charity in the work of the Savior in restoring supernatural life to souls. For this reason she is a mother to us in the order of grace (*LG* 61).

Mary, thus defined by her most important role, is the woman with whom God made a covenant. By dedicating herself to this covenant she collaborated in a decisive way in the formation of a new human race. By believing and accepting the proposal made to her by God she collaborated actively and effectively at every point in the Savior's mission and thereby contributed to communicating the divine life that comes from God and was obtained for humankind by the sacrifice of Christ (Jean Galot).

The Virgin Mary played an exceptional part in the regeneration of the human race in several ways. There was the universality of her influence, inasmuch as her "Yes" marked the beginning of the new economy; her unique functions as Mother of the Life that renews all things; and the exceptional nature of her role, since she was united to Christ by close and indissoluble bonds.[58]

---

58. See Stefano De Fiores, *Maria nel mistero di Cristo e della Chiesa. Commento al capitolo mariano del Concilio Vaticano II* (Rome: Ed. Monfortiane, 1984³) 105–6.

From cradle to grave, in childhood and in old age, on joyous days and during sad nights, Christians owe everything to Mary: the blessings of baptism and a religious education, the blessings of conversion and perseverance, of strength and courage in struggles, of protection and defense in trials. She is a refuge and source of consolation in misfortunes, a source of counsel and wisdom in the choice of a state of life and in the performance of duties, and the source of grace to do good and avoid evil. In short, everything that has for its purpose to preserve and revive in us the life of Jesus Christ comes to us from her tender maternal love.[59]

IIc) Mother of Individual Sons and Daughters

In becoming Mother of Christ, Mary became the spiritual mother of all human beings who come into this world, in order that these might become children of God under her maternal guidance and protection. It is an uncontrovertible truth, says St. Bernard, that the life of Christians develops under the shadow of Mary's maternal protection; for each and every one of them she remains an open and always reachable door, and her womb remains spiritually open. This maternal womb, says St. Irenaeus, which the Infinitely Pure One made pure by taking flesh from her, is the permanent source of the rebirth of human beings in God, provided they accept him in faith as "God with us through the Virgin," that is, as Savior (see *TMPM* I, 155).

Mary's spiritual motherhood does not signify simply a maternal care or sensibility that calls for a response of filial trust and love. It signifies, first of all, her most fundamental task, which is to cooperate in giving birth into the Christian life, as well as in developing this life in each soul (Jean Galot). Mary is present, and plays a real maternal role, to all who have become sons and daughters in the Son through the

---

59. See G. J. Chaminade, *La conoscenza di Maria*, 75.

power of grace. As a result, Christians who become children of the Father become children also of Mary, just as Christ himself did. We could not be brethren of Jesus if we did not have Mary as a mother. Montfort: "All the true children of God, the predestinate, have God for their Father and Mary for their mother. He who does not have Mary for his mother does not have God for his Father.... Alas! God the Father has not told Mary to dwell in them, for they are Esaus" (*True Devotion*, no. 30).

As Mother of divine grace, the Virgin encounters human creatures in a completely transparent way, at the root of their being, in the heart of their hearts, in the place in which they are accepted by the Son in order that they may be presented to the Father and may receive the gift of life in the Son and for his sake (Bruno Forte). Mary fulfills this role especially at the moment of baptism, where she is present as a mother at the spiritual birth of each member of the Church.

At the very moment in which human beings are about to be incorporated into the mystical Christ through baptism, at the moment in which their potentiality for a supernatural life, received at the Incarnation of Christ, is about to be actuated, at that moment the mystery of Nazareth is repeated for them. Thus Mary repeats her consent and her motherhood for the human beings whom she births individually into the supernatural life through the working of the Holy Spirit. She renders explicit their membership in the Body of Christ, which was already implicit from the moment of the Incarnation.[60]

In the rite of baptism, for example, the priest asks the candidate "Do you wish to be baptized?" and receives the answer "Yes, I do." This "Yes" is a repetition of Mary's *fiat*. There is but one difference: Mary uttered her *fiat* on behalf of the entire human race. This new "Yes" is from the individuals who receive baptism at this moment and whose

---

60. See L. H. Marvulli, *Maria Madre del Corpo Mistico* (Rome: 1948) 49.

rebirth into the Christian life really coincides with their birth from Mary. They become Christians because they become brothers and sisters of Christ and because at the same time they become the sons and daughters of the very Mother of Jesus, who recognizes and loves her own Son in each of her adoptive children.

Just as the Virgin's activity in the Incarnation was to form Jesus Christ, so too, in her mystical motherly role in relation to other human beings her task is to form Jesus Christ in them, in cooperation with the Holy Spirit.[61] Thus the motherhood which became hers at the moment of the virginal birth achieves its ultimate effect when, mirroring the divine paternity and in cooperation with the Father, she gives birth to a new human race in Christ.

As we all know, the role of a mother does not end when she gives birth to a child; a true mother sees to the growth and full development of her child. The same is true of Mary as a mother. She does not stop at an affective relationship but is committed to forming the children of God as they develop the grace given them at their baptism and live as true brothers and sisters of Christ.

The Final Puebla Document, issued by the Latin American Church, reminds us: "Mother Mary awakens the filial heart that lies sleeping in every human being. In this way she prompts us to develop the life of baptism" (no. 295). The aim of her spiritual teaching is "producing in the children the spiritual characteristics of the first-born Son" (*MC* 7). To be the mother of Christians and to form Christ in all the members of his mystical body are one and the same thing. She "longs to form her own Son in all her adoptive children.... She gives birth to them daily with ardent desire and solicitous affection as long as they have not yet reached

---

61. Roberto Masi, in *Lo Spirito Santo e Maria Santissima*, 116.

maturity in her Son"; they are the "good fruit which her heart ceaselessly produces."[62]

St. Augustine says that all the predestined in this world are hidden in the bosom of the Most Holy Virgin, where they are preserved, nourished, protected, and brought to full maturity by this good Mother, until finally she gives birth to them into glory after death. Indeed, with good reason and with even greater validity and truth, we can apply to the Virgin Mary the thought of the Apostle: "I have a mother's affection for them [the children of God] until Jesus Christ is formed in them in a fully mature way."[63]

In this context I cannot pass over in silence some interesting words of Archbishop Carli that are filled with meaning and truth: "The individual faithful have an even greater need of Mary's permanent motherhood, because they are always 'little children' (Mt 18:3; Lk 10:21) requiring rebirth in the spirit ... growth in truth and grace, and repeated reconciliation with God because they are exposed to the forces of dissolution (Gal 4:19)."[64]

As the holy Virgin Mary nourished, formed, and educated Jesus, so too she must nourish the soul with the milk of her grace, form it with sensitivity, and educate it. At her knee the soul must learn to know and love Jesus. From her heart it must derive love of him and even learn to love him with her heart and to become like him through love (St. Maximilian M. Kolbe).

Why the Motherhood of Grace?

When we ask why Mary's motherhood in the order of grace was established for the growth of every Christian, it is important to recognize in it a sign, especially accessible to the

---

62. Guerric of Igny, PL 184:205A, in *Marianum* 54 (1992) 250.

63. See Eph 4:13. The verse was dear to Montfort: *AES* 214, 226; SM 67; *True Devotion*, nos. 119, 156, 164, 168.

64. Archbishop Luigi Maria Carli in *DME*, cited in *Marianum* 38 (1976) 475.

human psyche, of the fatherhood of God. In order to make his fatherhood better understood, the Father created a maternal face to be present in the communication of grace, and he made this motherhood an image of his own fatherhood.

It is only too obvious that "mother" is one of the most deeply rooted symbols in human psychic experience.

> Human beings are very sensitive to the presence of a maternal face; in such a face they can more easily see the face of the Father. They know from experience the unlimited devotion and indulgent kindness of a mother; when they look to Mary they sense that in their spiritual life they are guided and protected by a love that is full of compassion. In this way they are led to discover the deepest reality of grace, which is the merciful goodness of God, who stoops to them to bring them to the happiness of the divine life. In his inscrutable plan the Father willed to give humanity the most moving image of his fatherhood, namely, the motherhood of Mary. He willed, as it were, to allow human beings to experience something of his divine fatherhood.[65]

God gave Mary to all human beings as a solicitous mother in the realm of grace in order to help them acquire the grace of eternal salvation, and so be reborn and sanctified in a more human way and in a way that is easier and more suited to their condition. By her tender maternal presence she helps make Christians feel the warmth of the Father's divine love. Thus the role of the Virgin Mother cannot be regarded as simply an addition to an already complete economy of grace. It is in no way superfluous because it is meant to reveal and express what is most essential in grace itself: the goals sought by the Father in his goodness. Thus understood,

---

65. Galot, *Maria, la donna*, 377–78.

Mary's role is part of the fundamental nature of grace (Jean Galot).

Max Thurian has written: God the Father has given us Mary as a Mother in the order of grace, because Christianity would seem to be really intolerable without the feminine, virginal, and maternal tenderness of Mary, who gives Christ to us. Another reason: because the Church would be seen as an arid, shut-in structure in both its authority and its ministry, were it not permeated by and, as it were, included in the warmhearted and reassuring image of Mary. In this sense, the Lord Jesus reveals himself as affectionate: he is God, the Son of Mary (in *Avvenire*, March 26, 1987, p. 3).

As we end these reflections, it is useful to remind ourselves that Mary is not a substitute for the Father in the latter's proper activity. "It is he himself who wills this motherhood to be an expressive image of his fatherhood. The motherliness of Mary does not dispense Christians from turning to the Father; on the contrary, it bids them to turn to him and discover his fatherly face" (Jean Galot).

The Virgin's maternal activity in the lives of her children is concerned not with herself but with them and, behind them, the Father's plan.

IId) A Motherhood of Example

Holy Father, in your limitless goodness
you have given your Church, in Mary
   of Nazareth,
a mirror and model of the worship that pleases
   you.... In her school may we find
the model of evangelical life ...
and learn to love you above all things.

(Preface from the Italian Sacramentary)

"When we gaze on Mary, we are meant to see ourselves reflected in a model which God has given to us for our advancement and our sanctification" (John Paul II). Christians, whose task it is to translate the Creator's plan into historical action, must necessarily encounter this luminous model. For, according to biblico-Judaic teaching, spiritual fatherhood or motherhood essentially involves exemplarity; that is, spiritual fathers or mothers are examples, models of life, for their children.[66]

Now, it is undeniable that this aspect of spiritual motherhood has its highest expression and complete effectiveness in the spiritual motherhood of Mary, who exerts a strong influence on believers by her example; in her God has shown us, on the scene of history, what he wants from all of us. Every aspect of her person (virtues, privileges, and so on) has an ecclesial dimension and implication. That is, she is a "type," a "model," a "prefiguration" of what the entire Church is called to become both on its pilgrimage and in glory.

The Virgin, who gives free rein to the Lord, becomes for believers a perfect paradigm of Christian life and a paradigm of humanity's behavior toward God. She gives each of us the impulse and the strength to go to God with our whole being: intellect, will, heart, affections, sentiments, and actions. In a few words, she tells us what it means to make a place for the Lord. As a supreme model of faith, charity, and complete union with Christ, her life shines out as a model of virtue for the whole community of the elect and illumines all the faithful (see *LG* nos. 53, 63, and especially 65). The children will put on all the virtues of their Mother if they keep their eyes on her example in order to follow it in their own lives (see Paul VI, *MC* 57).

Just as every mother in the natural order passes on something of her own character to her children, so in the supernat-

---

66. By way of examples see 1 Cor 4:15 and 1 Thes 2:7, 11. For comment and explanations I refer the reader to A. Serra, "Bibbia," in *NDM* 289–90.

ural order there is and ought to be a likeness between Mary, the Mother, and Christians, her children. In fact, if they are to be authentically her children, they must commit themselves to being like her.

Her magnificent example urges us on not only to a deeper experience of God but also to an active involvement in the world through concrete activities and choices. Only those who become like Mary, the handmaid of the Lord, will be able to become truly like Christ, our supreme model and inspiration.

As a complete model of evangelical life, the Virgin Mother can say with Paul, and with better reason than Paul: "Be imitators of me, as I am of Christ" (1 Cor 11:1; see also 1 Cor 4:16). In her "the entire Church in the incomparable variety of its life and activity attains to its earliest form of the perfect imitation of Christ" (Paul VI). If we love, we will imitate.

It has been written that in the future it will not be the intellectuals who speak of Mary, but the witnesses, those who after her example commit themselves to bringing about the reign of God.[67]

IIe) The Most Far-reaching Extension of Motherhood: A Motherhood Proclaimed from the Cross

At the foot of the cross,
through her Son's testament of love,
Mary extended her motherhood
to all the human beings
who are reborn from the death of Christ
for a life that will have no end.

(Preface for Marian feasts in the Italian Sacramentary)

---

67. S. De Fiores, "Mariologia," in Pifano, *Tra teologia e letteratura*, 218.

1. A Universal Motherhood

Mary's motherhood in relation to humanity was confirmed by the irrevocable words of Jesus on Calvary, during the moments when he was completing his redemptive sacrifice. "One can say that if Mary's motherhood of the human race had already been outlined, now it is clearly stated and established. It emerges from the definitive accomplishment of the Redeemer's Paschal Mystery" (*RM* 23), as a universal motherhood, in keeping with the universality of the work of redemption. On Calvary Mary received a motherhood that was limitlessly open in its extension and in the mystery it contains, a motherhood that extends to all human beings, all the heirs to the new covenant, all the children of the cross, who are reborn from the redemptive death of the Savior. Mary, then,

> is not only the mother of every disciple who adheres to Christ through faith but also the mother of every human being, since each is called to accept the grace of Christ. Analogously, she is not only the mother of the Church that presently exists in a visible form, but the mother also of what may be described as the Church that is "becoming," that is, mother of the progressive unification of humankind in faith in Christ. This motherhood with its limitless boundaries enables her better to represent the spiritual paternity of the Father, since it is a motherhood in the order of grace (Jean Galot).

The blood of the crucified Christ covers the whole of creation and has reconciled all things with God (Col 1:20; Heb 2:14–16). These universal, indeed cosmic dimensions of the salvation wrought by Christ's sacrifice foretell the sovereign dominion of the Father, which will reach its fullness at the end of time. Against this background, we see that beneath the cross Mary is called upon to cooperate more closely, by her maternal activity, in the extension of God's fatherhood in the world. Here, looking back to what had been said at the time of the virginal birth of the Son, we see a fuller development of her role as representative of God's fatherhood and as cooperator with this fatherhood.

The cooperation of Mary in the Incarnation through her motherhood implies her association with the divine love with which the Father gives his Son to humanity. Moreover, this love of the Father takes its most sublime form in the drama of the passion. Given these two truths, we cannot fail to admit that it is first and foremost here on Calvary that in virtue of her active participation in the sacrifice of her Son Mary enters into the mystery of God's fatherhood at a depth hitherto unknown. At the very moment in which the earth was rendered fruitful by the precious blood of the man-God and in which all were washed and cleansed by that blood, the fruitfulness of Mary was also emphasized. "She offered the Son to the eternal Father on Golgotha, making a complete sacrifice of all her maternal rights and of her motherly love.... Thus she who was the bodily Mother of our Head could become the spiritual Mother of all his members for new reasons of suffering and glory" (Pius XII).

J. Galot comments that it is helpful to determine, in the redemptive sacrifice, the element of Mary's co-merit by analogy with the merits of Christ. Jesus, though he was God, humbled himself through obedience even to the point of death on a cross; thereby he merited his power as glorified Savior. Analogously, Mary, though she was Mother of God, devoted herself to a perfect obedience that meant a complete sacrifice of her maternal affections; she merited thereby a spiritual motherhood in relation to all human beings. This motherhood, while being a result of her being Mother of God, flows more directly from her participation in the redemptive sacrifice.[68]

---

68. Galot, *Maria, la donna*, 292.

In her "Yes" to the Incarnation of the Word Mary represented the whole human race. By her consent to the sacrifice of her Son, the representational character of her motherhood of that Son reached an even higher level. Now, the close and exceptional relationship that united her to her Son associated her with the representational role of the Savior himself.

As Mother of him who is God, the Totally Other and the Savior of the world, Mary now acquired a motherhood capable of influencing the whole of humankind. She is the only created person who has a universal role in the divine economy of salvation.

2. The Hour of Birth

> Though blessed, you one day wept,
> nor will a day come when you forget those
> tears; every day will speak of them,
> and the many centuries that have passed.[69]

Love impels one to work together with others. If this is true of everyone, it is extraordinarily true of two inseparable persons: Jesus and Mary of Nazareth.

It is not by chance that at the hour of the crucifixion the gospel mentions the presence on Calvary of the Mother of Jesus, of her who was "in a singular way the generous associate ... of the Lord" (*LG* 61). She was too closely bound to her Son not to be with him even (and I would say above all) during this fateful time so full of mystery and of universal salvation. "God brought her to this point in order that she might give the supreme proof of love" (Rene Voillaume).

We know very well that if the greatest proof of love is to give one's life for those one loves, then the greatest suffering is also the greatest proof of love. So it was with Mary. As a result of her complete obedience on Calvary, her love was

---

69. A. Manzoni, *Il nome di Maria*, vv. 57–60.

expanded to the point of becoming the source of a new motherhood. At the Annunciation the "Yes" of Mary's heart led to the conception of Jesus; now the time for the pains of birth had come.

Odo of Morimond is one of so many who have perceived in Mary's sufferings beneath the cross the element of universality and of redemptive value (a value obviously different from that of the Son's sufferings). He has written some especially enlightening words that contain a whole theology of the Virgin's spiritual motherhood: "She was mother of all and therefore had to suffer for all, and, in keeping with her name, had to drink the cup of bitterness for all."[70] St. Alphonsus M. Liguori, for his part, says that by her sufferings the Virgin gave birth to all of us into eternal life, so that all of us can describe ourselves as the children of Mary's birth pangs (*The Glories of Mary*). We can apply to her the words of the Apostle: "My children, for whom I am again in labor until Christ be formed in you!" (Gal 4:19).

Moreover, the sorrowful Virgin gives reality, in an especially intense way, to the image which Jesus had used, on the previous evening, to foretell the participation of the disciples in his suffering: "When a woman is in labor, she is in anguish because her hour has arrived; but when she has given birth to a child, she no longer remembers the pain because of her joy that a child has been born into the world" (Jn 16:21).

The scene of Mary at the cross (leaving John aside) takes on a true and proper salvation-historical meaning that cannot be grasped in isolation nor in purely historical and symbolic terms. It must be seen rather as the very heart, the culminating moment, of the mystery of salvation. Calvary was the place and time when Mary offered to the Father her most valuable possession as a mother: her only-begotten Son. For her, as for Jesus, this was the moment of supreme love,

---

70. In *Marianum* 54 (1992) 248.

the moment in which "in order to save many souls Mary offered up to death Jesus who was her own very soul" (St. Alphonsus).

She made this offering by uniting her own intentions with those of her Son, thus associating herself most completely with the sacrifice that was to win the salvation of the human race. Her own "Yes" arose to the Father along with the "Yes" of the Son. Mary was there on Calvary because she wanted to be there and share in her motherly heart all the sufferings of the crucified Jesus. She was there in order to give the ultimate expression to her love for humankind and to ratify here on earth the mystery of invisible love that was being accomplished. Dying, the one beside the other, and supporting one another with mutual, reciprocal, deep, and intense love, Mother and Son were, both of them, pure, holy, spotless victims. They thus inaugurated a new era: from the love of the Son in the womb of the Mother arose a new human race; there arose the Church that would always call itself "the Body of Christ."

Beneath the cross, Mary was heroic in her faith-inspired obedience (see *RM* 18) and in her love. In her giving up of Jesus and of herself it is difficult not to see a reflection of the magnanimity of the Father, with whom she is especially associated in the supreme sacrifice of the Only Son. Mary was there on Calvary with the Father in order, with one and the same intention, to hand over the same only-begotten Son to the world; she was there to give her consent to the sacrifice of the Son and imitate the action of the Father, who "so loved the world that he gave his only Son" (Jn 3:16) and "did not spare his own Son but handed him over for us all" (Rom 8:32). Jean Galot remarks that "in the person of the mother pierced by sorrow we can discover the face of the Father who is committed to the redemptive tragedy; her compassion suggests the mysterious suffering of the Father, which is united to that of Jesus."[71] Her suffering is the human reflection of the Father's, the beginning of Christian participation in the affliction felt by the divine Father at the death of his Son.[72]

But let us listen to the living and eternal words of the gospel and let us allow them to lead us step by step:

> Standing by the cross of Jesus were his mother and his mother's sister, Mary the wife of Clopas, and Mary of Magdala. When Jesus saw his mother and the disciple there whom he loved, he said to his mother, "Woman, behold, your son." Then he said to the disciple, "Behold, your mother." And from that hour the disciple took her into his home (Jn 19:25–27).

We are on Mount Calvary and there arises before our eyes the scene so feelingly described by John the Evangelist. The description is concise, just a brief reference but enough to make us grasp what an abyss is hidden here. There is a cross. Jesus is nailed to it, and there beside him is Mary, his Mother, accompanied by some women. Also there is John, the beloved disciple.

This is the "hour" which Jesus has mentioned so often (Jn 7:30; 8:20; 12:27; 13:1; Mk 14:35, 41; Mt 26:45; Lk 22:53). It is their hour: the great hour of the Son and the Mother, the hour that had not yet come at Cana, the hour which, according to the teaching in John, signifies the moment determined by the Father in which the Son is to complete his work and be glorified (Jn 7:30; 8:20; 12:23,27; 13:1; 17:1; 19:27).[73] It is also the hour of darkness, from which will emerge the light of the resurrection and of new life for every human being: the hour in which the human race is saved and redeemed.

---

71. Galot, *Maria, la donna*, 275; see also 268.
72. See Moltmann, "The Motherly Father" (note 13, above).
73. See John Paul II, *RM* 21.

That hour was the most tragic of her life, the most painful to her mother's heart. She had always kept in her heart Simeon's prediction: "And you yourself a sword will pierce" (Lk 2:35), and now she experienced the sharpest wound that sword could inflict, although it had always pierced her soul and tested her faith. The son whom she had brought forth, loved, and educated and for whom she had hoped the promised messianic royalty, she now saw in the depths of rejection, crucified, and in agony on the cross, as though he were a criminal: "spurned and avoided by men, a man of suffering" (Isa 53:3).

Standing at the foot of the cross she witnessed what was, humanly speaking, the complete refutation of the angel's promises: "He will be great and will be called Son of the Most High, and the Lord God will give him the throne of David his father, and he will rule over the house of Jacob forever, and of his kingdom there will be no end" (Lk 1:32–33). What an interior tragedy for Mary! What faith could not but doubt the angel's word and fail to understand once again that Glory willed to dwell in the most complete poverty? The soul of this mother and believer was pierced more than ever before by the painful sword, which now required of her an act of purest faith: to believe, against all the evidence, that God would be faithful to his promises, to believe in the triumph of the Son, in the resurrection he had foretold, and in the final victory of the Savior.

It is written in the Bible that when Judith returned after endangering her own life for the sake of people, the inhabitants of the city went out to meet her, and the high priest blessed her saying: "O daughter, you are blessed by the Most High God above all other women on earth.…Your praise will never depart from the hearts of those who remember the power of God" (Jdt 14:18–19 NRSV). We would apply the same words to Mary: "Blessed are you among women! The courage you have shown will never depart from the heart and memory of the Church!"

The heroic faith of the Mother of Jesus sheds a great light on the inevitable trials that befall us every day. For Christians of every age Mary's presence on Calvary is a sign that faith is necessarily subjected to struggles and testings. Associated as she was with the tragedy of the Passion, she had to face the hostility of those who rejected Christ, the spectacle of the Church's seeming failures, the sufferings and persecutions inflicted on believers. It is not possible to persevere in faith except by overcoming difficulties and temptations (Jean Galot).

Beneath the cross Mary is a prefiguration and model for the Church and Christians who, though persecuted and in utter anguish, believe and hope against all hope. Here, more than in any other situation, Mary became capable of standing by the cross of every human being and of every one of her children in order to console them on their journey and in the labors of each day. "Wherever the Christian community is committed to painful struggles, it receives strength from her who was so radically associated with the Passion of Christ and who helps all Christians unite themselves with that Passion."[74]

While the Virgin always takes motherly care of her children, this is especially true when they enter times of trial. Not to be forgotten in this context is the trial of trials, "the hour of our death," during which "she will be there as she was at her son's death on the cross" (*CCC*, no. 2677), ready to free us from the anxiety that seizes us at this final, fateful moment of our earthy life. She will change that anxiety into a luminous hope of the resurrection and true life and into a serene,

---

74. D. Hrusovsky, "Beata Virgo Maria coredemptrix et passiones atque dolores actuales Mystici Corporis Christi," *ME* 9:29–42.

clear-eyed passage, a calm leap as it were into the infinite, into the radiant dawn of an endless new day.

3. *Christ Makes His Mother the Mother of All His Disciples*

Let us return to the cross and remain there with Mary as intensely as we can, Let us lovingly recall the words of Jesus, his last will and testament, which we must never forget but always carry with us, as children recall and preserve their father's final words.

The real extent of Mary's motherhood are seen there, at the foot of the cross, where according to our limited way of thinking she should have been isolated and suffering. At this very moment, at the culmination of the Paschal Mystery, the unthinkable happens: Jesus makes his own Mother the mother of all his disciples in every age. The Mother of Jesus of Nazareth becomes the mother of John and, in him, the mother of the Church, just born from the open side of Christ. As Savior of all humankind, Jesus willed to give Mary's motherhood its greatest possible extension. Here on Calvary she is asked to open her heart to the entire world, in utter reliance on her Son's testamentary words: "Woman, behold your son" (John 19:26).

Such are the mysterious and surprising words with which Jesus, amid the agony of the cross, proclaims Mary to be the mother of the human race, mother of all the disciples, who are represented here by the beloved disciple. In virtue of this love-inspired testament Mary receives a limitless number of children in place of a single one. The words of Jesus reveal an intention that looks beyond the narrowly domestic world of mother and son and reaches out to the entire Christian community. Mary, the Mother, is here addressed as "Woman" and asked to raise her motherhood to a higher level; this is the level created by the "hour" of Jesus, and on it the boundaries of her motherhood are extended to the entire human race.

"Woman, behold your son!" Jesus is asking his Mother to accept the loss of her one Son and to become the mother of every disciple. In other words, he is asking her to complete her sacrifice as mother, by agreeing that her one Son, in whom divine infinity was bodied forth, be replaced by another. "What an exchange!" St. Bernard exclaims, addressing Mary: "You are given John in place of Christ, a servant in place of the Lord, a disciple in place of the Teacher, the son of Zebedee in place of the Son of God, a mere human being in place of the true God. Was this not more than a sword, these words that pierced your soul and divided soul and spirit?"[75]

Mary is convinced that this exchange is necessary, for Jesus belongs to all, even if her maternal heart must be torn apart. In her there is no thought of self, no effort to defend the object of her love from the desire of others to possess him. Quite the contrary! As the sacrifice of her Son perdures down the centuries, she, together with the Father, constantly renews, in solitary and silent love, the Son's self-offering for the salvation of the world. Never has self-denial and altruism reached such sublime heights in the heart of any other woman. "Woman, behold your son!"

It is clear that the primary purpose of the words of Jesus from the cross is not to entrust Mary to John but to entrust John to Mary; it is she who is asked to treat John as her son. Consequently, it is she who receives a new responsibility, that of watching over the disciples of Jesus and devoting a motherly care to them. In choosing John as the symbol of all the disciples whom he loves, Jesus shows that the gift of his Mother is the sign of a special love that embraces all those

---

75. In *Meditazioni mariane*, 118.

whom he desires to draw to himself as disciples, that is, all Christians, all human beings, all those who want him.

The majority of modern exegetes hold that the expression "the disciple whom he loved" signifies not so much a personal preference on the part of Jesus as it does the state of those who obey the gospel and thereby find themselves in the sphere of the love of the Father and the Son. Thus interpreted, "the disciple whom Jesus loved" is the type of every other complete disciple whom Jesus loves because of his or her faith.

After entrusting this new motherhood to his Mother, the dying Jesus turns to John and asks him to respond to Mary's maternal love with his own filial love: "Behold, your mother." We may undoubtedly see in these words an expression of the Son's special solicitude for his Mother, whom he was now leaving behind in her great sorrow. But the "testament of the cross" says something more about this solicitude. As recent exegesis has insisted, the scene on Calvary cannot be taken as dealing with the simple familial relationship of a son to a mother. After all, if Jesus had wanted to provide for his Mother in time to come, he would simply have commended Mary to his disciple. In fact, as we have seen, his primary concern was to entrust the disciple to Mary.

In short, the event on Calvary must be interpreted in relation to the completion of the work of salvation and be seen as marked by the Redeemer's great act of giving to his Mother a motherhood in the plan of salvation; this he does by entrusting all of the redeemed to her as her children. This fact becomes even clearer when we consider that the Savior utters his words of commendation at the moment when he is completing his redemptive mission. As the evangelist tells us, Jesus was aware that, after speaking these words, all was now completed (Jn 19:28); the gift of his Mother was the Son of God's final gift to the human race. With this priceless gift of love he completed the work entrusted to him by his Father.

4. Personal Nature of the New Motherhood

"And so this 'new motherhood of Mary,' generated by faith, is the fruit of the 'new' love which came to definitive maturity in her at the foot of the Cross, through her sharing in the redemptive love of her Son" (*RM* 23). At this point we must make it clear that the universal scope of this new motherhood did not in any way detract from its personal character, which, in fact, is very much accentuated in the scene on Calvary.

The fourth evangelist gives us a valuable basis for attributing to Mary an operative spiritual motherhood not only toward all human beings in general but also toward each individual human being. The very fact that Jesus entrusts John alone to her as a son (Jn 19:25–27) is a clear sign that he does not directly proclaim her to be Mother of the Christian community. He acts in this way because he wishes to stress the point that Mary's maternal love will be a personal love of each human being: a love that will be poured out on all Christians but in an individual and special way and will be marked by the same concern with which she turns to John.

By naming a single disciple Jesus would have us understand that Mary's maternal love is not something vague and nonspecific. No, every Christian will receive from Mary all the individualized affection that mothers give, nor will the limitless number of children detract from the attention given to each. Christ wants to assure his disciples that this boundless love will be bestowed on each as if he or she were the only one. In fact, if maternal love is to retain its value, it must focus on individuals and may not forget anything that concerns each of them.

But what is to be the scope and quality of Mary's individualized maternal love? What will be its special characteristic? Here again, the gospel is clear: John is the Lord's
beloved disciple and is assigned to be Mary's son in place
of Jesus (Jn 19:36–37). Two very important implications
emerge during this scene on Calvary and lead to two
astonishing results:

a) The motherhood of Mary that began beneath the
cross due to the Savior's creative words signals a motherhood in relation to *every* beloved disciple of the Lord, that
is, to every disciple insofar as the latter is loved by Christ.

b) Mary is asked to pour out on this disciple the maternal love she had always given to her Son; she is asked to
have for us, her adoptive children, the same tender solicitude that she had for her own Son.

At this point I think it important to focus our attention
on the response of the "beloved disciple" to the Master's
request as the latter entrusts his sorrowing Mother to the disciple's care. The gospel tells us that the response is quick,
decisive, and immediate: "And from that hour the disciple
took her into his home" or "with him." The Greek text reads:
took her "among his own things" (*eis ta idia*), that is, among
his own possessions or as his property. Many commentators
interpret "his own things" as the disciple's material possessions or, more concretely, his home, and translate the passage accordingly.

But a careful analysis of John's vocabulary, confirmed by
not a few patristic witnesses, suggests that we read *ta idia* at
a deeper level. The words "his own things" refer in essence
to the disciple's faith in the Master and to the life-giving setting in which he will henceforth live. Beginning with the
paschal event (the hour of Jesus), the followers of Christ
considered Mary as one of the treasures that constitute the
"property" of their faith. And, as one of their treasures, they

made a place for her in their acceptance of Christ (see *NDM* 291–292). Here again many of the spokesmen of the tradition have intuited the wealth hidden in the phrase *ta idia*. There was, yes, a material house, but above all there is the mystical dwelling in a heart that opens itself to Christ the Lord. Sophronius of Jerusalem commented: "The preeminent disciple took the spotless Mother of God into his home as his own mother.... He became a son of the Mother of God" (*NDM* 292).

Much more was involved than John giving hospitality to the Mother of Jesus. Rather, she was a treasure which he received as a trust, precisely in order to reach the stature of an authentic "disciple" of Christ. Not only did he "take Mary" into his own material dwelling; he also introduced her into his own vital setting, "beginning a relationship of spiritual intimacy (with her) that helped to intensify his relationship with the Master, whose unmistakable features he saw on the face of the Mother" (John Paul II). Mary, the Mother, entered into the depths of the disciple's life and was henceforth an inseparable part of it, as a blessing, riches, and a priceless inheritance; in short, as an inalienable value.

"From that hour." For us Christians that hour was and will always be a very important moment in history. The "hour" is the moment in which Mary began her motherly presence in the life of the Church. "From that hour" the Church learned that Mary is a constitutive part of its creed. "From that hour" onward, Mary and the mystery she embodies would be indissolubly linked to the mystery of the Church, to the Church of every age as it continues to recall and delve ever more deeply the words which Christ himself spoke to it from the cross: "Behold, your mother!"

By taking Mary with him the beloved disciple anticipated, in a fashion, the action asked of all those who wish to cling fully to Christ, our brother, as he continues to show

Mary to us as our mother. For, like John, we are all called upon to take Mary with us; that is, we are asked to receive her among our dearest and most precious possessions. John Paul II suggests that "taking Mary with us" means giving her a place in our lives by remaining habitually united to her in our thoughts, our affections, and in our zeal for the reign of God and for devotion to her. It means entrusting ourselves to her and developing a close loving relationship with her as Jesus wants, who willed to crown his saving work with the gift of a mother, his very own Mother. Today he keeps on saying to us: "Behold, your mother!"

IIf) Mother of the Church

During his address marking the end of the third session of Vatican II (November 21, 1964) Paul VI solemnly declared Mary to be Mother of the Church. These are his authoritative words: "For the glory of the Blessed Virgin and our own consolation, We declare Mary Most Holy to be the Mother of the Church, that is of the whole Christian people, both the faithful and the bishops, who call her a most loving Mother. We decree that from now on the whole of the Christian people should use this sweetest of names to pay more honor to the Mother of God and to pour out their prayers to her."

As a matter of fact, the title "Mother of the Church" was not something new for devout Christians. Long before it was expressly used in the Christian community, the doctrine it represents had begun to take form in the patristic period as a reflection on or, better, a flowering of thought about the divine motherhood. Since that time and throughout the history of Christian tradition, this teaching has continually been formulated in various ways. For if the Virgin of Nazareth is the Mother of God, mother of the restoration of the universe, and mother of everything involved in the salvation given to the human race, then we must logically assert her motherhood in regard to the Church in which salvation and grace are made available to all human beings.

That Mary is Mother of the Church can be gathered beginning in the very first pages of Luke's narrative. In the passage on the Annunciation (ch. 1) we are told that the angel revealed to Mary the coming of a definitive kingdom (v. 33), the messianic kingdom, which is the Church. Since Mary is asked to accept the entire content of the angelic message, her "Yes" to the coming of the Messiah implies a "Yes" to the formation and spread of this kingdom; her role of Mother will culminate in the birth of this kingdom. Continuing to follow Luke's account, "the ecclesial thrust of Mary's motherhood is confirmed at the presentation of Jesus in the temple, in which she offers her Son for the rise of many in Israel" and accepts the sword that was to pierce her soul (Lk 2:34–35).[76]

Moreover, in his description of the messianic motherhood the third evangelist gives us a glimpse — surely not by chance! — of a by no means weak analogy between the moment of the Messiah's Incarnation and the moment of the Church's birth. For the action of the Holy Spirit in Mary for the formation of the infant (1:35) is presented as a prelude to his action on Pentecost for the formation of the Church, the latter being born of the little group gathered with Mary in prayer (Acts 1:13–14).

Luke had begun his gospel by telling of the Virgin Mary and her unique role in the coming of Christ. When he mentions the presence of the Mother of Jesus in the group awaiting Pentecost, he suggests a prolongation or continuity between the birth of Jesus and the birth of the Church. In both births, which are the work of the Holy Spirit, Mary has a very important role to play: she exercises her maternal action on Pentecost (the birth of the Church) as she had at the begin-

---

76. Galot, *Maria: itinerario spirituale*, 102.

ning of the life of Jesus (Head of the Church). "Thus she who is present in the mystery of Christ as Mother becomes — by the will of the Son and the power of the Holy Spirit — present in the mystery of the Church" (*RM* 24). Mary at Nazareth and Mary in the upper room in Jerusalem: in both cases her unobtrusive but essential presence points out the path of "birth from the Holy Spirit."

When John, for his part, recalls the presence of the Virgin Mary at both the beginning and the end of Jesus' public life, he too was highlighting the maternal cooperation in the work of the Church. The public life, Golgotha, and the upper room: three stages in which Christ, a Head who had himself been born, built his Church, three stages in which Mary played a part as mother. "Let us, therefore, not separate the Son from the Mother or the Mother from the Son! In the Mother and the Son we find the Church, and in the Church the Mother and the Son."[77] Wherever Mary acts, the Church is born and acts. Wherever Mary extends her presence, the Church is enlarged. The Church has the same boundaries as the maternal mission of Mary, and Mary's maternal mission takes concrete form and becomes "historical" in the Church.[78]

As the Virgin had a prayerful and active presence at the beginning of the new-born Church, so she, with her motherly heart, continues to be present in the Church of every age and in all its vital operations, inspiring its expansion and development in the world. "Today as yesterday she is an operative presence in the Church, giving support to faith, words to apostles, and strength to martyrs, because all of them, everywhere, proclaim and bear witness to the Christ whom she has given to them" (E. Toniolo). Her presence in

77. L. Da Castelplanio, *Maria nel Consiglo dell'Eterno, ovvero la Vergine predestinata alla missione con Gesù Cristo*, I, preface to Part 1 (Naples, 1872).
78. Francesco Franzi, in *Maria Santissima e lo Spirito Santo*, 125.

the drama of Calvary makes us think of the great desire she must currently have of assisting the Church in its trials and persecutions (Jean Galot).

"Mary, who gave us, in Christ, the wellspring of grace, will not fail to help the Church.... And our confidence is still further enlivened and strengthened when we think of the very close bonds that bind this heavenly Mother of ours to the human race" (Paul VI). The Father desires to unite the whole of humanity in his love. Mary's maternal heart is driven by this universal aim. The Virgin's entire ambition is that all her children, to whom, after Jesus, she gave birth by her love, be completely united so as to form with him a single Son, a single Jesus Christ,[79] to the praise and glory of God the Father.

D. The Father Constantly Shows the Son to Us
(The Testament of Mary)

In ending this chapter I want to emphasize a significant point that is by no means of secondary importance. I refer, on the one hand, to the Synoptic treatment of the words spoken by the Father during the theophany on Mount Tabor: "This is my beloved Son ... listen to him" (Mt 17:5) and, on the other, to Mary's instruction at Cana:

"Do whatever he tells you" (Jn 2:5).

Here we see the wisdom of our holy Mother: like the Father, she calls attention to the Son, urging us to obey him and be guided by him. "She does not hide Jesus from us but always puts him in the limelight and points to him to be loved by the faithful" (S. De Fiores). In any case,

---

79. G. J. Chaminade, *Lettres* III (Nivelles, 1930) 390.

who could better direct us to him than the Mother who, herself formed by the supreme love of the Father, gave him to us?

"Do whatever he tells you."

Such is the Mother's gentle instruction that is intertwined with the words of the hidden Father, to the point of becoming one with them, identical with them: "This is my beloved Son … listen to him." At Cana Mary is simply interpreting and reflecting the Father's will, his compelling desire regarding the Son.

"Do whatever he tells you."

These are the strong words spoken by the "Mother of Jesus," and indeed the last words of Mary that are recorded in the gospel. They constitute, as it were, "the testament" of the Mother of God. This is an unforgettable testament that contains riches still unexhausted and will remain a part of the history of the Church as an invitation to gather up the eternal words of Jesus. It is a testament that seems to include not only everything that Mary said but, even more, everything she was and still is: a white flower always open to the rays of the divine sun, "a fertile soil, entirely open to the sun" (liturgical hymn). "Through a new and sublime joy she gives enchanting delight to our souls; she does not fasten our gaze on herself but impels it to look further" to where her own gaze is turned: the "miracle of the light, holiness, and life"[80] that issue from Christ.

Cardinal Suenens asked: "What does Mary mean to us?" and answered: "She is the one … who claims our lips, our hands, and our arms for the service of her Son, in order that with her we may bring Christ to human beings who are dying

---

80. Paul VI, *Insegnamenti* II (1964) 525.

because they do not know him."[81] She is the one who faces humanity as spokesperson for the will of the Son (see *RM* 2) and who, when she is preached and honored, refers believers to him (see *LG* 64).

Yes, in the history of the Church Mary, like the Father, is and will always be "she who shows us the 'light from the East': Jesus Christ, her Son and the Son of God" (Paul VI). Her entire life is devoted to Christ, to manifesting him, to making him known. This is her task, her purpose, her mission, and the meaning of her intervention at Cana, where we see that after the miracle is worked she disappears, and it is Jesus who has made his glory known (Jn 2:11).

"Do whatever he tells you."

Words ancient and everlasting, filled with life; words that seem new each time we hear them; sublime words that in the past and henceforth Mary utters to all her children and each of us.

> Father of life,
> Beginning without a beginning,
> supreme goodness and eternal light,
> who have stooped to see the distress of
> humanity and have given us Jesus, your Son,
> born of a woman,
> as our Savior and friend,
> our brother and redeemer:
> grant to all your children to know
> that on the journey to you,
> humanity's final haven,
> Mary Most Holy,

---

81. Cited by Terenzio De Poi, *Mese di maggio con Padre Kolbe* (Padua: Ed. Messaggero, 1983) 5.

icon of pure love,
in her kindness walks with them.[82]

We glorify you, Father,
because you have made Mary
the mother and "faithful spouse
who lovingly follows your Word;
the perfect model
of those who receive your word by faith
and keep it in love.
To you be glory through all ages!"[83]

82. John Paul II, *Prayer for the Third Year of Preparation for the Great Jubilee of 2000* (Rome, 1999).
83. Italian Episcopal Conference, *In Preghiera con Maria Madre di Gesù* (Marian Year 1987; Rome: Vatican Publishing House).

Chapter Four
Mary in Relation to the Son

A. Mary Is Completely Ordered to the Son and Closely United with Him

> The mystery of Mary finds its full meaningonly in the mystery of the Son, from which it is inseparable.

In the Virgin Mary everything is ordered to Christ and everything depends on him. It was in view of him that God the Father, from all eternity, chose her as the supremely holy Mother and adorned her with gifts of the Spirit that were not granted to anyone else (*MC* 2).

"Redeemed, in a more exalted fashion, by reason of the merits of her Son, and united to him by a close and indissoluble tie" (*LG* 53), she received everything for the sake of the Son: Christ was her reason for existing. As a result, Mary can be understood only in the light of Christ. Her profound, unique, and unmistakable mystery as Mother of God, "her marvelous greatness, her holiness, and her sublime beauty can be understood only in the light of the Son because all are reflections of him; all come from Christ and all are oriented and ordered to him."[1] It can be said that the more deeply we penetrate into the mystery of Christ, the better we understand the singular dignity of the Mother of the Lord and her role in the history of salvation.

---

1. G. M. Sartori, "Incarnazione e maternità divina," *L'Osservatore Romano*, September 14–15, 1992.

Grignion de Montfort justly observes that whether he looks to time or to eternity, he always finds Mary at the side of Jesus: "Thou, Lord, art always with Mary, and Mary is always with Thee, and she cannot be without Thee, else she would cease to be what she is.... She is so intimately united with Thee that it were easier to separate the light from the sun, the heat from the fire" (*True Devotion*, 63).

We cannot think of Christ our brother in his real humanity and mystery without thinking of her who conceived him, gave birth to him, and was his close and faithful "companion on the journey." The infinite difference between Christ and Mary must not make us forget the no less infinite likeness between them; otherwise we would end up denying that Christ is truly human, and would fall into docetism. "The humanity of Christ and the motherhood of Mary are so linked that to be mistaken about the one is necessarily to be mistaken about the other as well" (St. Thomas Aquinas).

United to Christ as no other human being is, Mary, more than any other, resembles him in his physical and spiritual traits. "No one else has been more like Jesus, not only with the natural likeness between mother and son but also with the likeness bestowed by the Spirit and by holiness, and no one in the history of the world has been more centered on Christ or been a more complete Christ-bearer" (John Paul II). She is the image which, better than any other, mirrors the Lord; she is the most perfect instance of conformity with Christ, because more than any other she was able to achieve the divine likeness in herself. The poet perceives this truth when he sketches her with a quick stroke of his pen, calling her "the face that most resembles Christ's" (Dante).

Pius XII asked: "Do you not think that the face of Jesus, the face that the angels adore, must have in some measure resembled the face of Mary?"[2] Theodore of Studios gave voice to a similar thought: "We venerate the holy image of Mary in order to worship Christ himself, who is pictured in her" (in *TMPM* II, 659).

A Profound Communion of Life with Her Son

Motherhood by its nature is a new and sublime combination of knowledge and love; it presupposes an entire loving relationship of which it is itself the fruit. If this is true of every motherhood, it must be all the more true of the Mother of God. In fact, what is most attractive about Mary's life is her close and complete union with her Son and her God, as well as the journey she completed at his side as a strong woman who persevered at all times and in every event. We see in the Virgin, as never elsewhere in the history of humanity, a profound, intimate relationship, a marvelous exchange of tender love between her and her Lord. It can be said that her life was wholly absorbed by a complete communion with her Son, by a divine interlocking love that marks her historical existence and is prolonged in eternity.

What could Mary say about her mystical union with Christ? How was her life really affected by being Mother of God? What kind of deep understanding was there between her and her divine Son? How he must have amazed her, and how great must have been her desire to contemplate him and adore him! How are we to explore their intimate spiritual union, the divine and human dimensions of which escape an impersonal theological discourse and of which nothing is greater in this world?

At Nazareth the Virgin Mother lived for thirty years in the sweet intimacy of a family where she was in an unbroken physical, moral, psychological, affective, and spiritual con-

---

2. From his "Address to Catholic Youth" (December 8, 1953), in *Meditazioni Mariane*, 166.

tact with her Son. During this time there was established between them a reciprocal influence on all levels, a set of interpersonal relationships that were concrete and invigorating, tender and warm. Mary gave Jesus the best of herself: human life, her blood, her milk, her most affectionate care, her time, her toil, her collaboration, her joys and sorrows, and, above all, the purest and most ardent maternal love. "What joy Jesus must have experienced from knowing himself to be so loved by Mary! After the incomprehensible joy produced in him by the beatific vision and by the infinite satisfaction with which the heavenly Father contemplated him, nothing must have given him greater joy than the love shown him by his Mother" (Don Columba Marmion).

Jesus in turn gave himself wholly to Mary through his divine sanctifying work in her. Following upon his entrance into the world, the infinite, thankful love with which he faces the Father, expands to embrace also the Mother from whom he is born into a life in time.

As biological science suggests, Jesus must have had even a physical influence on his Mother during the months in which he lived within her. A fetus acts on the mother's blood and impresses on the maternal organism some of the biological and therefore also the psychological qualities it inherits from its father. But Jesus did not have a natural father; therefore what he did not derive from his Mother came from his humanity as united to the divinity. Jesus must have transfused into his Mother something of his perfect human humanity-united-to-the-divinity. She therefore had even a physical bond with Christ of which no other creature could ever boast. Thus from whatever angle we think about the situation, we see the most sublime harmony and most perfect union between the Mother and the divine Son.

St. Ephraem sought insight into what happened at the Incarnation; a perfect symbiosis, he thought, a sharing of life through a reciprocal giving between Mary and the Incarnate Word: her gift of the flesh, his of the Spirit.

> The Holy One dwelt in his mother's womb corporeally and in her spirit spiritually…. He impressed himself on his mother's spirit as in a temple and even after his birth he was no less in her, for he radiated forth from her members. His splendor was conveyed by the beauty of his mother; the anointing of his body spread out upon her. She had woven the garment for him; the Son spread his splendor over all her senses.[3]

This mutually advantageous relationship between Mother and Son established the closest possible union with God after the hypostatic union. In the hypostatic union a single divine Person lives in two natures; during the gestation of the incarnate Son in his Mother's virginal womb, there are two persons living the same human life, which is communicated by the Mother to the Son. This was a conscious and therefore sanctifying union. If during the public life a power went forth from Christ that healed all (see Lk 6:19) — the woman with a flow of blood was healed simply by touching his garment: Mt 9:21ff. — what must we say of the sanctifying influence which Jesus the priest exerted upon the Mother who had become the temple in which he offered himself to the Father for the salvation of the human race (see Heb 5:1ff.)?

Mary, for her part, was conscious of carrying the Savior of the world in her womb, as the angel had told her; therefore she lived in union with him, not only physically but also contemplatively (see Lk 2:l9, 51) in response to his sanctifying action. "She is so transformed into Thee by grace that she lives no more, that she is as though she no longer existed. It is Thou only, my Jesus, who livest and reignest in her more

---

3. St. Ephraem, *Hymns on the Nativity*, 130 (CSCO 186, p. 37, Syriac; 187, p. 33, German translation).

perfectly than in all the angels and saints" (*True Devotion,* no. 63).

Mary's life could not but be marked most deeply by holding the Son of God in her arms, living and eating with him, and enjoying his company for many years. Her will acted in agreement with his; her heart beat in complete harmony with his; she "shared the thoughts of Christ and his hidden wishes, so that she could be said to live the very life of the Son" (Pius X). If Paul with his lively eloquence could say: "To me life is Christ" (Phil 1:21), and "I live, no longer I, but Christ lives in me" (Gal 2:20), with how much greater right could Christ's Mother say this! Even after giving birth to him she carried him within her; to find him she needed only look into her own heart, which was filled with him.

These overwhelming thoughts flow from the inexhaustible pen of St. Bernard, one of the greatest of the Marian teachers, who himself draws in turn upon the rich patristic tradition. In his writings we find the most enlightening explanation of the divine work of transformation in Mary and of the suprahuman effects produced in the Virgin of Nazareth because she was Mother of God; these effects gave her, in turn, a unique ability to show forth the Son.

In various writings we find Bernard convinced that while, in a sense, Mary conceived God first in her mind (*De Divers.* 52, 3), God present in her maternal womb also imbued and permeated her with his divinity. If the Madonna's heart was filled with charity, it was because "in her womb the Charity that comes from God dwelt bodily for nine months" (*Sermons on the Assumption* 1, 2). By the power of this Charity Mary's soul was not only "wounded" but even pierced by love of Christ, so that every part of her soul overflowed with it. Mary was the only creature whom God united physically with himself, and, although there was no union of her person with the divinity, she seemed to have been

immersed, as it were, in the inaccessible light of the divinity. "She merited not simply to be merely touched by that fire, but to be wrapped in it, penetrated by it, and, as it were, enclosed within it" (*Sermons on the Assumption* 3). Her human nature, being permeated by the divine nature, was strengthened and exalted by it.

Immersed as she was in the love and light of God, Mary calls to mind the image Bernard uses in his *The Love of God* to describe the state of those who reach the highest degree of love for God:

> As a little drop of water placed in a large amount of wine seems completely to lose its own nature to the point of taking on the taste and color of the wine; as iron thrust into fire and becoming incandescent loses its original form and becomes wholly like fire; as air filled with the light of the sun takes on the brightness of this light, so that it seems not only lightsome but itself light: so it is with the saints as they are transformed by God (*The Love of God* 10, 28).

The closeness of Mary to the divinity transcends that of any other creature. She alone became so familiar and so close to God because she alone was his mother. The abbot of Clairvaux says to Mary: "He dwells in you and you in him; you clothed him and are clothed in him; you clothed him in flesh, he clothes you with the glory of the divine majesty" (*Sermons on the Assumption* 6). When Mary allowed the Word to become flesh, the Word communicated to Mary the splendor of his presence. As a result, second only to the human nature of Christ, the Virgin Mary is the creature most permeated by the divine nature; she is, par excellence, the new creature who has put on the Lord Jesus Christ (see Rom 13:14). This divine brightness makes Mary the great sign of God's presence and the instrument of his redemptive action:

"Having been made all to all, she regards herself as owing a limitless love to the wise and to the ignorant ... so that no one is beyond the reach of her fervent and merciful heart" (*Sermons on the Assumption* 6).[4]

B. In Mary the Son of God Acquires His First Personal Relationship with the Human Race

In revealing the mystery of the Father
Christ makes humanity fully known to itself
and unveils the sublime vocation of every
   human being.[5]

Every human being born into the world is connected with the entire human race because he or she possesses the same human nature. This law applies even to Jesus, Son of the eternal Father, since he became a human being for our salvation. Thanks to the divine and utterly human motherhood of Mary, "Jesus ... is a true son of man. He is 'flesh' like every other man; he is 'the Word (who) became flesh' (see Jn 1:14). He is of the flesh and blood of Mary" (*RM* 20). "God with us" could be seen, heard, and touched with our hands (see 1 Jn 1:1) because God first became incarnate in him.

As the place where the divine and the human meet, Mary is not indeed the center, but she is central to Christianity. For she is the one who by putting herself at the service of the divine action linked Jesus to the whole human race as by an umbilical cord. She anchored God to the earth and to humanity; she made God be forever Emmanuel, God with us (Isa 7:14); she turned Christ into our brother.

In becoming the son of Mary, the Son of the Most High entered the human community as one of its members; he

---

4. "Il Pensiero Mariologico di San Bernardo," *Marianum* 54 (1992) 137–38 and 172.
5. International Theological Commission, "The Theology of Redemption," *Il Regno*: Documenti no. 3 (1996) 104.

lived on our planet and took on the burden of our earthly life with all the sufferings, limitations, and kinds of impoverishment which this life inevitably brings with it. He breathed the same air, quenched his thirst at the same wells, worked with human hands, and loved with a human heart. In short, he lived a real, down-to-earth human life that ensured the Word's complete membership in the human race. It was this life that Mary, his Mother, gave him. It is she who for the endless ages to come gave birth for our sake to Jesus, the supreme human being.

The eternal Son of God willed to approach us and even to be lost in the human crowd: "He willed to be one of us through the blessed and never adequately praised presence of Mary. We received Christ from her; we meet him as the flower of humanity that blossomed on the spotless and virginal stalk that is Mary; that is how this flower came into existence. It is from her that we have him, in his very first relationship with us."[6] With us he forms the human race, the one, same human race in the sight of God.

Through the human nature which the divine person of the Word assumed in the spotless womb of Mary, "the nature shared by every human being is elevated to the highest possible dignity" (John Paul II). This principle, which has been accepted by theologians in every age, was put as follows by the International Theological Commission in 1966: "The Incarnation of the Logos affects human nature in its entirety. Because the Son of God is a member of the human family, all the other members have been raised to the new dignity of being his brothers and sisters."[7] This astonishing mystery, like all the mysteries of God's immeasurable wisdom and goodness, makes the heart leap for joy.

---

6. Paul VI, *Insegnamenti* XV (1977) 763, and in *Marianum* 33 (1971) 411.
7. "Teologia della Redenzione," 104.

C. The Unparalleled Pedagogical Task of Mary

If it be true — and it is — that Jesus Christ became like us in every way and shared our human condition in every way except sin (see Heb 4:16), then he was a child like all of us and, again like all of us, had to be reared and educated; in short, he, like every other human being, was inevitably influenced by his mother in every aspect of his life. "We must see in Mary the educator of the Son of God during his human childhood" (Jean Galot).

After becoming a tiny baby the eternal Word rested on Mary's knees and on her heart, was nourished with her milk, sought her loving embraces, stayed at her side, and listened docilely to her. Like every other child he was unable to stand on his own or provide for his needs, and therefore he allowed himself to be cared for, fed, and clothed by a creature who carried out all the duties of a mother. We can imagine Mary's feelings of joy as she reared this divine Son. But how many questions she must have asked herself about this unique being whose mother she was!

Experience tells us that in every mother-child relationship the task of educating is certainly a basic one and more important than simply giving birth. The child not only grows within his mother but he also develops in constant reference to her as he models his behavior on hers; she is the first world that he discovers and explores. We must therefore admit with Jean Galot that in her there was a "preformation" of the attitudes which Jesus would develop. This preformation,

> which was inspired by the Holy Spirit, rendered the mother especially suited to educate her child and promote his growth in accordance with the special requirements of his person and mission; it made her able to have on her Son an influence fully in conformity with the divine plan.

When the Holy Spirit descended on Mary in order to effect the conception of Jesus, he began a continuous action in her that would ensure the harmonious development of the child. Led thus by God, Mary was able to educate her Son in an irreproachable manner. Hers was the lofty collaboration of the Theotokos ("Bearer of God") in the Incarnation.[8]

In the gospel we see the fruit borne by Mary's education of Jesus. We are told that Jesus was fully open to the maternal influence of Mary: he "was obedient to them" (Lk 2:51) and "retained the obedience and submission of the most perfect child toward the best of all mothers" (*True Devotion*, 27). The completeness of this submission gave an even greater effectiveness to the influence of Mary and Joseph on the boy, and forces us to admit that no other mother ever had so great an influence on her child.

The ideal goal sought in the education of a child is the full integration into the child's personality of that which one wishes to teach him or her. In that sense, the fruits of an education can no longer be seen as separate since they are part of the riches proper to that person.

The assimilation by Jesus of all that his Mother gave him in her educative work was so profound that we can no longer perceive the degree of the influence she had. But certainly hidden in the personal riches which the Christ gave and gives to the world is the result of his mother's deeply penetrating action. Later on, his disciples will testify that Jesus went about doing good to all (see Acts 10:38). There can be no doubt that his behavior bore traces of his mother's influence, even if we cannot identify these traces in a detailed way. But a comparison of the attitudes of Jesus with those of

---

8. Galot, *Maria, la donna*, 107–9.

his mother allows us to measure some aspects of this influence.

Among the gospel narratives that seem to show more clearly the influence of Mary's training we may cite the washing of feet at the Last Supper (Jn 13:4–17), an action by which Jesus wanted to place before his disciples a vivid symbol of humble service. He chose a gesture which he had seen the Virgin of Nazareth perform for visiting guests and which he had learned to perform himself after her example. In Mary the action manifested a deep-rooted disposition (at the Annunciation she described herself as handmaid of the Lord; then she went off to Elizabeth in order to serve her). Christ then used this same gesture to make clear his own readiness to serve. Through the Model whom she gave to the future Church, Mary's training continues to influence the disciples of Christ.[9]

D. In Mary the Life of Jesus Is Lived in Advance

In Jesus we find much of Mary.
We see her prolonged and reproduced in Jesus.

(Leonardo Boff)

In the form which the Virgin's consent took we can see "preformed" as it were some distinctive aspects of the life of Jesus. She had already begun to form in herself the interior dispositions that would later characterize the Messiah in the carrying out of his work: service, docility to the Father's will, consecration to virginity, establishment of a covenant, and so on. In Mary these dispositions were the fruit of an exceptional grace that sought to involve her entire personality and behavior in the mission of her Son; her vocation was to offer to God a human model that would later be found

---

9. See ibid.

again in Christ. By agreeing to be a mother in God's plan she brought into being a maternal image that would be reflected in the Savior; the divine intention was to involve the mother of Jesus in his fortunes.[10]

At this point the likeness between a mother and her son takes on a new dimension: beyond the physical and psychological likeness we find a moral likeness that is due precisely to Mary's acceptance of the divine plan that was to reach its fulfillment in Jesus. Consequently, it was not by a simple consent that the Virgin Mary cooperated in the accomplishment of the mystery of redemption; rather her "Yes" was matched by a profound attitude that contributed to forming the attitude of her Son.

1. Servant of the Lord and Mother of the Servant of the Lord

> In your womb, O Virgin Mary,
> God takes the form of a servant.
>
> (Byzantine Hymn)

The preformation in the Mother of the spiritual face of the Son is clear from the words of her answer to the angel: "Behold, I am the handmaid of the Lord" (Lk 1:38).

When chosen to be a mother, Mary calls herself a servant, signifying her status as a humble creature before her creator and interpreting her maternal mission as one of service. She thus situates herself in the religious tradition of the servants of Yahweh, a tradition that finds its supreme expression in Christ Jesus, the "servant of Yahweh" par excellence (Isa 53). Her self-description as "servant" anticipates the description Jesus will give of his own fundamental outlook: "The Son of Man did not come to be served but to serve"

---

10. For a more detailed study of the " preformation" of the life of Jesus in Mary see the reflections of Jean Galot in *Maria: itinerario spirituale*, 74–5, and in *Maria, la donna*, 75–87 and 106–09.

(Mk 10:45; Mt 20:28). Jesus rejects any claim to be served; he has come only to serve.

It is indeed surprising to see that the spiritual revolution caused by the words of Jesus about the Son of Man having come to serve had already begun in Mary. If we set side by side the declaration of Jesus with that of his Mother we find a harmony between interior dispositions. Christ will always be conscious of being a "servant of the Lord" according to the prophecy of Isaiah (42:1; 49:3, 6; 52:13). For her part, from her first moment as Mother of God, the Virgin of Nazareth plays a part in Christ's messianic service, for the ground of everything she will do is her complete self-giving to the service of the divine plan and kingdom as represented by her Son (Lk 1:32–33, 38).

We can therefore justly say that the attitude of service, which is a manifestation of supreme love, marks the entire historical activity of both Mother and Son. The likeness between the two is crystal-clear. Indeed, the term "servant," which Mary uses to describe herself, takes on a still greater value when seen as a response to the lofty role offered to her by the angel (to be mother of the Messiah who is destined to sit on the throne of David and to rule for ever). The Virgin of Nazareth, while conscious of her high dignity, was bathed in the mentality proper to a messianism that was not concerned with glory but was characterized by *kenosis* (self-emptying, hidden life, obedience). Instead therefore of demanding her rights as mother of the Messiah, she allowed herself to be "emptied" of them and to seem in the sight of all to be just one woman among many. She did not cling to her privileges, did not claim an important position, but chose the way of service.

Her animating basic disposition as a servant helped Jesus grow in his own mission of service and avoid the idea of an overly self-centered and triumphalist glorious Messiah, that

was typical of the contemporary Jewish mentality. If Mary
had shared that mentality, she would have thrust her Son into
a life of triumphalism. On the contrary, however, she contributed to the formation of one who chose to avoid being
served (Jean Galot).

Sacrifice and Service

Even the element of sacrifice that was implied in the
coming of the Savior was linked by Jesus with service; his
condition as a servant brought with it a commitment to a
redemptive self-sacrifice. "The Son of Man did not come to
be served but to serve and to give his life as a ransom for
the many" (Mk 10:45; Mt 20:28). Although Mary could
not have grasped all the implications of the servanthood
that described her, she nonetheless accepted all the consequences of service according to the divine plan.

As we know, the mission of the handmaid of the Lord, like
that of the Servant of the Lord, was hidden, laborious, and not
without poverty and painful trials. No less than her Son, Mary
experienced temptation and the suffering inflicted by interior
trials. It would be a great mistake to think that the life of this
woman filled with grace was an easy, comfortable life. Far
from it: her holiness matured during a difficult journey of
faith; hers was the holiness of a "strong woman," burdened by
painful experiences that included poverty, flight, and exile.

The Mother of the crucified Savior shared every aspect of
our earthly condition with its demands and sufferings. With
full confidence and deep consolation we can say of her what
is said of her Son (here I paraphrase what Heb 4:15 writes of
him): "We do not have a mother who is unable to sympathize
with us in our weaknesses, our labors, and our trials, for she
herself was tested in every way like us, but was without sin."
We must constantly remind ourselves of this truth lest we
risk making her unreal and placing her off in an ethereal, dis-
embodied world.

The Most Radical Kenosis or Self-emptying of Faith in the History of Humanity

In the Encyclical *Redemptoris Mater* which John Paul II wrote for the Marian Year (1987), he very fittingly applies to Mary's life the great concept of *kenosis* which Paul used in explaining the events of Jesus' earthly life ("Christ Jesus, who, though he was in the form of God, did not regard equality with God something to be grasped at. Rather he emptied [*ekenosen*] himself, taking the form of a slave": Phil 2:6–7).

The pope says: "Through ... faith Mary is perfectly united with Christ in his self-emptying" (*RM* 18). Her self-emptying was completed beneath the cross, but it had begun long before, during the hidden life of Jesus in the home at Nazareth, when Mary's life was likewise "hidden with Christ in God" (Col 3:3). It is not difficult to observe, from that point on, a "particular heaviness of heart, linked with a sort of 'night of faith' ... a kind of 'veil' through which one has to draw near to the Invisible One and to live in intimacy with the mystery" (*RM* 17).

Until the day of her passage into heavenly glory Mary's poverty would consist in her generous devotion to the person and work of her Son, this always in the obscure light of faith (Lk 2:34, 34, 48–50; Acts 1:14, 23–30; 8:1b, 3; 12:1; 28:22).[11] For from the beginning her faith was not so enlightened that she was dispensed from every effort at inquiry; she was not granted from birth such a fullness of faith as to exempt her from having to make progress. On the contrary, her entire life was a journey of faith, a constant and radical perseverance in this virtue which is so indispensable and life-giving for Christians.

In short, Mary's "Yes" was not a "Yes" which she uttered once and for all as an "amazing young girl" who foresaw

---

11. *Acta Ioannis Pauli PP. II*, in *Marianum* 46 (1984) 397.

what was to come. Rather, day after day and moment by moment, her "Yes" became the substance of her life. The person and work of her Son were for her a real mystery; the events in which he was involved amazed her, so much so that she had to make an effort to grasp their meaning. An example of this is the painful search for the boy Jesus and the discovery of him in the temple (Lk 2:41–50).[12] As a sharer in the *kenosis* of Christ (which ranged from his choice of a messianism that excluded earthly immunities and privileges to his passage through death) the handmaid of the Lord "moved forward on a life-long 'pilgrimage of faith,' while her beloved Son, misunderstood, calumniated, condemned, and crucified, traced out for her, day after day, a painful path to follow" (John Paul II). At Nazareth and during the public life of Jesus Mary advanced in faith to the point of sharing, in her role as loving Mother, in the universality of her Son's mission.

Just as the fact of being the Son of God did not serve to spare Christ any suffering or humiliation, so the fact of being Mother of God did not serve to spare Mary any kind of humiliation and suffering. In the gospel we read that once Jesus left Nazareth and began his ministry, he had "nowhere to rest his head" (Mt 8:20). We can add that Mary had nowhere to rest her heart, not even during the most painful and heart-wrenching moment of her life, on Calvary. Standing beneath the cross she too drained the bitter cup of her Son's passion, for this was a necessary step toward the glorification of which she had sung in the Magnificat: "from now on will all ages call me blessed" (Lk 1:48).

Christ, the Servant of Yahweh, entered into the kingdom of the Father after having endured extreme poverty, extreme

---

12. On this subject Origen comments in his *Homilies on Luke* 19–20 (text and French translation in SC 86, 272–88): "As Mary and Joseph searched for the lost boy Jesus they experienced the wearisome toil required for finding the 'Word' contained in the Scriptures and hidden in events."

humiliation, and a complete stripping of the self that was sealed by death and, indeed a death on a cross, which was the most humiliating and shaming means of torture. Beside the cross, like a supporting pillar, was Mary, the handmaid of the Lord, who "shares through faith in the shocking mystery of this self-emptying" (*RM* 18). There she was pierced by a pain that reached the deepest point of a mother's suffering; "This is perhaps the deepest 'kenosis' of faith in human history" (ibid.).

Out of this night of faith, which resembled that of Abraham on Moriah, came Mary's glory. As Mother of the suffering Servant who was to be honored, exalted, and glorified at the Father's right hand, Mary shared in every way the mystery of abasement and greatness, merit and glory.

> No one was so humiliated in this world as
> Mary; and this shows that no one has been
>   raised higher than she.
> The Lord grants glory in the degree of one's
>   humility;
> he made her his Mother, and who is like her in
>   humility?
> If there was a soul purer and gentler than she,
> he would have dwelt in that soul.[13]

Mary, "the handmaid of the Lord" (Lk 1:38a), is both chronologically and qualitatively the first model of the attitude that the disciples of Christ must possess. She teaches the men and women of today that to enter into the mystery of Christ means becoming servants. "It is precisely this service which constitutes the foundation of that Kingdom in which 'to serve ... means to reign' " (*MDig* 5).

---

13. James of Sarug, in *TMPM* IV, 145–46: 8, no. 5.

2. Docility to the Will of the Father

Una tibi placendi movet voluntas[14]

In the extraordinary event of the Annunciation, which makes known to us the inner truth of the Virgin of Nazareth, docility to the will of the Father is one of Mary's characteristics. She comes before us as one who abandons herself completely to the living God and docilely allows him to lead her, giving full service of intellect and will to him who spoke to her through his messenger (see *DV* 5).

The Annunciation is illustrative of the Virgin as a creature "poor in spirit," who with her "Yes" opens herself with complete docility to the will of God. Her entire life stands under the sign of that "Yes," as Christ's entire life would stand under the sign of the cross. To the divine messenger Mary first declares herself to be "the handmaid of the Lord," an expression that clearly describes her readiness to carry out the Father's will with complete docility and love. She then makes the divine plan her own, desiring that it be fulfilled in her: "May it be done to me according to your word" (Lk 1:38).

We do not have here a simple acceptance of the divine will as made known by the angel. The desire which is the form her answer takes, shows the full conformity of Mary's will to that of God and the commitment of her whole being with all its aspirations to the carrying out of the message. She desires only what her Lord desires.

Here again, therefore, we see immediately and with utter clarity the "preformation" in Mary of Christ's fundamental outlook and habitual way of acting. As the gospel teaches us, the spiritual food of Jesus, the energizing source all his actions, consisted in doing the will of the One who sent him;

---

14. "A single determination to please you motivates them" (the Mother and the Son are one in their will to please the Father).

his personal ambition was to be a docile Son. He wanted to bring to completion the work the Father had entrusted to him: "My food is to do the will of the one who sent me and to finish his work" (Jn 4:34).

But the express desire of Mary at the moment of the Annunciation was the same as his, so that her acceptance was in complete harmony with that of her Son: "She was determined to seek satisfaction and joy in her life in the same way as her Son was to do: the doing of the divine will was already her food" (Jean Galot).

It must be accepted that the deepest maternal bond between Mary and her Son flowed from this shared dedication to the supreme plan of the Father. The meeting of these two wills, that of the Word and that of the Virgin, occurred at the very moment of the Incarnation, when the divine "Yes" of the Word: "Behold, I come to do your will, O God" (Heb 10:9; Ps 40:8–9) is completely echoed in Mary's joyous "Yes": "May it be done to me according to your word" (Lk 1:38). On this point Calabuig remarks that at Nazareth these two wills began to act as one and would continue to be one throughout the entire life of Christ until its completion on Easter and its eschatological fulfillment.

Beyond a doubt, submission to the Father's will played a decisive role in the redemptive sacrifice, as Christ's prayer in Gethsemani bears witness: "Not what I will but what you will" (Mk 14:36). The same conformity of Mary to the Father's will finds its first expression in the words used by the Virgin in her reply to the angelic message.

Mary was always open to the divine will, without ever placing the least obstacle in the way, but the submission reached its high point during the time of suffering on Calvary when Christ Jesus became "obedient to death, even death on a cross" (Phil 2:8). During this time which was so decisive for the human race, when the gift of self reached its supreme embodiment, Mary stood, erect and fearless, as though turned to stone, "enduring with her only begotten Son the intensity of his suffering" and associating "herself with his sacrifice in her mother's heart" (*LG* 58). There she remained courageous in the presence of the Son who was dying before her eyes in agonizing pain; she abandoned herself more than ever to God, "lovingly consenting to the immolation of this victim which was born of her" (ibid.) This splendid model of maternal fortitude seemed to be repeating: "Behold, I am the handmaid of the Lord. May it be done to me according to your word" (Lk 1:38).

After all, what does "standing beneath the cross" signify if not this commitment of the Virgin Mother, this steady, determined will to entrust herself with abandon to the Father? *Stabat Mater* (Jn 19:25): the Mother of the crucified Messiah "was standing" there: in her own sacred, adoring silence she accepted the silence of God; forgetting herself, she accepted the mysterious, disconcerting plan of him who always remains the "Wholly Other."

Raniero Cantalamessa reminds us:

> We are not told that Mary cried and lamented, as did the women who accompanied Jesus on the way to Calvary (Lk 23:27); we are not told of any words she spoke as she did at the finding in the temple or at Cana in Galilee. We are told only of her silence. In the gospel of Luke Mary is silent at the moment of the birth of Jesus, and in the gospel of John she is silent at the moment of the death of Jesus.... The wisdom of the world is through words and discourses; the cross finds expression through silence. Silence is the language of the cross! For God, only silence emits the sweet perfume of sacrifice. It keeps suffering from

being wasted, from seeking and finding its reward here below.[15]

"God reigns where he is obeyed. God dwells in those who do his will," says A. Martinelli in an eloquent address at an international Marian congress. He goes on to say: "At no moment in human history was God's will done with such love and accepted with such submission as on Golgotha." At this time which was tragic yet was also so laden with meaning and with salvation for all of us, Mary and her Son were partners in filial obedience to the Father and open to him in the depths of their being.

"They entered into the circle of his decrees and penetrated into the sphere of his holiness and his glory; they belonged completely to him as they experienced the complete holocaust of themselves." Their wills were wonderfully united to the point of merging in a single redemptive offering, a single self-surrender, a single Yes. There was but

> a single victim, a single heart, one and the same movement of giving, one and the same holocaust. A single altar but also a single spiritual temple in which the Father received the most perfect filial worship. In virtue of this sacrifice offered with such great love and heroic dedication, the Father received the most sublime praise and saw his reign over the world reach its supreme degree. Is there anything more glorious than to comply with the will of God?[16]

Thanks to the generous obedience of Jesus, which was anticipated in Mary, the Father's work had come to be done in its entirety, with a human collaboration that took the form of a pure docility to the will of God.

---

15. Cantalamessa, *Maria uno specchio per la Chiesa*, 116–17.
16. Martinelli, in *Maria Santissima e lo Spirito Santo*, 91–98.

In the Son a love superior to every other love was at work. At work in the Mother was a love to which no other save Christ's can be compared (St. Bernard).

3. The Virginity of the Mother
Foretells the Celibacy of the Son

> The child born of the Virgin is the stone that
> though not pushed split off the mountain (Dan
> 2:34); that birth was not the work of a man
> nor did concupiscence play a part in it;
> there was only a faith on fire,
> and the result was the conception of the Word.
> If you do not believe that it so happened,
> you, too, are an unbeliever.
>
> (St. Augustine)

Looking still at the account of the Annunciation, so pregnant and rich in teaching, we learn that the consent given by the young girl of Nazareth was deliberately conditioned by her virginity, for she did not hesitate to speak of this as a difficulty in carrying out the angel's message: "How can this be, since I have no relations with a man?" (Lk 1:34).

If we study her words carefully, they bear witness to Mary's mature decision to remain a virgin. In fact, the words "I have no relations with a man" express directly a state of being, but with the intention of persevering in that state, since they express an obstacle to the planned motherhood revealed by the angel.

When Mary asks "How can this be?" she is not casting doubt on the fulfillment of the announced plan but is inquiring into the "how" of it. That is, she thinks that the difficulty raised by her virginity can be overcome in the divine plan, but she does not know how. Once the angel has made known to her how God will accomplish the "great thing" that is the virginal conception, she moves on from "How can this be?" to "May it be done to me according to your word."

Her decision to remain a virgin was in sharp opposition to ideas dominant in the Jewish tradition, which said that Mary had an obligation to contribute through a fruitful marriage to the vigor of her people. Her virginity was, therefore, very much a novelty that foreshadowed the novelty of voluntary celibacy which Jesus introduced. It also allows us to glimpse an important aspect of the preformation in Mary of the future reality of her Son. Thus, to the great surprise of his hearers, he in his turn praises the virginal state of life. But he also specifies the fundamental motive for a voluntary renunciation of what was regarded as the most valuable privilege of a human being, that is, fatherhood and motherhood: some are eunuchs "for the sake of the kingdom of heaven" (Mt 19:12).

With this statement Jesus made clear that he was dealing not with the kingdom of Israel, which sought its strength in the numbers of its people, but with the kingdom of God, which spreads through a spiritual fruitfulness. At the same time, however, he was aware that the qualitative leap he had made was not only a novelty for the Jewish mentality but also meant overcoming the deepest demands or natural tendencies of human beings. Therefore he adds: "Not all can accept [this] word, but only those to whom that is granted.... Whoever can accept this ought to accept it" (Mt 19:11, 12b). Only a special gift of God can make human beings appreciate properly the state of consecrated life.

The novel idea, voiced by Jesus, of celibacy for the sake of the kingdom sheds light back on Mary's determination to remain a virgin. The young girl of Nazareth was able to commit herself to the way of virginity because the kingdom of heaven inspired all of her actions.

Mary thus began a way of life that was destined to become widespread in the life of the Church; down the centuries thousands have devoted their lives to purity and virginity.

They have renounced marriage and family, which are two of the highest values of the created world, in order to place themselves at the disposition of God's ultimate plan, which is that human beings should live with him, in him, and for him in the most radical and unconditional way.

According to John Damascene's splendid image, Mary is the fruitful plant of virginity because it is thanks to her that the concept of virginity as a value spread (*TMPM* II, 507). In the history of the Church she is, and will always be, the First-Fruits of female virginity as Christ is of male virginity (Origen). In this sphere, the young woman of Nazareth will be a reminder to all that virginity means indeed a liberation from the desire that turns love into dependency but also that it is not a renunciation of love. On the contrary, it means the attainment of love: of that authentic love that is undivided, all-absorbing, and universal.

In Mary, the virginal icon of the Son, human beings contemplate their own dignity because they realize that they too can, through their graced freedom, become the icons of Jesus Christ.

4. *In Mary the Redemptive Sacrifice Was Preformed*

As a first pointer toward the sacrifice on Calvary, the incident of the presentation of Jesus in the temple (Lk 2:22–35), as illumined by Simeon's prophecy, becomes very important, for it tells us that Mary's life as mother was from the very outset oriented in a painful way toward the redemptive drama. In this light we can say that her co-redemptive role (of which we shall speak further on) consisted not simply in her participation in a moment of tribulation but also in an interior disposition which guided her maternal mission toward the final sacrifice.

In the divine plan, long before the sacrifice was completed in Jesus, it had become a reality first and foremost in the heart of the Virgin who would live out this faith-reality in her maternal flesh. According to Max Thurian, the Virgin Mother lived for the sake of her Son's "hour"; hers was therefore a life dominated by a spirit of sacrifice. Her action of presenting the fruit of her womb in the temple was a sacrificial gesture (letters of St. Paul). She was the first to fill out in her own flesh and for the Church what was lacking in the sufferings of the Whole Christ which is the Church.[17]

The reference to Mary in Simeon's prophecy is not unimportant, since it is spoken directly to her. It involves her in an incomparable way in the painful lot of her Son and in the opposition to him that will develop. Ahead of him lies a road strewn with thorns; this obscure plan with its death and resurrection the Mother will likewise accept in her heart.

Driven by the Spirit, as Luke the evangelist tells us, Simeon went to the temple and spoke to Mary, the child's mother: "Behold, this child is destined for the fall and rise of many in Israel … and you yourself a sword will pierce" (Lk 2:34–35).

This prophetic announcement gives the appearance of being a "second annunciation," in the sense that it develops and modifies that of the angel at Nazareth. It links Mary and her child so closely that in speaking of the sword that will pierce the mother's heart it also makes known the coming suffering of Jesus. If Simeon had not referred to this sword, his prophecy would not have brought into focus the drama of the passion; it would have pointed ahead to the opposition encountered by the Messiah but not to his tragic end.

In his writings, Vinandy emphasizes the fact that the account of the Presentation tells us, first and foremost, of the destiny shared by Mother and Son.[18] It is a sharing that includes the suffering of Mary, so clearly announced in the

17. Max Thurian, *Mary Mother of All Christians* (N.Y.: Herder & Herder, 1960).
18. See *La prophétie*, 349.

holy old man's image of a sword. Jesus will be rejected and struck; Mary will be rejected and struck with him. Every opposition to the Messiah, every rejection of him by Israel — even after Easter and down to our day — will pierce deeply the heart of his Mother.

After Simeon's prophecy, Mary knows that a sacrifice lies ahead for her Son and that she herself will experience its terrible suffering. She knows that she is presenting her child for a sacrifice that will torment her as well. Unlike other mothers, who cannot know in advance the sufferings their children will cause them, she knew, from these early days on, that she was on her way toward the most difficult trial a mother could face.

The ransom to which Luke refers in the passage on the Presentation in the temple was only a symbol or an image. Here, however, it becomes a reality. In order to ransom her first-born, Mary could not simply pay the priest a sum of money (as was customary among the Jews). She won his deliverance only by offering him for the proposed sacrifice; it was by accepting the sword which would pierce her soul that she could continue to have her Son.

As a mother, Mary offered her Son before he could offer himself; she performed the action of offering that Christ the priest was to make later on. It can be said, therefore, that Mary was the first to offer the redemptive sacrifice; in her is "preformed" the redemptive act par excellence which was already centered on Christ. We do not have here simply an offering which Mary makes of herself; it is her Son whom she offers, and it is he who is leading her on to the redemptive sacrifice.[19]

---

19. See Galot, *Maria, la donna*, 254–60.

E. A New Adam and a New Eve
Giving Rise to a New Human Race

It is beyond question that in the handing on of the faith and in Christian reflection on it through all the generations the pairing of Adam and Christ has been accompanied by the pairing of Eve and Mary. Mary is the "new woman" who is always closely associated with Christ, the "new man," in the work of salvation, which is to give rise to new generations. Beginning with the Fathers of the Church, many scholars, theologians, and churchmen, in their efforts to give Mary her proper place in the divine plan of salvation, have provided clear and tested arguments for the doctrine of the New Eve. This doctrine describes her vocation by reference to the New Adam. Cignelli comments: at the first creation there were a man and a woman: Adam and Eve. At the beginning of the new or second creation there were a New Adam and a New Eve: Christ and Mary.[20]

It was fitting that a woman be associated with Christ in his mission of salvation. According to the prophecy in the Protevangelium, it was in response to Eve's part in the first sin that God decided a woman should play a role in the struggle against the demon (see Gen 3:1–15).

> If sin came about through the complicity of the man and the woman, then redemption ought likewise be accomplished through an association of a man and a woman. That is, alongside the new Adam there ought to be a new Eve who collaborates with him in extending the reign of grace, just as the first Eve had contributed to extending the reign of sin. In the origin of a new human race a new Eve ought to play a decisive part in union with the new Adam. Thanks to this collaboration of a woman the victory over sin can achieve its complete extension in the human race.

---

20. See L. Cignelli, *Maria nuova Eva nella Patristica greca* (Assisi, 1966).

The redemptive plan thus shows its harmony with
the work of creation. God created the human race as
man and woman (Gen 1:27) in order that the race
might be marked by his image. The human couple
came into being as a reflection of the community of the
divine persons. But the likeness between humanity and
God ought to be reinforced by redemption. It was
fitting, therefore, that redemption be accomplished
through the association of a man and a woman. The
first community, which gave rise to the whole human
race, is matched by a community that is the source of
the spiritual rebirth of humanity.[21]

On this point St. Bernard writes: "There is no doubt that
Jesus Christ, all by himself, was more than able to redeem
us, but it was more fitting that both sexes should play a part
in our salvation, since both played a part in our ruin-
ation."[22] "It was right that life should return by the same
path by which death entered" (*TMPM* I, 126).

Among the early Fathers of the Church who brought out
the profound meaning of the New Adam-New Eve pair, St.
Justin and St. Irenaeus deserve special notice. Both men
added to the thinking of Paul by contrasting the obedience
of Mary and the disobedience of Eve, just as the Apostle
had contrasted the obedience of Christ and the sin of
Adam. Parallel with the path followed by the obedient new
Adam was the path followed by the new Eve, who was obedient to the will of God.

A mysterious bond connects and, at the same time, distinguishes the scene of the Annunciation in Luke and the scene
of seduction described in Genesis 3:1–20, the two scenes
representing two actions, each of which begets a history (a

---

21. Galot, *Maria, la donna*, 272.
22. Cited in St. Alphonsus Liguori, *The Glories of Mary*, 177.

history belonging both to God and to humanity). Human beings destroy, God rebuilds; human beings sin, God saves; human beings introduce death, God restores life. But a unique entity guides both processes: a virginal woman. By means of Eve, still a virgin, Adam sinned; by means of Mary, a virgin, Christ, God incarnate, is born. "When Eve was still a virgin and unblemished, she allowed the serpent's words into her bosom and brought forth disobedience and death. In contrast, Mary, a virgin, brought forth faith and joy when the angel Gabriel brought her the glad tidings."[23] "Thus the knot of Eve's disobedience was untied by Mary's obedience; what the virgin Eve bound through her disbelief, Mary loosened by her faith."

"The disobedience of Eve, which flowed out over the whole human race, was answered by the obedience of Mary, which had the same universal echo, but with diametrically opposed results. In the drama of the fall the woman had entered the path of disobedience and evil, thereby "becoming the cause of death for herself and for the entire human race; in the plan of salvation a woman enters upon the path of obedience and the good, thereby becoming the cause of eternal salvation for herself and for the entire human race."[24]

The age-old doctrine of the New Eve emerges with all its freshness and vitality in the teaching of Vatican II, which confirms that "the Father of mercies willed that the Incarnation should be preceded by assent on the part of the predestined mother, so that just as a woman had a share in bringing about death, so also a woman should contribute to life" (*LG* 56).

Given this teaching, we find the deeper reason why in specific circumstances Jesus turned to his Mother and called her

---

23. St. Justin, *Dialogue with Trypho*, ch. 100 (PG 6:709–12).
24. The two passages are from St. Irenaeus, *Against the Heresies* III, 22 (PG 7:958–59; SC 34 [1952] 378–82). The first is cited in *LG* 56.

"Woman" (Jn 2:4; 19:26). Used within the mother-son relationship the word may seem strange, but Jesus certainly did
not think so, for in using it he intended to attribute to his
mother all the greatness which the word conveyed. It is true
that "Jesus used the same word when addressing other
women; but when he called Mary (his Mother) 'Woman,' he
was giving the word a special, more pointed meaning, since
he would normally have addressed her as 'mother' " (Jean
Galot). By replacing "mother" with "woman" he intended to
make clear to Mary that he was moving beyond their familial
relationship and thinking of her as the "New Eve" or "New
Woman," who was collaborating with him in establishing a
new race and "taking part, as a mother, in that 'monumental
struggle against the powers of darkness' which continues
throughout human history" (*RM* 47).

The moments or historical contexts (wedding feast at
Cana, Calvary: the former foretelling the new or messianic
age, the latter fulfilling the prophecy) in which Christ,
according to John the evangelist, used "Woman" in addressing his Mother were very important ones. They tend to suggest that the word did not have simply a generic sense, much
less that it signified a distancing of himself from her, but
rather that it conveyed Christ's intention of universalizing
the figure of his Mother.

With good reason Chaminade writes: "It is certain that
Jesus behaved toward Mary as a very affectionate, loving,
and respectful Son. If he nevertheless addressed her simply
as 'Woman,' even at the supreme moment of his life, that is,
on the altar of the cross, it meant that he could not find a title
more reverential and true, and better suited to the place in
relation to humanity and to himself."[25]

---

25. Chaminade, *La conoscenza di Maria*, 63.

F. Co-redemptrix

Introduction

> Knowing ... that the death of the Son was for the bene-
> fit of all, the Mother hastened to see whether she too
> might contribute to the common good by her own
> death.... At the foot of the cross she gazed with com-
> passionate eyes on her Son's wounds, from which, she
> knew, would come the redemption of the world.
>
> She stood erect, providing a sight not unlike that of
> her Son, for she did not fear those who might kill her.
> The Son hung on the cross, the mother offered herself
> to her persecutors.[26]
>
> Who can penetrate the mystery of the look that
> passed between Mother and Son at such a moment?
> They had become one with the suffering and sin of the
> entire world.

The doctrinal elements underlying the ancient patristic
parallelisms: Eve-Mary and Adam-Christ, have as it were
solidified and flowed together in a more recent, spacious
conception that draws its inspiration from theology: the
concept of co-redemption. This doctrine, like that of the
New Eve, says that in a mysterious, eternal, divine plan of
love the Virgin Mary is associated with the person and
saving action of the Redeemer. It says that Mary was too
closely linked to her Son for there not to be also a mystery
of collaboration. Her greatness is connected not only with
the mystery of the Incarnation but also with that of
redemption. In fact, the two mysteries form a single
whole, since the Son of God became a human being in
order to obtain salvation and divine life for humanity.

---

26. Ambrose of Milan, *Training of Virgins* 6, 49 (PL 16:318).

In the realization of this sublime mystery, which embraces all of us, Mary became not only the "nourishing mother" of the "Son of Man," but also "in a singular way the generous associate" of the Messiah and Redeemer (see *LG* 61). She participated in the highest possible way in the mystery of Christ both as incarnate Word and as Savior. In the eternal plan of God for humanity her entire life can be seen as essentially a work done together with Christ for the human race. Karl Rahner makes the careful statement that in the entire history of salvation the human being we call Mary is as it were the individual upon whom the salvation of the living God falls directly from on high in order then to reach out to the whole human race.[27]

From the very instant of the Incarnation Jesus adopted the dispositions of a victim, thereby anticipating his bloody sacrifice. In the womb of Mary he was already the redemptive mediator, the priest and victim who by his sacrificial obedience would sanctify the human race (see Heb 10:5–10). Thus, in the Virgin's spotless womb as in a perfect sanctuary pleasing to God the first sacrifice of the messianic age was offered. And from that moment Jesus closely associated his Mother with himself in the accomplishment of our redemption; as a result, she developed an ever closer relationship with the Son of God and her Son. From then on, she would not be separated from his person and his work.

Theological Foundations of Co-redemption

The doctrine of co-redemption has often been given varying interpretations and been the subject of sometimes impassioned debates among theologians and scholars. It has its roots in the medieval period when, as devotion to the passion

---

27. Karl Rahner, *Maria Madre del Signore. Meditazioni teologiche* (Fossano: Ed. Esperienze, 1962) 39.

of Christ was growing and teaching on redemption was being developed, theologians began to bring out not only Mary's association with the sufferings of her Son but also her direct cooperation in the work of redemption. In other words, the theologians realized that the Mother suffered with her Son for the salvation of the world in virtue of the Father's plan which willed that there be a New Eve as a "suitable partner" (Gen 2:18) for the New Adam. Through her compassion ("suffering with") she contributed not only to making the drama of the cross more deeply human but also to "meriting" the deliverance and sanctification of humanity. The result of her maternal association with the sufferings of the Son was to effect salvation for all of us.[28]

Indeed, the presence of our Mother on Calvary seems to have been inspired by the intention of sharing in the sacrifice of her Son. The uninterrupted series of "Yeses" which she had spoken to the Redeemer throughout her life, even when they cost her a martyrdom of soul and spirit, reached its culmination on the altar of the cross in the sacrificial offering of herself with the Lamb, which was the price paid for the ransom of the world.

On the other hand, when Jesus himself asks Mary to consent to his death just before commending his spirit into the Father's hands (Jn 19:25–38), he emphasizes the close association of his Mother with his sacrifice. He also shows that he regards her presence on Calvary not simply as evidence of her maternal sympathy but as an involvement in the work of redemption. God has arranged that the redemption of humanity should come about not only through the merits of Christ and the satisfaction he offers but also through the

---

28. See Galot, *Maria, la donna*, 239–92; and *Maria, itinerario spirituale*, 91–92, 268–74.

merits of Mary, so much so that without the latter we would not have redemption as God decreed it in his eternal plan.[29]

Redemption: Objective and Subjective,
Direct and Indirect

In order better to understand the special character of Mary's co-redemption, we must bring up some important points established by the theologians.

First and foremost, it must be pointed out that Mary's cooperation in objective redemption is beyond doubt, since the divine maternity constitutes a fundamental aspect of such cooperation. That is, by bringing the Redeemer into the world, the Virgin Mary had already contributed in an eminent way to the overall work of salvation. "The very name *Theotokos* [Mother of God] contains the entire mystery of salvation" (St. John Damascene). Jesus is the "Son of Man" and has saved us thanks to this Mother: "the beautiful lamb, pure and innocent, who gave birth to the Lamb for the sacrifice" (*NDM*, 1050). It was in her womb that Christ took the first fruits of our flesh, which were the material for this sacrifice. "He could not have died for us if he had not taken mortal flesh from her" (St. Augustine): the redemption of the world is tied up with the body received from Mary and offered in the sacrifice of the cross.

This form of cooperation with objective redemption, namely, the divine maternity of Mary or the act of giving the human race its Savior, is by its nature mediate or indirect, as defined by the theologians. We know, however, that the cooperation of the Mother of Jesus went further, beyond her simple role as Mother, and was a cooperation in the redemptive work itself. In practice, Mary did not simply give us the Savior but personally collaborated in the redemptive sacrifice which acquired all the graces of salvation. "We

---

29. S. Meo, "Nuova Eva," in *NDM*, 1022–23.

must therefore speak of a 'direct or immediate cooperation' in objective redemption; this implies Mary's meritorious association with the redemptive sacrifice. Only when thus viewed does co-redemption, in the case of the Mother of Jesus, acquire its proper features, its true identity, and take on its full meaning and value."[30]

Regarding this conceptual guide, some testimonies of not a few scholars, outstanding theologians, Fathers, and churchmen can be useful and enlightening, stimulating and incisive.

The first member of the throng of those who have directly reflected on Mary's cooperation with the sacrifice of Calvary was Arnulf of Chartres, an enthusiastic disciple of St. Bernard and a man described as the first champion of Marian co-redemption. In connection with the cross he distinguishes two altars: one in the heart of Mary, the other in the body of Christ.

> Christ sacrificed his flesh, Mary her soul. She wanted to die with her Son, but the death on the cross was the privilege of the high priest, a dignity which Christ could not share with anyone. Yet Mary's maternal affection did cooperate, at the highest level and in its own way, in rendering God propitious, since in his love Christ brought to the Father both his own desires and those of his Mother, and since what the Mother asked, the Son approved and the Father bestowed.[31]

Developing these ideas elsewhere, St. Bernard's disciple says:

> In the presence of the Father, the Mother and the Son ... in marvelous union take measures for the accomplishment of human redemption.... The

---

30. Galot, *Maria, la donna*, 243–45.
31. Arnulf of Chartres, *De septem verbis Domini in cruce* 3 (PL 189:1694).

Mother's affection moved Jesus, so that Christ and Mary were one in will, and the two, in like manner, offered but a single holocaust: she in the blood of the heart, he in the blood of the flesh. As a result, Mary obtained with Christ a shared effect, the salvation of the world.[32]

Like Arnulf, many others have described the Mother's participation in the immolation of her Son, using touching and stimulating images that were dictated by the heart under the movement of the Spirit. "All the sufferings and wounds of the Son were felt in the Mother's heart. The insults leveled at the Son pierced the Mother's heart like arrows, and the nails inflicted on the Son wounded her heart like spears. The sword that pierced the side of Jesus struck her heart as well."[33]

She suffered in her heart what the Son suffered in his flesh. Who could think otherwise if they but knew what it means to be a mother? As Christ cried out: "My God, my God, why have you abandoned me?" so the Virgin Mary must have been pierced by suffering that corresponded, for a human being, to that of the Son.[34] It can even be said that "she ... suffered an even greater torment than if her body were being tortured, because she loved in an incomparably greater measure him on whose account she was suffering."[35]

In a true sense she died with him even while remaining alive, and as a living woman endured suffering more cruel than death itself (St. Bonaventure). Blood no longer flowed from the Lord's wounds, nor did the Virgin's eyes weep tears; and the heart of Mary was buried with the dead

32. Arnulf of Chartres, *De laudibus B. M. Virginis* (PL 189:1726–27).
33. Maximus the Confessor, *Vita Mariae* (CSCO 478 and 479).
34. Soren Kierkegaard, *Diario* XII A 45.
35. A. of Lausanne, *Homilia V* (SC 72:148; in *TMSM* III, 293).

body of Jesus.[36] "True enough," says St. Bernard, addressing the Madonna,

> once your Jesus had breathed his last, the cruel spear
> could not reach his soul. When, not respecting his dead
> body, it opened his side, it could no longer do your Son
> any harm. But it could indeed harm you. It pierced your
> soul. His soul was no longer there, but yours could not
> withdraw. Your suffering drove its way into your soul,
> so that we can rightly call you more-than-martyr, since
> your sharing in the suffering of your Son was far more
> intense than the physical torments of martyrdom.[37]

As the Byzantine liturgy contemplates, with deep feeling, the suffering of Mary at the foot of the cross, it says: "She had to be associated with her Son in everything having to do with our lot. As she had given him his flesh and his blood while receiving in return the gift of her graces, so too she had to share in all his sufferings and in all his afflictions."

All these keen and penetrating intuitions of faith have been confirmed in the ordinary teaching of the Church. Beginning with Leo XIII, quite a few pontifical documents have given voice to the doctrine of the co-redemption, although without claiming to impose it on the theologians or the faithful as a teaching that must be followed. The pope who issued *Rerum novarum* dealt with the doctrine in three encyclicals. In *Nella iucunda semper* (1894) he wrote that though absent in body from Gethsemani and the pretorium, Mary was present in spirit, because "when she consented to be the Mother of this redeemer-God and presented him in the temple, she became associated with him in the harsh expiation that redeemed the human race." But it was on Calvary

---

36. Charles Drelincourt, cited in Thurian, *Mary Mother of All Christians.*
37. St. Bernard, *Sermon for the Sunday after the Assumption*, 14–15 (*Opera* 5:273–74).

that, "inspired by her immense love and desire to receive us as her children, she offered her Son to the divine justice."

The teaching of Pius X developed along the same lines. In the encyclical *Ad diem illum* (1904) he proclaims:

> Not only did Mary give the world the victim required for our salvation; she also had the duty of protecting him, nourishing him, and, at the appointed moment, offering him on the altar of sacrifice. Thus the sharing of life and sufferings between Mother and Son was never interrupted. Because of this communion in sentiments between Mary and Christ Mary merited to become, in a worthy manner, the repairer of fallen humanity.

Benedict XV reflected on co-redemption in his apostolic letter *Inter sodalicia* (1918). In his contemplation of Mary at the foot of the cross, the pope wrote that she suffered and, in a sense, died with her Son in order to save the human race and satisfy the justice of God. It can therefore rightly be said that, as far as this was in her power, she sacrificed her Son and, with him, ransomed the human race.

In the encyclical *Miserentissimus Redemptor* (1928) Pius XI asserted that because the Virgin and kindly Mother of God gave birth to Jesus the Redeemer, raised him, and at the cross offered him as a victim for our sake, she became, through her mysterious union with him and by his extraordinary grace, repairer of the human race along with him.

Pius XII took up the question of co-redemption on several occasions. In the encyclical *Mystici Corporis* (1943) he wrote:

> As true queen of the martyrs, Mary completed what was lacking in the sufferings of Christ for his body, the Church.... Herself free of every stain, whether personal or inherited, and always most closely united

to her Son, this New Eve made a holocaust of all her maternal rights and her maternal love and on Golgotha offered him to the eternal Father on behalf of all the children of Adam, now stained by the wretched sin of their first parent.

In *Marialis cultus* (1974) Paul VI explained the Marian feasts in their connection with the mysteries of Christ. The memorial of the Mother of Sorrows (September 15), he wrote, is "a fitting occasion for re-living a decisive moment in the history of salvation and for venerating, together with the Son 'lifted up on the Cross, his suffering Mother' " (no. 7). Pope John Paul II dealt extensively with this subject, especially in the Apostolic Letter *Salvifici doloris* (1984). Here he had this to say, among other things:

> The many intense sufferings of Mary combined to form a massive linkage that not only proved her indestructible faith but were also a contribution to the redemption of all.... On Calvary the suffering of the Blessed Virgin Mary, along with that of Jesus, reached a peak, the loftiness of which is difficult for human beings to imagine. But that suffering was certainly mysterious and supernaturally fruitful for the purpose of universal salvation.

During a general audience on November 23, 1988, the same pope sums up: "Mary willed to share completely in the sufferings of Christ, for she did not reject the sword prophesied by Simeon but instead accepted, with Christ, the Father's mysterious plan."

As is easy to see, all the documents mentioned above give expression, though covertly, to what the theologians call the immediate or direct cooperation of Mary in objective redemption. Though they do not use the word, the texts assert the truth in question in equivalent and often very strong terms.

For example: "Mary sacrificed her Son"; "she offered him to the Father"; "she is restorer or repairer of humanity"; "with Christ she ransomed the human race"; "she shared in redemptive merit"; "she was associated with the acquisition of salvation"; "she contributed to the redemption of all."

Vatican Council II did not use the word "co-redemptrix" in order to avoid any possible misunderstanding in the areas of pastoral life and ecumenism. But it adopted the same perspective when it described Mary's association with all the mysteries of redemption, including Calvary (see *LG* 57–59) and when it summed up the whole matter in a few especially felicitous words: The Blessed Virgin was "here on earth ... in a singular way the generous associate and humble handmaid of the Lord" (*LG* 61).

Following in the Steps of the Mother of Jesus,
   the Entire Church Is a Co-redemptrix

The title "co-redemptrix" allows us better to understand and make the most not only of Mary's special role but also of the role proper to Christians in the one economy of the history of salvation.

The Mother of Jesus, who was the first to share in the redemptive sacrifice, will always be an inspiration and perfect model for all who courageously accept to be unreservedly associated with the redemptive self-offering of Christ. "She does not simply draw us into her feelings during the drama of the cross; the Sorrowful Virgin also enlightens us about the value of our own sufferings, for, when united with the sufferings of Christ, they are meant to contribute to the building of a better world. She urges us to accept the cross with generous hearts and to believe in the fruitfulness which every participation in the sacrifice of Christ adds to the work of salvation." Thus when St. Paul refers to his apostolic activity, he does not hesitate to write: "We are God's co-workers" (1 Cor 3:9).

Now, the word "co-redeemer" is certainly not more daring than "co-worker" or "cooperator"; rather it is an equivalent. Every baptized person, who has been grafted onto the paschal mystery of Christ and made a participant in his priestly ministry, is thereby called to collaborate with him, as a living stone (1 Pt 2:5a), in the establishment of his kingdom. All of the baptized are called to think of themselves as cooperators in Christ's saving work and to become, in the final analysis, co-redeemers in the footsteps of Mary, even while realizing, of course, that her more excellent co-redemption has a unique and exceptional value.

In addition, when we speak of co-redemption in connection with the Church of God or Christians generally, we are dealing, strictly speaking, with cooperation in subjective redemption. That is, all good Christians are urged to play a part in the spread of the life of grace in themselves and in others: through their striving for personal holiness, their exemplary manner of life, and their apostolic endeavors.

This kind of cooperation was clearly a reality in Mary's life. She welcomed grace with subjective dispositions that made possible its full development. In addition, in her contacts with others and by the witness of her life she encouraged in them a docility to God's will.

> But the Virgin of Nazareth not only cooperated in the application to the human race of the fruits of Christ's redemptive activity. Although she herself had benefited from the redemptive grace of her Son, she was to be celebrated in the world of the redeemed as the one who cooperated directly in the completion of the redemptive sacrifice, in the sense that she collaborated with Christ in the overall work of redemption and in the acquisition of salvation for all human beings, whatever their race or location in the world.
>
> Therefore the degree of co-redemption in the Mother

of God cannot be measured by the same standard as that of other Christians. It is coextensive with the entire redemptive work of Christ; her extraordinary participation in the priesthood of her Son makes this Mother the sole co-redemptrix of the human race.[38]

Mary's Co-redemptive Action in Light of the Eucharistic Sacrifice

The eucharistic sacrifice is a commemoration and renewal of the sacrifice of the cross; it has the same content as the latter and differs only in the manner of its offering. On the cross the sacrifice is a bloody one, while in the Eucharist there is no shedding of blood, but the victim is the same both on the cross and on the altar at which the Eucharist is celebrated. Consequently, the sacrifice of the Mass contains all the fruits of Mary's cooperation, and in it is actualized everything that Mary did at the side of Christ her Son and in dependence on him; her presence in the mystery being celebrated is connatural. "She who participated in the historical mysteries of her Son is now present in the mysteries made present in the memorial."[39]

Every Mass brings us into close communion with her, the Mother, whose sacrifice "becomes present again," just as the sacrifice of the Son "becomes present again" when the words consecrating the bread and the wine are pronounced by the priest (John Paul II).

In the framework of the Mass one element is eucharistic communion, which consists in receiving the victim immolated in the sacrifice. If Christ, the victim, includes in his sacrifice all of Mary's cooperation, then, when he gives himself in communion, he gives himself in that precise form and in no other. A communion in which the salvific influence of

---

38. Galot, *Maria, la donna*, 244.
39. Jesús Castellano Cervera, "La Presenza di Maria nel Mistero del culto," 401.

Mary is not actualized and does not share is impossible, because, in the final analysis, it would involve a contradiction; that is to say, we would have to think that when Christ gives himself as food in communion, he ceases to be the one who, as victim, immolated himself in the sacrifice. "The identity between victim immolated and food received ensures the influence of Mary in communion, an influence which she exercises through the grace of the Spirit and the merits of her divine Son. That grace is implicit in the fact that her Son willed to associate her with his own sacrifice."[40]

Co-redemption and the Uniqueness of Christ's Mediation

In response to what we have been saying, a spontaneous question may well be asked: "But is not Christ the sole mediator, as the Scriptures say (1 Tm 2:5–6)?" In order to answer this reasonable question, it will be enough to explain what is meant by the "uniqueness" of Christ's mediation.

Both the authoritative teaching of the Church and theology teach that Christ is sole mediator or that his mediation is unique, not in the sense that it does away with all other mediation, but in the sense that every other mediation depends on his and derives its entire value and meaning from his. In fact, it is the inexhaustible mediation of Christ that gives rise to other, subordinate mediations. "No creature could ever be counted along with the Incarnate Word and Redeemer; but just as the priesthood of Christ is shared in various ways by both his ministers and the faithful, and as the one goodness of God is radiated in different ways among his creatures, so also the unique mediation of the Redeemer does not exclude but rather gives rise to a manifold cooperation which is but a sharing in this one source" (*LG* 62).

---

40. Cardinal P. Palazzini, in *Maria Santissima e lo Spirito Santo*, 162–63.

It is clear, of course, that in her exceptional role as co-redemptrix Mary depends completely on the Son: from him she receives the disposition to share in his mediation; from him she has everything that she is and seeks to communicate to other human beings. Her maternal mediation is not autonomous but subordinated to the mediation of Christ, because it implies a collaboration, a secondary contribution to the redemption. Far from detracting from the unique role of the redeemer, it reveals all his greatness.

Here again the conciliar document is very explicit: "Mary's function as mother of men in no way obscures or diminishes this unique mediation of Christ but rather shows its power.... The Blessed Virgin's salutary influence on men originates not in any inner necessity but in the disposition of God. It flows forth from the superabundance of the merits of Christ, rests on his mediation, depends entirely on it and draws all its power from it" (*LG* 60).

Mary's cooperation is essentially maternal and, as such, substantially distinct from the value of Christ's sacrificial offering and his priestly activity. "What Mary really merited is her maternal power in the order of grace, her power to collaborate as mother in the flow of redemptive grace" (Jean Galot). The sharing of Mother and Son in sorrows and sufferings has allowed the holy Virgin to be, alongside her Son, a most powerful mediator and reconciler of the entire world (Pius X).

G. Mary Reigns Forever with Christ in Heavenly Glory

O Mother of God, you have moved from
wonder to wonder (*LM*, 91).

1. Introduction

The path which the Father traced for the Son, the Word
Incarnate, he traced also for the Mother. "She had to travel
the entire way which the Savior had trodden" (Nicholas
Cabasilas).

The limitless love of the Father for Mary invaded her and
took possession of her in a continuous crescendo: eternal
predestination, immaculate conception, divine maternity,
and finally the transfiguration of her entire person in heavenly glory and her anticipatory participation in the full fruits
of redemption.

As the sun, after traversing the great arc of its daytime
journey, in the evening plunges into the sea amid fiery
flashes, so Mary, after completing the period of her great
mission on earth, entered, glorious, into heaven "to shine
refulgent as Queen at the right hand of her Son, the immortal
King of ages" (*MDig*). Then, when she shall have also completed the heavenly period of her saving work, she, together
with Christ and all the blessed, shall be absorbed into God, in
order to sing his glories and celebrate his mercies through all
eternity. "If as Virgin and Mother she was singularly united
with him in his first coming, so through her continued collaboration with him she will also be united with him in
expectation of the second" (*RM* 41), when "God will be all in
all" (see 1 Cor 15:28).

This history of intimate, holy, and truly unique love
among all the members of the human race, the love which
existed between Mary and the Son of God on earth, has its
culmination in the Assumption. For of all her gifts bestowed

on her the Assumption is the supreme and crowning privilege.

A note introducing the Mass in honor of the Immaculate
Heart of Mary reads: "For nine months the life of the Son of
God made flesh was attuned to the life of his Mother;
that bond was never broken but was even strengthened
by Mary's presence, body and soul, in heaven" (Italian
Sacramentary).

2. The Assumption:
Brief Historical and Theological Explanations

The Assumption of Mary into heaven is a dogma solemnly defined by Pius XII in these words: "By the authority
of our Lord Jesus Christ, of the blessed apostles Peter and
Paul, and our own authority, we proclaim, declare and define
as a dogma revealed by God: the Immaculate Mother of
God, Mary ever Virgin, when the course of her earthly life
was finished, was taken up body and soul into the glory of
heaven" (Apostolic Constitution *Munificentissimus Deus*,
November 1, 1950).

The words "was taken up ... into the glory of heaven"
immediately signal a difference between the Ascension of
Jesus and the experience of Mary: Mary did not raise herself
up or ascend, but was taken up by the power of her risen and
glorified Son.

A complete reading of the document just cited allows us
to maintain that the subject of the Assumption was not so
much the body or the soul of Mary as her person in its
entirety. In other words: Mary understood as Mother of God,
without blemish and always a virgin: these are incomparable
prerogatives that by themselves justify the extraordinary
privilege of the Assumption. But in its theological explanation the papal document does not base the truth of the
Assumption solely on these two prerogatives but on Mary's
entire life and the mission which she carried out at Christ's

side. Even though in the definition proper she is described only as "Immaculate Mother of God" and "ever Virgin," in the theological exposition that precedes the definition she is also described as "the noble companion of the divine Redeemer," as though this were a further reason for her assumption into heaven.

We can say that the fundamental theological principle underlying this profound mystery is the complete actuation of the one, identical decree of predestination that links the life, privileges, and cooperation of Mary not only with the historical life and work of Christ but also with his complete victory over sin and death and with his kingship and glory.

a. Beginnings

Scripture contains no explicit and direct testimony regarding the assumption of Mary into heaven; nor is there any kind of reference in the tradition of the first three centuries to the final destiny of the Virgin (one reason is that no sure eschatological teaching had yet emerged). As a result we do not know precisely how Mary's earthly life ended: whether in a calm sleep of death, followed immediately by a resurrection and glorification like that of Jesus; or in a direct transferral to heaven and a transformation of her present life, inasmuch as that life had already been conformed mystically to the death of Jesus on Calvary. Nor do we know just when in historical time the Assumption occurred during the period after Pentecost.

The teaching of the Church passes over these questions, regarding them as nonessential for the purposes served by the truths of the faith. Instead, the Church has simply asserted the fact of the Assumption: "When the course of her earthly life was finished, [she] was taken up body and soul into the glory of heaven."

We must accept that the belief in the Assumption of the Blessed Virgin belongs among those truths regarding which

Scripture, but not reason, is silent. The belief is not based on historical accounts but on an intuition of the faith of the Church, which, guided by the light of the Holy Spirit, has become progressively aware of Mary's supreme dignity. We might say that the Holy Spirit has led the Church to read between the lines that which the text of Scripture does not expressly say.

The solemn definition of the dogma was not a sudden or arbitrary act of the extraordinary papal magisterium, but rather a final stage that ended a centuries-long journey of faith on the part of the entire Church. It was a goal that crowned and proclaimed a faith long and universally professed by the entire people of God. One example: at the end of the seventh and the beginning of the eighth century St. John Damascene clearly taught the resurrection of the Mother of God and her glorious assumption into heaven. "The most holy and incorruptible body born of her and united hypostatically to the Word rose from the tomb on the third day. But it was necessary that the Mother be reunited to the Son. And just as he had come down to her, so this beloved Mother had to be carried up to a broader and more beautiful dwelling place, to heaven itself" (*Homilies on the Dormition* 2, 14).

b. Theological Explanation of the Assumption *in* Lumen Gentium

The truth of the Assumption, as found in Vatican II, appears with an entirely new freshness in the eighth chapter of *Lumen Gentium*, where it is reexamined in a christological and an ecclesiological setting. By means of a fine theological and pastoral synthesis it is placed within a fuller vision of Mary's life and mission, to the point that it takes on a full and complete meaning never reached in previous magisterial documents.

In particular, as though crowning the relationship between Mary and Christ, Vatican II harks back to the formula of the dogmatic definition. It sets forth, once again, the two aspects, personal and christological, which the document of Pius XII finds in the Assumption and queenship of Mary, both connected with the work and victory of the Son. But it also introduces a new doctrinal enrichment: "Finally, the Immaculate Virgin, preserved free from all stain of original sin, was taken up body and soul into heavenly glory, when her earthly life was over, and exalted by the Lord as Queen over all things, that she might be more fully conformed to her Son, the Lord of Lords (cf. Rv 19:16) and conqueror of sin and death" (*LG* 59).

The Assumption, then, brings eschatological completion to the progressive conformity with Christ, which during the stages of Mary's historical journey had found expression in the suffering inflicted by her faith and her full acceptance and openness to the saving will of God. It brings to completion, in all its ontological and moral fullness, the glorious conformity of Mary with her risen Son.

To put it briefly, according to Vatican II the Assumption is but the final stage of the lengthy journey, marked by a responsible commitment, of Mary's motherhood of and cooperation with the Savior.

3. Biblical Foundations of the Assumption

We have seen that from the viewpoint of the faith the Assumption is but the full effect of the utterly unique bonds linking Mary and her Son in the flesh and even more in the spirit.

The Scriptures tell us of this close, privileged union between Mother and Son, for they show us the loving Mother of God closely united with her divine Son and always sharing his lot. It is here, in Revelation, that we find a wonderful confirmation, even if veiled and implicit, of

Mary's glorification. *Munificentissimus Deus* appeals to this unmistakable fact when it says: "This truth is based on Sacred Scripture ... and has been lucidly developed and explained ... by theologians." In the final analysis, the teaching of the Apostolic Constitution derives its life-giving power from the pure wellsprings of God's word and the teaching of the Fathers of the Church. The following considerations will help clarify this claim.

a) The Assumption: Required by the Divine Motherhood

Thinking in the light given by the entire biblical narrative of the history of salvation, the Church on its journey of faith has constantly expanded the horizons of its knowledge in Mariology as elsewhere. In light of a comprehensive reflection on the mystery of Mary, the Church has become increasingly aware that the concept of the divine maternity is not limited solely to the fact of conception and birth, but includes the entire lengthy process in which Mary became progressively more closely united with her Son, the Savior. Conception, birth, and nourishing constitute only the first essential and decisive aspect of the divine maternity. This motherhood matured and became more perfect to the point of establishing a close and unbroken union between Mother and Son in the work of salvation: from Nazareth to Bethlehem, from Cana to Jerusalem, from Calvary to her Assumption into heaven.

In this dynamic process, from becoming Mother to working for salvation, the divine maternity had its cornerstone in the Incarnation. It was completed by the entire earthly lives of Mother and Son and reached its perfection in the Assumption, when the face of the Mother achieved its full likeness to the face of the Son. Thus the "complete biography" of the Virgin Mother is part of the "complete biography" of her Son, Jesus Christ.

Early Testimonies

The first sermons on the Assumption already give evidence of doctrinal thinking that links the glorious entry of the Virgin into heaven with her divine maternity and everything that went with it: virginity, holiness, and intercession for humanity. A number of proofs were offered:

* The divine maternity created a spiritual and corporal connection between Mary and Christ, a union that ought to be continued in heaven through the presence of the soul and glorified body of Mary. St. Germanus of Constantinople has Christ speak thus to Mary: "Where I am, you too must be, a mother inseparable from your Son" (*Homily 3 on the Dormition*).

* The divine maternity turned the body of Mary into the dwelling place of the body of Christ, the place of the incarnate presence of God among us. For this reason the body of Mary ought to have been exempt from any corruption. We are revolted by the thought that this body of the Virgin, so closely connected with the humanity of Christ by reason of her biological motherhood, should then be separated from the Son and be subject to the corruption of the grave. It was impossible that this house of God, this living temple of the all-holy divinity of the only Son, should become the prey of death in the tomb. St. Germanus again: Jesus says to his Mother, "Entrust your body to me as I entrusted my divinity to your womb…. You became the place where I stayed; this place will not experience the decay caused by deterioration in the tomb" (ibid.).

* Because of the oneness of Mary's body with that of the Savior, it ought to share the latter's glory. St.

John Damascene writes: "It was necessary that she who had God, the Word, as guest in her womb should have a dwelling in the tents of her Son" (*Homily 2 on the Dormition*).

* Mary's motherhood elicited the affection of Jesus for her; this affection called for the reunion of Mother with Son. "As a child seeks longingly for the presence of its mother and as a mother loves the company of her child, it was fitting that you, of whose maternal love for your Son and God there was no doubt, should return to him. And was it not fitting that this God who had such a truly filial love for you should take you into his company?"[41]

* It was right that the Mother of Life should share the dwelling place of that Life. The close bonds between Mother and Son are not to be thought of as something purely private, for the Assumption is not a privilege bestowed within a family but is a demand of the economy of salvation: "How could the corruption of the tomb have been allowed to reduce to dust and ashes she who through the Incarnation of her Son has delivered humanity from the complete destruction of death?"[42]

* The heart of Mary, next to which the heart of the Incarnate Word was formed, could not be allowed to be destroyed by the corrupting activity of death. Even as a physical organ and the vehicle of a love that touches the world of the Infinite and embraces the whole human race, it ought to have remained

---

41. St. Germanus of Constantinople, *Homily 1 on the Dormition* (PG 98:347).
42. Ibid. (PG 98: 348 and 345).

intact as the expression of a love that knows no interruption or waning.

* The divine maternity implied a holiness and unlimited purity of body and spirit: The Immaculate One, the Virgin, the completely pure and holy Mother, "the uncorrupted one could not undergo corruption."[43] Her body, rendered holy by the touch of the Spirit and brought into the divine realm of the hypostatic union, could not be subject to the corruption of death, which is historically the wages of sin.

b) Some Particular Biblical Texts

When the Apostolic Constitution *Munificentissimus Deus* enters into the detailed theological explanation of the mystery of the Assumption, it mentions various texts of Scripture cited by the Fathers, theologians, and sacred orators. The latter, in order to explain and justify their faith in the Assumption, appeal to these texts and show the wonderful harmony between that privilege and the truths taught us in Sacred Scripture. The most important passages they cite are the following (in the present order of the biblical books):

* **Genesis 3:15:** "I will put enmity between you and the woman."

    The New Eve is closely united with the New Adam, though subordinated to him, in the struggle against the enemy from hell: "As the glorious resurrection of Christ was an essential part and final sign of this victory, so it was fitting that Mary's share in this struggle be crowned by the glorification of her virginal body" (*NDM*, 163).

---

43. Cited in E. Toniolo, "Spirito Santo e Maria nei primi Padri," in *Maria e lo Spirito Santo*, 241.

* **Exodus 20:12:** "Honor your father and your mother" (see Leviticus 19:3).

  From the very moment in which our Redeemer became the son of Mary, being a most perfect observer of the divine law, he could not fail to honor not only his eternal Father but also his earthly Mother. Since, then, he was able to bestow on this Mother the immense honor of preserving her from the corruption of the tomb, we ought to believe that he actually did this.

* **Psalm 132:8:** "Advance, O Lord, to your resting place, you and the ark of your majesty."

  The ark of the covenant was made of wood that could not rot, and many have therefore seen in it a kind of image of the most pure body of Mary as preserved from the corruption of the tomb and raised to great glory in heaven.

  As the ark built by Moses stood in the temple of the Lord because it was a sign and instrument of God's covenant with his people, so Mary is in heaven in her human completeness as a sign and instrument of the new covenant.

  In addition, the transfer of the ark from Kiriath-Jearim to Jerusalem calls to mind the Assumption of the Virgin into the heavenly homeland, the new and eternal Jerusalem.

* **Song of Songs 3:6D** (see 4:8 and 6:9). The spouse of the Song of Songs, who comes up from the desert like a column of smoke filled with the perfumes of myrrh and incense in order that she may be crowned, is a prefiguration of Mary, the heavenly spouse who, together with her divine Spouse, is raised up to the palace of heaven.

* **Isaiah 60:3:** "to … bring glory to the place where I set my feet." The body of the Virgin, "the sanctuary in which the Lord sets his feet," is the real place meant here. In the Assumption God willed really to glorify this "place" which had been forever uniquely consecrated to him.

* **Apocalypse 12:1:** "A great sign appeared in the sky, a woman clothed with the sun, with the moon under her feet, and on her head a crown of twelve stars."

    The Scholastic theologians saw the Assumption foreshadowed not only in various Old Testament figures but also in the "woman clothed with the sun," whom John the Apostle saw on the island of Patmos. In addition to the Scholastics, many others in the ecclesial tradition have seen the "great sign" of the woman as celebrating the Assumption of Mary at the side of her Son.

* **Luke 22:28–29a:** "It is you who have stood by me in my trials; and I confer a kingdom on you."

    How extraordinarily rich in content these words of Jesus are! They apply most fittingly to Mary, "the generous associate … of the Lord," who in an entirely special and indeed unique way always stood by Christ, especially in "the hour of trial."

* **Romans 8:17:** " … joint heirs with Christ, if only we suffer with him so that we may also be glorified with him."

    This revealed truth, which is closely connected with the preceding, is one of the clearest testimonies to the glorification of Mary. No one suffered with Jesus as the Virgin did, who at the foot of the cross endured in her maternal flesh the torments of her crucified Son. Therefore no one else is more fully glorified with Jesus.

According to Giulio Bevilacqua, the entire profound meaning and logic of the paschal mystery persuades us that Christ, having become the "first fruits of those who sleep" and having entered "into the glory that was his from the foundation of the world," willed to have with him as first fruits of the resurrection the sublime creature who shared most closely in his sacrifice.[44]

A point to be emphasized: the glorious triumph of the Savior had its source in the Incarnation, but it resulted more immediately from his redemptive passion, by which he merited his elevation to the heights. "In Mary, too, her glorification had its source in the divine maternity, but she merited it in a more direct way by her participation in the redemptive sacrifice. It was in her soul, pierced by the sword, that she merited the Assumption" (Jean Galot).

* **John 6:63:** "The words I have spoken to you are spirit and life."

We can say that the ultimate root of the glorification of the Blessed Virgin to a place beside her Son lies in the life-giving and pregnant power of these words of the gospel, which are a marvelous summing up of all the Scriptures and of Mary's being.

After all, what is the Assumption concretely if not the manifestation of the radical transformation which the seed of God's word produced in the Mother of Jesus, she "whose vocation was to feed upon and be filled by the

---

44. Cited in Thurian, *Mary Mother of All Christians.*

divine words"? (St. John Damascene, in *TMPM* II, 505). As Origen attests, she possessed knowledge of the law; she was holy and, through daily meditation, knew well the oracles of the prophets (*Homilies on Luke* VI, 7).

Having become in body and in spirit the dwelling of Wisdom made flesh, Mary drew down on herself the favor of God and came to share immortality or incorruption. According to the Old Testament, this is a gift bestowed by wisdom, that is, by the loving acceptance of God's plan as expressed in the Scriptures (see Ws 6:17–20; 8:17; Prv 8:35; etc.).

4. The Ecclesial and Universal Dimension of the Assumption

Mary, not withstanding her importance as an individual person, is never to be viewed in isolation. The privileges she had in her relationship with Christ and the mysteries that marked her life should never be separated from the mission of salvation that she carried out and continues to carry out for the benefit of the entire human race.

It is in this light that the "miracle" of her bodily assumption into heaven is to be interpreted, that is, as a salvific event with universal relevance. It has its place in the overall economy of salvation as a reality that closely relates to us and involves all of us, being as it is the first instance of what will be our glorious destiny at the end of time.

The state of glory granted to the Virgin is not something unconnected with us but rather a gift to the entire race. It is a gift granted to the Mother that belongs also to her children, a gift which the children are intended to share and enjoy.

a) The Assumed Virgin: Eschatological Icon and Beginning of the Risen Church

> The preredeemed is also the prerisen:
> after Christ and before us!
>
> (*NDM*, 182)

"In the meantime the Mother of Jesus in the glory which she possesses body and soul in heaven is the image and beginning of the Church as it is to be perfected in the world to come. Likewise she shines forth on earth, until the day of the Lord shall come (cf. 2 Pet 3:10), a sign of certain hope and comfort to the pilgrim People of God" (*LG* 68).

These incisive and quite felicitous words of Vatican II brought out the ecclesial significance of the dogma of the Assumption. This was an entirely new theological perspective. The glorious state of the Virgin here takes on an important ecclesial meaning and purpose: that is, the events which God accomplished in her are eschatological events that show the ultimate plan of God for the entire human race and the beginning of the eschatological destiny to which God is calling the Church and every human being.

The Assumption, though a special gift of the Risen Lord to his Mother, is not simply something private or personal to Mary, something that gives her life a harmonious end. It is a saving event that is paradigmatic for all of us. In it we see the radiant fulfillment of the divine plan for the human creature and the radiance of a redemption that has reached its ultimate fulfillment in a first, privileged member of the great throng of the redeemed.

We may say that the Assumption is simply the effect of the resurrection of Christ the head on the most eminent member of his body and, at the same time, a pledge of what the community of believers is called to become. It is the luminous assurance that human bodies will rise and that every human being will be saved, because, as in the

Virgin, so in all of us, the Spirit of the risen Christ will complete his mission: the victory over sin and death.

The fact that Mary, one of us, has entered the full glory of heaven gives us the sure pledge that the promises of Christ can be kept. The Virgin is already what we shall be; she is where we too shall be; she is our sister who has already reached the finishing line; she has outstripped us and gone before us, but in her destiny we see our own, and how joyous the prospect! In Mary, the glorified first fruits of believers in Christ, not only is the bodily glorification of humanity already announced: it has begun! Our hope is already realized, our flesh is already saved. In her the Church knows and joyfully anticipates the happy end of its history; it knows that in her it has reached its own ultimate goal and perfection. In the Virgin, now risen with Christ, the Church on its journey to the parousia sees the completion of its own mystery. In this first member, who ceaselessly goes before it, the Church has reached its end, its rest, and its fullness, which is its definitive bodily presence with the risen Christ.[45]

We must indeed say with Paul VI: "The glorification of Mary is for all of us a consoling proof of our future" (*NDM*, 183), a concrete sign of the hope offered to the entire human race, one of the "great deeds" by which God, who does not waste his wonders, gives signs to his Church. "Surrounded by dangers and difficulties" (*LG* 62) on its laborious journey toward its goal, the Church needs to see that someone has "made it through"; it needs to know that someone is lovingly extending a reassuring hand to it.

---

45. See R. Laurentin, *La Vergine Maria* (Rome: Ed. Paoline, 1970).

With good reason Dante could write in his prayer to the Virgin:

> To us here [in heaven] you are
> the noonday blaze of love,
> and to mortals on earth
> a living wellspring of hope.
>
> (Paradiso XXXIII, 10–12)

> Mary, you are indeed a living fountain of hope,
> an inexhaustible fountain that does away
> with thirst, needs, anxieties, and fears....
> Mother, give us always this saving water;
> the fountains of this world are all polluted.
> Do not allow the river of our days
> to run far away from you,
> in a sad and dreary desert without life.
> There is no other water
> that can make our desert bloom
> and forever satisfy our quest,
> save that which comes from you,
> from the blessed fruit of your womb.

b) The Assumption Forecasts the Final Splendor of the Christian's Body

Having been taken, whole and entire (soul and body), into heaven, the Virgin now shows forth the nobility of the body, the harmonious embrace of body and soul, matter and spirit. She personifies as it were the secret and profound yearning of humanity for God. In this perspective theologian Jean Galot has some very meaningful and profound remarks:

> The Assumption follows from the consecration of the Virgin's body when it became the temple of the incarnate Word. But while the dwelling of the Word in her was a unique privilege, it has a striking analogy in

Christian life, especially in sacramental life. Because they possess the life given by grace, Christians have already become temples of God, and their bodies share in this dignity. But through eucharistic communion their bodies become, in a more direct and more concrete way, the dwelling place of Christ's body. The Assumption forecasts the final splendor awaiting the bodies of Christians because they have been such dwelling places. The promise of resurrection that attaches to communion (see Jn 6:54) becomes clearer in the perspective afforded by the Assumption. The lowly matter which God accepts as a dwelling place is destined for the highest glory.[46]

The person of the Virgin Mother taken up into heaven thus represents the present and future dignity of the human beings whom God has created and redeemed. She is the great proof that God's glory is not based on the ruins of his creation and that, on the contrary, he is glorified in the glorification of his saints.

c) Mary Assumed into Heaven Is a Synthesis of Creation

The glorified body of the Blessed Virgin is a synthesis of the created world because it has been formed out of all the elements of the universe (air, water, the manifold energies at work in the cosmos, and so on). Therefore we can say that Mary's Assumption of body and soul into heaven has an eschatological meaning:

It is as it were an enthronement of creation within the final glory of God. Because of her Assumption Mary anticipates and preludes the ultimate destiny not only of human beings but of the cosmos as well: the entire

---

46. Galot, *Maria, la donna*, 324.

material universe has begun its resurrection in her. In her and through her the whole of creation has been led into the sacred space of trinitarian love. The entire creation, purified and clearly manifesting God, is symbolically contained in the glorified Virgin.[47]

In her "the universe speaks as it attains its fulfillment."[48] As the Fathers would say, the whole earth exults at her glory.

To creation, which lives "in hope that [it] would be set free from slavery to corruption and share in the glorious freedom of the children of God" (Rm 8:20–21), Mary, now taken up into our common blessed fatherland, reveals its destiny, which is to be set free and "recreated" by the Spirit of the risen Lord. She reveals what is to be the universal transfiguration of the entire cosmos at the end of time.

Human beings are afflicted not only by the thought of approaching suffering and the dissolution of the body but also, and even more, by the fear that everything will simply cease to be (see *GS*, no. 18). "The assumed Virgin is in herself a message containing immortal hopes. The journey of humanity does not end on these shores but is moving toward the seventh day of history, when all alienation will be overcome and creation will be restored to the original freshness it had in Eden. Even the body, which is either disregarded or exalted in modern culture, will be drawn into the stream that is eternity."[49]

As Patriarch Athenagoras used to say, "everything will be transformed, everything. All that we have loved, all that

---

47. See, among others, Leonardo Boff, *Il volto materno di Dio*, 22; 230; 126–30.
48. H. Hulsbosch, *Storia della creazione storia della salvezza* (Florence: Vallecchi, 1967).
49. Paolo Pifano, *Tra teologia e letteratura*, 222.

we have created, all joy and all beauty will have a place in the kingdom."[50]

d) Mary's Ever Strong and Active Presence among Us

> While a mother, you remained a virgin.
> When you fell asleep, O Mother of God,
> you did not abandon the world.
>
> (From the Typikon of the Byzantine Liturgy)

> Who takes such care of the human race
> as you and your Son?
> Even after your death
> you can offer life to human beings.
>
> (St. Germanus of Constantinople)

d1. Now Made Fully Like the Risen Christ, Mary Conquers Time and Space

When the New Testament writers speak of the resurrection of Jesus, they describe the mystery by saying that the risen Christ has acquired a new presence and a new way of acting within us and among us (see Mt 28:20). He is here and will never leave us because his spiritualized presence has taken on an extension and intensity which his earthly presence did not have. The same can be said of Mary.

Taken up body and soul into heaven, Mary is now made completely like Christ. This conformation is not simply a matter of propriety; there is also a theological reason: the radical transformation of her being. The Assumption is henceforth a key to a deeper understanding of the mystery of Mary's presence in the Church, and this understanding will be helpful in christology and pneumatology.

---

50. *Jesus 2* (1979).

In virtue of her bodily glorification, which allows her to rise superior to space and time, the Virgin can live and dwell among us, even if invisibly and spiritually. After due consideration G. Oggioni writes:

> Risen Mary is here with me and in me; she is here with the Church and in the Church. Time and space do not separate us from her, from her body and her soul. She is not present to us simply because of the communion of the saints, as is true of all the other faithful departed; we are separated from her only because we, being still in time and space, cannot fully grasp her real presence.[51]

"What an incredible mystery!" exclaims Montfort. "I carry her within me, / Beautiful, resplendent, and visible, / But in the darkness of faith."[52] The privilege of the Assumption brings Mary closer to Christ and closer to the human race here on earth: "She is in heaven, but she is not far from us. She is with Christ and she is there for us."[53] She is the adornment and joy of heaven, but also of the earth. Here on earth Mary had represented the whole of humanity insofar as it is united with her; now, in the "city of light" that union is deepened.

Odo Casel eloquently reminds us of this:

> On earth the Virgin was a silent but immense force, for she carried the Son within her and was a living ark of Christ present in the midst of the community. Now that she has been caught up into God and is resplendent at the center of the communion of saints and angels, where all contemplate and boast of her, she has not

---

51. "Maria presenza viva e segno di communione nella Chiesa," *Mad* 26 (1978) 3–4, 27–28.
52. *Cantico* 77, in *Opere* (Rome: Centro Mariano Monfortano, 1977) 836.
53. Paul VI, *Insegnamenti* XI (1973) 786.

disappeared into nothingness; indeed, only now, from heaven, does she truly fill the Church with her presence.[54]

What a source of great joy to know that she is always present to us with her whole being, with the spotless splendor of her soul, the virginal integrity of her body, and the maternal tenderness of her heart! Here again St. Bernard has striking things to say that shed light and fill the heart with enthusiasm. "Beloved, what a motive for festivity, what a reason for gladness, what a matter for rejoicing we have in the Assumption of Mary! The entire universe is brightened by her presence, so that even the heavenly homeland blazes with the light from her virginal lamp" (*Sermon I on the Assumption* [PL 183:415]).

The first doctrinal reflection on the spiritual presence of Mary in the life of Christians goes back to the patristic period. St. Germanus of Constantinople provides us with outstanding witness of that reflection. Using language that is both theological and experiential, he speaks at length of her presence in a homily on the Dormition, a homily that is also a "conversation" (one meaning of *homilein* is "to converse") with the Mother of the Lord here present in the assembly. The author interprets the Church's faith in the Virgin's presence not only during the liturgy but also in the life of the faithful. Some passages are especially enlightening:

> Most Holy Mother of God, you have left the earth behind but you have not distanced yourself from this world.... You draw near to those who call upon you, and you make yourself known to those who faithfully seek you.... As once you dwelt bodily with your contemporaries, so now you live with us through your spirit....

---

54. Odo Casel, *Il mistero dell'Ecclesia*, 443.

Your body is indeed no hindrance to the force and energy of your spirit, which, being immaterial, breathes wherever it wills.... Therefore, Mother of God, we believe that you journey with us....

Moreover, since now you still walk bodily among us, just as if you still lived here, the eyes of our hearts are drawn to look for you every day....

Just as when you lived on earth you were not unconnected with life in heaven, so, too, after your Assumption you are not unconnected with the life of human beings but are spiritually present to them....

Our eyes, it is true, cannot gaze upon you, Most Holy One, but you are nonetheless present in our midst.... Remain willingly among us and show yourself in various ways to those whom you judge worthy....

A clear sign of your presence among us is the great protection you afford us. All of us listen for your voice, and the voices of all reach your ears ... you visit all, O Mother of God. Watch over each of us ... let no one escape your compassionate gaze (*Sermon I on the Dormition of the Most Holy Mother of God*).

d2. The Maternal Mission of Glorified Mary

Having been united with the Savior in her earthly mission, Mary could not but likewise be united with him in her mission in heaven, where she shares the universal outlook of the Savior and the breadth of his care for all human beings. Thus the work of saving the human race goes on through Christ and Mary. The fruits of that work, far more precious and plentiful than the losses caused by the disastrous effects of sin (see Rom 5:20), bring to humanity a glorious triumph superior to that which it would have reached had it remained in the state of original justice.

As was true of Christ the Lord, once taken up into heavenly glory, so too, as we remarked elsewhere, the Virgin Mary in her glorified state began a new life. She now enjoys a spiritual presence that is not limited by conditions of time and space, an active influence capable of reaching her children here and now, without limitations imposed by time or place. She is therefore to extend to the maximum degree the range of her maternal action. Her spiritual presence is characterized by an attitude of loving communion with us and of intercession for us on the level of the individual person; it is thus different from other presences, such as that of the angels and the saints.

As queen at the king's side, the Blessed Virgin is associated with all the activity by which Christ leads the Church, guides its development, and spreads its holiness throughout the world. The Ascension marked for Christ the definitive establishment of his heavenly power and his kingship over the universe. Analogously, Mary's Assumption inaugurated her power as queen of the world. This power is directed essentially toward the actual communication of salvation to humanity; it is a mediatory power conferred on her for the carrying out of her maternal mission. "Taken up to heaven she did not lay aside this saving office but by her manifold intercession continues to bring us the gifts of eternal salvation" (*LG*, 62), becoming, in Christ, "a life-giving spirit" (1 Cor 15:45).

Here is how the Byzantine Liturgy celebrates this truth: "You have reached the Wellspring of Life, you who conceived the living God and who now by your prayers will deliver our souls from death" (Troparion).

The Virgin is present in us, not locally, as though she were ubiquitous, but through a communication of life and a sharing, on our part, in her fullness of grace (which in turn depends on that of the Son). If in the beatific vision she sees us, thinks of us, and loves us, then she cannot remain inactive because love is essentially operative and communicative. In the inevitable flow of time she accompanies us lovingly and with a mother's tenderness. She follows us, moment by moment, throughout our history and supports us so that we will not fail to achieve a happy arrival in our heavenly homeland.

The purpose God has in the Assumption shows that this glorious privilege of Mary does not put distance between her and the rest of humanity.

> Mary's elevation into heaven has for its purpose to place her at the disposition of all human beings and to intensify her influence within our universe.
>
> The perfect happiness of the Virgin does not disconnect her from human suffering. On the contrary, her glorified state makes her more able to sympathize with all earthly sorrows and, in her prayer to Christ, to bring to him all her concerns for each of those whom she loves as her own children. The Assumption enables her to be attuned to the joys and sufferings of every human being; it gives her the ability to be of help in all sufferings, not necessarily by obtaining the elimination of the painful situation, but at least by increasing the sufferer's courage and the willingness to accept trials as a means of redemption.
>
> She who herself passed from the sword of suffering to a higher joy helps human beings to accomplish the same passage.[55]

It is said of the risen Jesus that he lives to "intercede for us" with the Father (Rom 8:34). Like him, Mary, whose heavenly state allows her to know not only all our circumstances but also God's desires for us, always intercedes for

---

55. Jean Galot, *Maria, la donna*, 322.

us with the Son, "with the power of her desire, the fervor of her devotion, and the purity of her prayer that salvation may come to all" (St. Bernard). Her intercession is an "omnipotent supplication."[56]

St. Germanus of Constantinople, the great poet of Mary's living spiritual presence among us, addresses the glorified Virgin thus: "Christ willed to have your lips and your heart close to him; as a result, he agrees to all the desires you bring to him when you suffer on behalf of your children, and with his divine power he does everything you ask of him" (*Homily* 1; PG 98:348).

Consider, moreover, that the ceaseless prayer of an upright person counts for much; that Abraham, who pleased God by his faith, was asked to pray for Abimelech, because he (Abraham) was a prophet; that patient Job was bound to pray for his friends because he had spoken aright to God; that meek Moses by lifting up his hands won the battle for Israel against Amalech. Shall we then be surprised at learning that Mary, the only spotless daughter born of the seed of Adam, enjoys such an extraordinary influence over the God of grace? "It is not strange, is it, that the Mother has a power over her Son greater than of the purest angel and the most glorious saint?" (Cardinal John Henry Newman).

We may well apply to Mary most holy, assumed into heaven, the words which St. Therese of Lisieux said at the end of her earthly life: "I think that my mission is now beginning: the mission of making the Lord loved as I love him and giving souls my little way. If God in his mercy hears my desires, my paradise will be found on earth until the end of time. Yes, I want to spend my heaven doing good on earth."[57]

---

56. See Archbishop Luigi Maria Carli, in *Marianum* 38 (1976) 476.
57. *Novissima verba*, July 17, in *Gli scritti* (Rome: General Postulancy of the Discalced Carmelites, 1979) 338.

In what human soul or heart can such an ardent desire be felt more deeply than in that of Mary, mother of our salvation and cause of our joy? Does anyone surpass her in spending her heaven doing good on earth?

With the life-giving Lord and in the glory of the most holy and indivisible Trinity, the Virgin Mary is present with her whole being (soul and body) to all her children. She loves us with a heart of flesh; she looks upon us with eyes of flesh. With her loving gaze she reaches into the depths of our beings and welcomes all of us into her maternal heart. It is a heart that beats ceaselessly with intense love for each of us, a heart utterly pure, full of God, a pleasing refuge always open, in which it is sweet to rest.

No other creature is closer to, indeed within, the heart of every human being than she is, together with her Son Jesus.[58] She is the Mother par excellence, the Mother who awaits all of us in the kingdom of her Son, the Mother who, like a brilliant star in the heavens, shows us the way to her. The Virgin Mary, so closely one with her Son, is a single way, a single song.

> Jesus, Son of God,
> "most beautiful among the children of men,"
> we magnify you
> because you chose Mary
> to be your mother
> and your gentle and generous companion,
> and because you gave her to us
> as an immensely loving mother
> and teacher of life.
> To you be glory through all the ages![59]

---

58. See Leonardo Boff, *Il volto materno di Dio*, 172.
59. Italian Episcopal Conference, *In Preghiera con Maria Madre di Gesù* (Aids for Celebrating the Marian Year 1987; Vatican Publishing House).

Chapter Five
Mary in Relation to the Holy Spirit

As Mary journeys with the Holy Spirit,
she becomes ever more his reflection and
    masterpiece
Hail, most pure receptacle of the Holy Spirit!

(Theotokion, Ode V)

I. Overview

A. Preliminary Remarks

Within the mystery of the Trinity the Holy Spirit is essentially "gift." He is not *a* gift, but *the* gift: the gift which the Father makes of himself in love to the Son and, in turn, the gift which the Son makes of himself to the Father. The Holy Spirit is as it were the life-giving, warm environment in which the eternal exchange of love between Father and Son takes place, But, in addition to forming the environment, he is himself the love that consecrates the gift: he calls forth the gift and accompanies it.

In the Holy Spirit the Father gives himself to the Son totally, and this gift is infinitely holy. In response to the Father's offer of love the Son is totally open to accepting it and giving himself in return with the utmost possible fullness. This mutual exchange, this reciprocal belonging, is accomplished in love, which in God is subsistent and is a person: it is the Holy Spirit, the Spirit of love, the third person of the Most Holy Trinity.

In this context we must accept that just as the mystery of the Virgin of Nazareth is wholly related to the Father and the Son, so too it is wholly related to the Holy Spirit. For, in order to collaborate with the Father and become Mother of the Son, Mary had to make herself transparent to the mystery of the Spirit, whose icon she became. In other words, she had to become Spirit-bearer before becoming Christ-bearer or Theotokos.

In the Spirit Mary was united with the Father and the Son; in the Spirit she shared in the fruitfulness of the former and the receptivity of the latter; in the Spirit she became holy mother, virgin, and obedient servant. It can be said that her entire life and supernatural activity were lived under the sign of the Spirit who worked in her from conception to glorification.

Even and especially at the time of the death of Jesus, Mary was under the complete control of the Holy Spirit, who had her completely at his disposal (Mühlen). The fact that she associated herself as a mother in the sacrifice of the Son and gave her consent to it was possible only by the power of the one, identical Spirit in whom Christ offered himself to the Father. The glorious state of the Virgin reflects her assimilation to the Son but it does so precisely because of the continual presence in her of the Spirit whose action caused her to sink, as it were, into the depths of the divine perfections.

Apart from isolated exaggerations, the emphasis on the Spirit, which marked a defining theological shift in the postconciliar period, has confirmed anew that the relationship between the Panagion (the All-Holy God) and the

Panagia (the All-Holy Virgin) ran through the latter's entire life, from before the Annunciation, to the central event of Christ's virginal conception, to Pentecost, and on to the Assumption into glory.[1]

The pairing of the Holy Spirit and Mary, far from being arbitrary, is based on divine Revelation and is the substantive element of our argument, namely, that the life of the Virgin-Mother can be understood only if we see in it the special influence of the Holy Spirit, with whom she was united in an indissoluble way.

Despite the laconic language of Scripture, the sacred writers have supplied fundamental data for understanding the relationship between the Holy Spirit and Mary. This is true of both the stories of Christ's infancy (see Mt 1:18,20, and Lk 1:35) and the account of Pentecost (Acts 2:14). A straightforward reading of these passages shows the important presence of Mary to be closely connected with the Holy Spirit.

Relying on this belief, which was based on an ever deeper and clearer understanding of the sacred texts, the Fathers and Doctors of the Church, both eastern and western, have attributed all of Mary's privileges and prerogatives to the various missions of the Holy Spirit, which themselves come from the Father and the Son. As those writers entered more deeply into teaching on the Paraclete, they realized that from him as from a wellspring had come the fullness of grace (see Lk 1:28) and charity, the abundant gifts and fruits of all the virtues, and the abundance of evangelical beatitudes and special charisms which, like the trousseau for a heavenly marriage, adorned the predestined mystical spouse of the divine Paraclete (Paul VI).

---

1. See the extensive and well-documented study of G. M. Roschini, *Il Tuttosanto e la Tuttasanta. Relazioni tra Maria Santissima e lo Spirito Santo* (Parts I and II; Rome, 1976–77).

B. The Synergy of the Holy Spirit and Mary

In him we live,
in him we move,
in him we have our being (Acts 17:28).

In religious language the term "synergy" means the attunement or, better, the cooperation of God and the human person as a result of the mystery of the indwelling, that is, the close union of the human person with God, who in his infinite unmerited love never acts in us without us.

The inhabitation leads to marvelous results in the just: the Trinity present in them enlightens them in their inmost being and imprints itself on them like a seal on wax, thereby producing an image of itself, which is sanctifying grace. Now the very life of God goes on in our hearts; God lives in us the mystery of the Trinity. The One whom the heavens and the earth cannot contain dwells in the little space of our hearts. Like the Virgin, Christians carry God within them; they are the paradise of God.

Have we ever thought seriously about this magnificent, consoling mystery that envelopes all of us and snatches us up into the whirlwind of God's life-giving love? Are we truly convinced of it and fully conscious of it?

Although the inhabitation is common to the three Persons of the Most Holy Trinity, it is nonetheless attributed in a special way to the Holy Spirit since he is the power effecting communion between the Father and the Son (see 1 Cor 6:19). He is the most important of the divine gifts because he is the active source of the new life of grace, love, and filial liberty (Rom 8:1–17); he does away with life according to the flesh and brings about the conformity of the just with Christ the Lord.

St. Cyril of Alexandria writes that the Holy Spirit transforms souls, imprinting the divine image on them and engraving on them the image of the supreme substance (*On John* XI, 11). In proportion to their personal holiness, the redeemed, who are caught up in the dynamic movement of salvation and "share in the divine nature" (2 Pt 1:4), are united with the Holy Spirit in a joint activity. That is, they act in synergy, or communion, with the Spirit. As a result, all their conscious, free actions are "pneumatic," that is, spiritual in the sense of being moved by the Spirit.

Mary is a shining light on these hidden paths; she is the creature whose behavior during her lifetime was completely "spiritual." The restrained but pregnant information given in the gospels describes for us a spiritual life inspired solely by the interior power of the Holy Spirit. Especially attentive to this life is Luke the evangelist. He shows the Virgin in a close relationship with the Holy Spirit, first in the Incarnation and then, in a different way, at Pentecost. Thus he depicts her in accordance with the general conception he has of the action of the Holy Spirit; that is, he sees her as the spirit-guided creature par excellence, who acts always according to the movement in her of the divine Spirit. "In her we see 'spirituality' in its radical form"; "Her entire life was guided more by the Holy Spirit than by her own spirit" (*NDM*, 1347 and 1357). According to St. John Eudes, the Holy Spirit was the Spirit of her spirit, the soul of her soul, the heart of her heart.

Far, then, from resisting the divine action, Mary shows that she finds her personal fulfillment through and in the Spirit: "All of her movements, interior and exterior, had a single source, a single motivation: that of the love of God" (St. John of the Cross). In Christian life she is the supreme expression of docile collaboration with God's plan. For this reason, the loftiest witness of synergy with the Spirit comes from the Virgin of Nazareth.

The mystery of the Incarnation provides us with a crystal-clear example and manifestation of this synergy, for it

resulted from the action of the Holy Spirit and at the same
time (though at a different level of causation) from the action
of Mary, who, being united with the Spirit by an intrinsic
bond, acted with him in a perfect harmony of intention and
will. Thus the Spirit acted in synergy with Mary, and Mary
acted in synergy with the Spirit.

> He activated Mary's conscious and free powers of
> action (as he does those of individual Christians) as
> related to God's supernatural action, and he became, at
> the level of action (not of being), a single principle with
> Mary: the Holy Spirit and Mary in perfect synergy;
> two persons (one divine and one human) with a single
> action, since the same action is attributed to the Spirit
> and to Mary.
>
> Mary's prayer, for example, was at the same time a
> prayer of Mary and a prayer of the Spirit. There existed
> a kind of symbiosis between them: the Spirit prayed
> through the intellect and will of Mary, who united her-
> self with him, making herself his sanctuary, his stable
> dwelling; in her he lived his intimate relationship with
> the Father and with the Son.[2]

He himself is the love within her: the love between the
Father and the Son, the love with which God loves himself,
the love common to the entire Trinity, the fruitful love that
leads to conception (St. Maximilian Kolbe).

The synergy of Mary (and Christians) with the Holy Spirit
on the level of grace has to do not only with prayer and action
but also with the will (loving God and the good, hating evil,
and so on) and with the intellect (knowing the good and the
signs of the times, discerning the spirits, prophesying, and so
on). It can therefore be said that the entire existence of the

---

2. Domenico Bertetto, "La Sinergia dello Spirito Santo con Maria. Approfondimenti
teologici," in *Maria e lo Spirito Santo*, 291–99.

Virgin (and of Christians, to the extent that they open themselves to the action of the Spirit) became a "pneumatic" or spiritual existence. The Spirit not only led Mary to act, but he acted *in* her, as in every Christian: It is the Spirit himself who prays within us (Rom 8:26): "God sent the spirit of his Son into our hearts, crying out, 'Abba, Father!' " (Gal 4:6).

C. Transparent to the Holy Spirit

The Virgin Mary is a river
filled with the perfumes of the Spirit.

(St. John Damascene)

By acting ceaselessly in synergy with the Holy Spirit Mary became a luminous daily manifestation of his action, a clear and even transparent reflection of him who is holy and the sanctifier: "She was rendered incandescent by the divine fire, so that nothing was to be seen in her but the flame of the Holy Spirit" (Paschasius Radbert).

In the setting of the trinitarian mystery the Virgin became the image of the Paraclete through participation and grace. As Mother of the incarnate Word, she represents the Spirit in an incomparable way: in her alone and in the greatest measure are to be seen and combined all the graces and all the splendors of the Spirit that are the possession of her own Son; indeed, these two persons display one and the same beauty. For this reason the holy Virgin is as it were a pillar pointing to the hidden treasures of the Spirit.

When we speak of the union of the Spirit with Mary, we are evidently excluding any hypostatic union of the two. We are clearly dealing with two distinct natures and persons: the divine Person of the Paraclete and the human person of Mary, but "the two are so pellucid that the one begins to become a reflection of the other" (*NDM*, 1357). In the singleness of the action in which the two achieve a complete convergence, the work of the Spirit shines forth in the various aspects of the holiness of his spouse. Through her evident obedience and her special acceptance of the Paraclete at the Annunciation and on Pentecost, Mary became a privileged locus of the Spirit's presence, a locus of the encounter between Father and Son. Even in her creatureliness she "was changed into an expression, almost a personification, of the Holy Spirit" (De Fiores).

As Virgin and Mother Mary mirrors the mystery of the Spirit's role in the intimate communion within the Trinity, his creative and transforming power. She reveals the nuptial love that the Trinity has poured out on her and on the Church, the tender maternal love of which she has become the icon. From the Virgin, a living and efficacious sacrament of the Holy Spirit, we move on to adoration of the divine intratrinitarian love that accomplished the great works of salvation in her and with her. Mary, the woman full of grace or, we might say, full of the Holy Spirit, whose light shines out in her with an incomparable splendor,[3] is the face through which, more than through any other sign or any other person (except for Jesus Christ), the divine Spirit gazes out upon us (loves us and consoles us) (X. Pikaza). She is like a mirror that disappears in order to show the Spirit reflected in it.

D. God's Great Impression, Prepared by the Holy Spirit

"Mary is the great, marvelous, and divinely shaped ornament of the human race" (Photius).

"She is like a 'mirror' in which are reflected in the most profound and limpid way

---

3. Paul VI, Address to the International Mariological-Marian Congress, May 16, 1975.

'the mighty works of God' (Acts 2:11)"
(*RM* 25).

According to St. Mechtild, God devoted more care to forming the microcosm that is Mary than to creating the macrocosm that is the entire universe. She was sealed in the depths of her being and from the first beat of her heart by the touch of the sanctifying Spirit and was constantly united with him in a perfect synergy. As a result, she became a splendid masterpiece of the Holy Spirit, a living impression of God, the wonder of wonders, the loftiest prodigy that came from the creative mind of God: a dizzying miracle of created grace, sprung from the very heart of the Trinity and from its surprising and inscrutable wisdom. Montfort had good reason to write: " 'Eye has not seen, nor ear heard, nor man's heart comprehended' (1 Cor 2:9) the beauties, the grandeurs, the excellences of Mary — the miracle of the miracles of grace, of nature, and of glory" (*True Devotion*, 12).

In their comments on the angel's greeting (Lk 1:28: "full of grace") and on Elizabeth's beatitude (Lk 1:42: "Blessed are you among women") the Fathers and ecclesiastical writers make clear their conviction about Mary's greatness: "The glorious Virgin, for whom he who is mighty has done great things, is resplendent with such an abundance of heavenly gifts and such a fullness of grace and innocence that she becomes as it were God's supreme miracle, the pinnacle of all his miracles, and the worthy mother of God. Thus, being placed as close to God as is possible for a creature, she transcends all the praises of human beings and angels" (*NDM* 690).

It is true that the author of these inexplicable wonders is the Holy Spirit, but it is also no less true that the Virgin's being was as it were a malleable material at the disposal of the divine action. Tradition has made this thought its own when it describes Mary as a "waxed tablet" on which God could freely write whatever he wished. In her reply to the angel, says Origen, it is as if she were saying: "Here I am, a writing tablet: let the Writer write what he wishes; let the Lord of all make of me whatever he wants" (*Commentary on the Gospel of Luke*, fragment 18). In his time Antipater of Bostra likewise commented: " 'I am the handmaid of the Lord': I am the Lord's servant, I am his writing tablet; the material is ready, let the divine craftsman make what he wants of it" (*TMPM* I, 617).

This same characteristic of the Virgin is described by another incisive image that is no less meaningful and original than the preceding: Mary is "the book in which the Father wrote his Word" (Byzantine Liturgy), "a great new book in which only the Holy Spirit has written" (St. Epiphanius). Andrew of Crete says to the Virgin: "You are truly the living book of the spiritual Word, which was silently written down in you by the life-giving pen of the Spirit" (*Homily 3 on the Dormition of the Most Holy Mother of God*). St. John Damascene is even more specific in a homily on the Nativity of Mary: "Today the creator of the universe, the divine Logos, composed a new book, one which the Father poured out of his heart, for it was written with the tongue of God, the Holy Spirit, as with a stylus."

Nowadays we might say that Mary offered herself to God as a blank page on which the almighty Creator could write whatever he wished. She comes before us a "letter" written by the very hand of God: a letter written not with ink but by the Spirit of the living God, not on stone tablets as the old Law had been nor on parchment or paper but on the table of flesh that was her believing, maternal heart. It is a letter which all alike, learned and ignorant, can read and understand, a letter consisting of few thoughts and simple words, but these so precious that we cannot allow even a single one to be lost.

Due to her readiness to be completely handed over to the Spirit as his pliable instrument, Mary reached the highest pinnacle, the crown and perfection of all that is holy. Shaped by the Supreme Artist, this woman, who was humble and yet more sublime than any other creature, is seen by all the faithful as the greatest work of art to come from the Creator Spirit and as the prototype of what God's art can make of human clay that does not resist him. As the first fruit of God's embracing love, Mary leads us into the mystery of what the Church essentially is: a work solely of the tripersonal God.

II. Analysis

Presence of the Holy Spirit in Mary Before, During, and After the Annunciation

If we look to the most recent directions taken in Marian pneumatology and allow ourselves to be schooled by the Scriptures, the Fathers, and the Magisterium of the Church, we must admit that special moments of Mary's existence were marked by the extraordinary action of the Holy Spirit.

The synergy of the Holy Spirit with the Virgin of Nazareth "was marked by a continually increasing power ... that led her to an ever deeper existential and operative holiness" (D. Bertetto). Under the movement of the divine Spirit her entire interior world was directed toward the heights; it opened itself increasingly to the divine operations in her and penetrated ever more deeply into the world of God: "A sacred harmony existed between the Spirit of God and the spirit of Mary. Moment by moment God poured ever new graces into her soul, and with all her powers she constantly corresponded with these graces. This correspondence and perfect harmony raised her to the supreme level of grace" (Bérulle).

Let us analyze this astounding journey of the Virgin, breaking it down into three essential phases: before the Annunciation, the Annunciation itself, and after the Annunciation.

A. Before the Annunciation
(God Prepares His Spotless Dwelling)

When the time had come when God resolved to effect his incarnation before our eyes ... he created the Virgin Mary, that is to say he called forth on earth a purity so great that, within this transparency, he would concentrate himself to the point of appearing as a child.[4]

1. The Holy Spirit Communicated Himself to Mary from the Very Beginning of Her Existence

We know that apart from Jesus there has been only one human being whose life was of a different kind: Mary, the Virgin, the Immaculate, the ever-pure. In her something occurred which our hearts have great difficulty in believing, because we always have our own bitter experiences before our eyes. This is that a human being is capable of entering into eternity without having had to repent of anything.

Yet such a human being exists: it is Mary. There was not an instant of her life that she had to disown, or even an empty and barren instant. There was no action to make her blush, none wrapped in shadow, none that

---

4. Pierre Teilhard de Chardin, *Le Milieu Divin. An Essay on the Interior Life* (Collins: Fontana Books, 1964) 134.

fell into the abyss of the past without having lit an ever-lasting light.[5]

This marvelous doctrinal summary by Karl Rahner of the reality of Mary Immaculate serves as a good introduction to what we shall be saying here. Before the Son descended to earth, the Father willed to prepare a suitable dwelling for him: Mary, the supreme gift which the Father gives to the Son after the complete gift of Himself. Then in order that Mary might be worthy of him for whom she was intended, the Father sent his Spirit into Mary. He did so in order that by wrapping her in redemptive and sanctifying love from the very instant of her conception, he might bring her into the world as the first fruits of the new creation of which Paul speaks (2 Cor 5:17; Gal 6:15), and thereby make her ready for her future mission.

In a charming but also penetrating passage Ildephonsus Schuster wrote: "Just as the first Eve was taken, radiant with life and innocence, from the side of Adam, so Mary came forth, resplendent and immaculate, from the heart of the eternal Word. The Word willed that he himself, through the action of the Holy Spirit, should form this body and this soul which were one day to serve him as tabernacle and altar" (*NCM*, 1012). Especially important was the operative presence of the Holy Spirit in the immaculate conception of the preordained Mother of God: "In the history of the human generations Mary represents the most perfect example of the unmerited action of the Holy Spirit" (John Paul II).

In their glorification of Mary all-holy, the Fathers abound in "enhancing names," that is, honorary descriptive titles, that exalt her beyond original sin, thereby confirming the Christian people's longstanding idea of her. Thus Eadmer,

---

5. Karl Rahner, *L'homme du miroir de l'année chrétienne* (Paris: Mame, 1966) 224–25.

"the first theologian of the immaculate conception," wrote a
Treatise on the Conception of Holy Mary in which he not
only defended the insight of the Christian people in favor of
the immaculate conception but also showed that such a
conception was both possible and appropriate. He did so
by using various images to emphasize God's complete
sanctification of the Virgin. "If in fact both Jeremiah and
John the Baptist were sanctified in their mothers' wombs,
who would dare to say that the unique place of reconciliation
for the entire universe and the sweet dwelling of the Son of
Almighty God was not illumined by the grace of the Holy
Spirit? ... Therefore with sure faith we maintain that before
all the centuries Wisdom prepared and built a house in which
it might have its own special dwelling."

Using the well-known example of the chestnut that
emerges unharmed from its spiny casing, Eadmer argues:
"Was it not possible for God to let a human body ... remain
free of every sting even though it was conceived amid the
stings of sin? Clearly, God could do so and he willed to do
so; and if he willed it, he did it (*potuit plane et voluit; si
igitur voluit, fecit*)."[6]

Moses heard God say to him: "Remove the sandals from
your feet, for the place where you stand is holy ground" (Ex
3:5). If that ground was made holy because the divine Majesty appeared there, how much more was the place made
holy into which the Majesty was to enter in person? This was
the approach taken by not a few Greek and eastern Fathers
and ecclesiastical writers: they maintain that the Holy Spirit
was always present in Mary from the first instant of her life,
so that the evil spirit could never have a place in her. In other
words: she was conceived without original sin.

---

6. In *NDM*, 685 and 305.

Thus protected by the victorious grace of God and "filled utterly with divine light even in her mother's womb" (John XXIII), she never experienced a time without God (Kolbe). Sin never touched her; there was no shadow or trace of it in her: she was the Spotless One, entirely beautiful, entirely holy, entirely pure with a purity that presided over the very coming of her soul into existence. The influence of the Creator-Word and future redeemer permeated the most hidden fibers of this tiny being and did not allow any shadow to find a place there.

According to the *Dutch Catechism*, Mary lived in a sinful world and was affected by its sorrows but not by its wickedness; she was our sister in suffering but not in evil.[7] The Virgin Mother owed nothing to sin but everything to the redeemer, her Son. She was redeemed beforehand; in her evil met its first and definitive defeat.

Such was the conclusion reached by theologians after a lengthy, indeed multi-centuried history.[8] A very valuable and convincing part was played by the well-known argument about the "perfect mediator," in which Franciscan John Duns Scotus appealed to the salvific power of Christ as forestalling sin instead of removing it once it had been committed. The immaculate conception is thus not an exception to redemption (as some used to think) but is due to a perfect and completely efficacious saving action of Christ, the one mediator.

In other words, the immaculate conception is an example of an anticipatory and complete redemption that is the retroactive effect of the paschal mystery of Christ as applied to

---

7. *Il nuovo Catechismo Olandese* (Turin-Leumann: LDC, 1969) 322.
8. The immaculate conception played a part in the theological debate over original sin: how was universal redemption, which necessarily presupposed original sin, to be reconciled with Mary's immaculate conception? This difficulty was resolved by a Franciscan, Duns Scotus (1270?–1308), who developed subtle but persuasive arguments.

the Lord's Mother. Far from being an exception to or denial of the universal necessity of redemption by Christ, it implies that Mary "being of the race of Adam ... is at the same time also united to all those who are to be saved" (*LG* 53). Duns Scotus' thinking undeniably played a decisive part in the development of the doctrine of the immaculate conception, so that he was rightfully given the title "Doctor of the Immaculate One."

On December 8, 1854, Pius IX issued a dogmatic statement that was the result of a faith process involving all elements of the Church (people, theologians, the magisterium): "We declare, pronounce and define ... that the most Blessed Virgin Mary was, from the first moment of her conception, by the singular grace and privilege of almighty God and in view of the merits of Christ Jesus the Savior of the human race, preserved immune from all stain of original sin" (Bull *Ineffabilis Deus*).

As it plumbed more deeply the hidden riches of God's word, the Church increasingly realized that because Mary was filled with the grace of God and committed by her divine motherhood to the victorious struggle against evil, she must have escaped every touch of or connivance with sin, whether interior or structural. That is, the Church understood the complete personal purity implied in the divine maternity, for the sake of which she was conceived in a state of complete purity and holiness. Or, as Vatican II teaches, she was "enriched from the first instant of her conception with the splendor of an entirely unique holiness" (*LG* 56).

As often happens, the first to grasp this essential necessity were the popular writers who produced the apocrypha. They understood, almost instinctively, that sin of any kind is irreconcilable with the holiness of the Mother of God. We need only recall here the *Protevangelium of James*, which was quickly accepted by all the Churches and became the historical mold in which all the feasts of Mary's personal life were developed.

The author of this noncanonical work shows Mary's life to be so holy and her person so praiseworthy that no place could be found for her in a world corrupted by sin. The very foods which the land produces were incapable of nourishing her, and her place could only be in the sacred space of the Lord's temple and indeed in its most sacred part which was inaccessible to the many but suitable for her. By this symbol he intended to show how the Virgin was being prepared to become herself the temple and sanctuary of God; how she fed on the heavenly food of God's word more than on food for the body; and even how grace had in a way preserved her in her mother's womb. In fact, in the earliest copies of the work Mary's conception seems already to have taken place mysteriously when an angel tells Joachim to come down from the mountain because his prayers have been heard and Anna has already conceived a daughter who would be a blessing for all of Israel.[9]

What we have here is certainly not reliable historical information. But the story told in the *Protevangelium* does clearly contain theological positions and even though it does not expressly speak of the absence of original sin in Mary, it presents an intuitive and mythical awareness of a holiness that was perfect from the beginning, in her very conception. It would be under the influence of this work that the first assertion of the Virgin's primordial purity would be made.

In his homily on the Assumption (to be dated between 550 and 650) Theotechnus of Livias does not limit himself to describing Mary as "holy and very beautiful" or "pure and spotless," but speaks thus of her birth: "She who is made of a

---

9. *The Protevangelium of James*, trans. Oscar Cullmann, in *New Testament Apocrypha* I, ed. Wilhelm Schneemelcher (Cambridge — Louisville: James Clarke & Co. — Westminster/John Knox Press, 1991), 421–39.

pure and spotless clay was born as the cherubim were"
(*Eulogy on the Feast of the Assumption* 5–6). The image
used here of a pure and spotless clay reappears several times
in Andrew of Crete, who uses it more joyfully and more pro-
fusely as well as with some theological depth: "The body of
the Virgin is a soil worked by God, the first fruits of the
Adamic mass as divinized by Christ, the clay shaped by the
divine artist." Andrew stresses the point that this formation
prepared the way for that of Christ, the New Adam.[10] Herself
made of a new, pure clay, Mary could be the clay from which
the Savior was taken.

Immaculate Conception: A Proper Name of Mary

Inasmuch as Mary Immaculate is a reflection of the Holy
Spirit, she provides a rich material for theological development. In this setting a considerable importance attaches to the
keen and long-continued thinking of St. Maximilian M. Kolbe.
On fire with faith and with tender love for this splendid and
extraordinary creature, Kolbe endeavored, in an atmosphere
of prayer and awareness of the mystery she represents, to
gain insight into the meaning of the immaculate conception
in the light of the "Uncreated Conception" of the Holy
Spirit.

Kolbe was the first to give a truly original and at the same
time profound theological interpretation of the mysterious
relationship between the Holy Spirit and Mary. To the question: "Who are you, O Immaculate Conception?" he looked
for an answer by focusing his attention on the heart of the
Trinity, where he views the Holy Spirit, fruit of the love of
Father and Son, as an eternal "uncreated conception," the
prototype of any conception of life in the universe: an infinitely holy and immaculate conception. This theological
principle led St. Maximilian to a definition of Mary's being,

---

10. *Sermon I on the Dormition of Mary* and *Sermon I on the Nativity of Mary.*

as he developed the idea that a very special relationship exists between the conception of the Virgin and that of the Holy Spirit, namely, that among all created conceptions hers alone (like that of the Holy Spirit) is an immaculate conception.

According to Kolbe, God willed the Immaculate Conception and brought it about in time (a created conception) as the most perfect likeness to the essence of God that is possible to one who is wholly a creature. The words "Full of grace" signify that of all the existent beings that represent the divine perfections Mary is the one who perfects them most perfectly. She alone among all mere creatures can call herself the "Immaculate Conception." These two words properly describe the essence of Mary, because "her being is to be the Immaculate Conception."

St. Maximilian shores up his position with a persuasive and effective argument.

> There is a difference between Immaculate Conception and one who is immaculately conceived. It is the difference, for example, between white and whiteness: If a thing is white it can be dirtied, but when a thing is whiteness itself, it undergoes no change. We see, then, why the name "Immaculate Conception" belongs to Mary alone. In addition, at Lourdes she said "I am the Immaculate Conception" and not "I was immaculately conceived." It follows that she is immaculateness itself.

Then, harking back to the image of the Spouse, Kolbe concludes that the name of the Holy Spirit is also Mary's name.

> If among creatures a bride receives the name of her husband because she belongs to him, is united with him, becomes like him, and in union with him becomes a

creative giver of life, how much more will the name of the Holy Spirit, that is, (uncreated) "Immaculate Conception," be the name of her in whom he lives with a love that is fruitful throughout the entire supernatural economy?

In virtue of his spousal relationship with Mary, "the Holy Spirit dwells in her, lives in her, and is eternally joined to her in an ineffable, indescribable way."[11] No wonder, then, that Mary reflects the nature of the Holy Spirit in the most perfect way possible to a mere creature.

Why the Immaculate Conception?

> The ultimate reason for the Immaculate
> Conception is the unmerited love of God.

With a view to her task of bringing God into the human world, Mary was, as we said, possessed in a unique way by the Spirit of God. There could be no divisions within her spirit nor any shadows over her body, which was chosen to be the tabernacle of the marriage of the Word with human nature. Being Mother of Jesus included a holiness proportioned to her close union with the Son of God: "There was to be no shadow darkening her relationship with him" (John Paul II).

Although not an absolutely necessary requirement, the absence of sin in Mary is seen by the "sense of the faithful" as being the only state that can be harmonized with the holiness of Christ and with the person and exceptional mission of the Virgin herself. It is undeniable that the attribution of an immaculate conception to Mary is in full harmony with her holy divine motherhood as well as with her role as collaborator in the redemptive work of the Only Son. But it is not possible to assert a strict necessity:

----

11. St. Maximilian M. Kolbe, *Chi sei, o Immacolata?* (Rome: Ed. Monfortane, 1982).

It would not have been impossible for God to bring about the Incarnation with Mary's help, even if she had contracted the original stain and had been purified of it before the Annunciation. So then the Immaculate Conception was not necessary, but it was fitting.

Indeed, it was more than fitting that sin be completely removed from her who was to give mortal flesh to the eternal Word of the Father, receive this Word with exemplary faith, and cooperate with him in the salvation of the human race. Mary would have been more disposed to fulfill perfectly her mission as Mother of Christ if she were preserved from original sin from the very beginning. It was fitting that she who was to contribute to the glory of the Incarnate Word should possess the most perfect holiness possible for a creature, as well as a holiness that was complete from the outset.[12]

It was also fitting that the Most Pure One, the Teacher of purity, should have his human origin in a pure bridal chamber (St. Cyril of Jerusalem).

St. Augustine roundly asserts of Mary: "On account of the honor due to the Lord, I do not want to raise here any question about her when we are dealing with sins" (*Nature and Grace* 36, 42).

Her motherhood was intended to be a reflection of the fatherhood of the Father. The temporal generation of the Word was to be an image of his eternal generation and to give expression in flesh to the holiness of his divine sonship. It was fitting, therefore, that Mary's holiness be the most perfect possible image of the absolute holiness of the Father.

We must not forget, moreover, that Mary was

---

12. Galot, *Maria, la donna*, 217–18.

created immaculate in order that she might better act in our behalf. Thus the fullness of grace allowed her to carry out in a perfect manner her mission as collaborator in the work of salvation; that same grace gave the fullest possible value to her cooperation in the sacrifice of Jesus. When Mary presented her Son, nailed to the cross, to the Father, her sorrowful offering was entirely faultless.

A total purity befitted Mary all the more since at the time of the passion she was offering to the Father a sacrifice that, like that of Christ, summed up and recapitulated the gift of her whole being, the offering of her entire person and her entire life. This personal offering could not have had its full value in the eyes of the Father if it had not been completely spotless. In order to be fully pleasing to the Father and to receive its most abundant fruitfulness, the offering had to come from a person full of grace from the beginning of her existence.

If Mary had been, even for an instant, stained by sin and subjected to enslavement by the devil she could not have pleased the Father so much in her mission as co-redemptress. Thanks to the Immaculate Conception, her compassion reflected to a greater degree that of God and of Christ.[13]

The privilege of being immaculate does not cut Mary off from the human race or from the Church; rather, being completely removed from the torrent of sin that always accompanies the successive generations, she becomes more fully a member of the human race, which is "made for the Lord" (St. Augustine), and is more capable of having compassion on sinners. For the fullness of grace leads to a fullness of love

---

13. Ibid., 217–22.

and therefore to a refinement of sensibility and activity that has never been lessened by the experience of sin.

Even though she dwells in the splendor of the Spirit and possesses the wealth of wonderful prerogatives with which God has honored her in order to make a worthy Mother of the Incarnate Word, Mary is nonetheless very close to us. She is close to sinners, that is, to all of us for whose sake she received exceptional grace. She seeks a degree of participation in her motherhood for all her earthly children, for whose sake she was personally enriched. The unique privilege of the Immaculate Conception "places Mary at the service of all and brings joy to those who regard her as their mother" (John Paul II).

All this shines forth in a brilliant passage of Gratry that sounds like a discreet invitation to take pleasure in her great gift: "The Immaculate is a point of radiant light in the history of humanity: a brilliant light that by overcoming the darkness enlightens, strengthens, and helps. She is a lamp for all, a treasure for the entire earth."[14]

Indeed, for "nothing in the world is more intensely alive and active than purity and prayers, which are suspended like an unmoved light between the universe and God. Through their serene transparency the wave of creation, laden with natural virtue and grace, draws aside the veils."[15]

2. Mary Immaculate: Most Pure Icon of the Human Mystery

> You are our innocent voice,
> our voice before sin,
> and the only temple worthy of the Most High.[16]

---

14. Alfonso Gratry, *Commento al Vangelo secondo san Matteo* (1863).
15. Teilhard de Chardin, *Genèse d'une pensée*.
16. D. M. Turoldo, *Laudario alla Vergine, "Via Pulchritudinis"* (Bologna: EDB, 1992) 21.

As though inebriated by light and looking back with nostalgia, Turoldo celebrates with felicitous words the enchanting splendor reflected on the face of the immaculate Virgin. She is "the leaven of our new creation" (Severus of Antioch), the beginning of a new world enlivened by the Holy Spirit who bestowed on her in advance, and as the first recipient, the fullness of all the fruits of Christ's redemptive work and thereby "restored humanity to the freshness of the original graced creation" (Paul VI).

As Christ who redeemed her is the perfect image of the invisible God, so Mary Immaculate is the perfect image of divinized humanity (Jean Mouroux). At the beginning of the eschatological history inaugurated by Christ, she comes into existence as the first new being of a creation renewed by God. She is the "unpolluted earth" and in her there shines forth the omnipotence of God who recreates humanity, as well as the complete renewal of creation in God. Mary will forever remain at the side of the redeemed as "the first wonder" (John Paul II), the radically successful instance of redemption (Karl Rahner).

God's victory, already completely won in her, the victory of Christ and his redemptive work and the victory of the Holy Spirit and his sanctifying activity — these become the victory of humankind and of creation as a whole, which in Mary has recovered its dignity and beauty. After the long, dead centuries marked by the sin of the first parents, this morning star appeared, shining clear and pure, diaphanous and inviolate, while the heavens changed their color with the promise of the impending day. The blooming on our earth of such a brilliantly white flower that was a worthy prelude to Christ, the Sun of justice and the new creation par excellence, was a sure sign of the reconciliation of the human race with God. She was the glowing dawn of a day the like of which heaven and earth would never see again, apart from the day of the Incarnate Word himself. She thus made her radiant appearance on the horizon of our history (John XXIII) as the herald of life and hope and the prophet of new goals to be reached by creation once it experienced the embrace of grace.

The Fathers explicitly say that when Mary was formed to be entirely pure and immaculate, the harm done by sin was also repaired and a new creation began. "Mary was born for the rebirth of the universe" (Andrew of Crete). Nicholas Cabasilas calls Mary "a new kind of being and the beginning of a new race ... a new earth and a new heaven ... that did not inherit any of the ancient leaven" (*NDM*, 698). In a homily on the Nativity of Mary Andrew of Crete said:

> Today the human race in all its resplendent and spotless nobility receives the gift of its first formation at the hands of God and recovers its ancient beauty. The disgraces caused by sin had obscured the splendor and attractiveness of human nature; but when the mother of him who is the Beautiful One par excellence was born, this same nature, in her person, regained its ancient privileges and was formed according to a model that was perfect and worthy of God.... Today the reshaping of our nature begins and a world grown old is divinely transformed and receives the first fruits of a second creation (*Sermon* 1; PG 97–912).

In Mary Immaculate human generation recovers all the splendor that marked the original divine creation and rediscovers itself. It is once again capable of a radical new beginning in the reshaping of itself and in fully taking up the original plan once again.

> In her immaculate human conception, which corresponds in a marvelous way to God's mysterious idea of creatures as rulers of the world, Mary restores the

image of perfect humanity. She is the only human creature in whom God's creative idea is now faithfully
reflected within history. She is the only human creature who reflects in an astounding way the image of
God as God thought it and loved before the rupture
caused by original sin undermined the divine plan
(Paul VI).

"The event," the miracle of Mary Immaculate, "sheds a
supernatural light on our human life" (John Paul II) and
shows us, in a single person, the face of the new humanity
redeemed by Christ, a humanity in which God renews "in a
still more wonderful way" his plan for paradise (see the
Opening Prayer for the Feast of Christ's birth).

According to writers both western and eastern, Mary
Immaculate in her historical concreteness embodies the
longing for and restoration of that lost and rediscovered paradise. She is the springtime whose flowers will no longer
experience the risk of fading and death. She is the fruit not
poisoned by the serpent. She is the beginning of a new and
ineffable history for creatures and the creator: "In her,
the intimacy granted by God to Adam at his creation and
so quickly lost flourishes once again in its original perfection" (John XXIII).

In Mary, who is after Christ the holiest image of God, God
willed to anticipate the final state promised to the entire
human race: to be, some day, completely of God and for him.
In her the Church joyfully contemplates, as in a crystal-clear
image, what it desires and hopes to be (see SC 103). At the
head of the throng of the saved the Immaculate One proclaims "To God alone the glory." She "proclaims a merciful
God who does not surrender his children to sin" (John Paul
II), but in his loving wisdom wills from eternity freely to
love all human beings, regardless of their sins and merits.

The Virgin Mary is the "radiant flower of the Holy Spirit that springs from a lowly earthly stalk but is pure and spotless, a symbol, exemplar, and hope of innocence for all of us."[17] She represents a thrust or push that turns the movement of history towards its true object, which is Christ (*NDM,* 700). Acknowledgment of Mary as immaculate is a doxological act, that is, an act of praise to God for the "great things" he accomplished in her (Lk 1:49). It gives a reason for hope, because it points to the victory of grace over sin.

She who is free of sin leads her children on to the resolute, energetic war against sin (see *MC* 57) so that they may become new human beings amid the conquering and liberating flood of the Spirit. The splendor of the Immaculate One, which shines today before our eyes, tells us: "Look, this is what you ought to be."

> Spirit of Love, undying light,
> spring of grace, crown of glory,
> we magnify you for clothing
> the Immaculate Virgin in eternal brightness
> and outlining in her the perfect image
> of the Church "without spot or wrinkle"
> radiant with beauty.
> To you be glory for ever![18]

3. The Sanctifying Spirit Gradually Prepared Mary for her "Yes" and the Complete Dedication of Her Life to God

> As God cleansed his people from every sin and
>   weakness
> so that it might be ready to say "Yes"
> to its espousal at Sinai,
> so too he preserved Mary from every stain

---

17. Paul VI, *Insegnamenti* XIII (1975) 1499.
18. Italian Episcopal Conference, *In Preghiera con Maria Madre di Gesù* (Rome: Vatican Publishing House, 1987).

> so that her "Yes" at the Annunciation
> might be freer and more joyous (*NDM*, 695).

The absence of sin made it easier for Mary to exercise faith but did not do away with the need of it. The fullness of grace from God was matched by a fullness of faith in Mary: "full of grace" was met by "full of faith." Day after day Mary would repeat her "Yes" in a free and docile cooperation with him who is essentially Love. "He constantly directed and led her by inspiring the right attitude in her at each moment, dwelling within her being, and supporting her fidelity and faith, so that at every moment her response to God was serene and filial."[19]

The Holy Spirit acted in Mary before the Annunciation not only to enable her to bestow a human nature and form on the Logos, but also to prepare her step by step for the complete consecration of herself to the Lord. As A. Serra explains, the Holy Spirit used his creative and sanctifying power to produce the humanity of the Word in the womb of a virgin who did not know a man. But in addition, and before that, he disposed the mind and heart of the young girl in Nazareth to consent to the plan of the Incarnation with all her heart and all her soul and all her strength (see Dt 6:5).[20]

It was the Holy Spirit who prepared Mary for the most important, the key action of her life: for her great "Yes" at the Annunciation, the divinely inspired words to which he himself gave rise in the depths of her soul. It was a marvelous "Yes" that crowned the greatest act of faith in the history of the human race; a total "Yes," such as God had looked for in vain from the chosen people; a "Yes" that would echo down the centuries and be remembered by following generations as the paradigm and idea of faith in and obedience to

---

19. Pierre Guilbert, "Marie des Ecritures," *Marianum* 58 (1996) 532.
20. A. Serra, "Aspetti mariologici della Pneumatologia di Lc 1, 35a," in *Maria e lo Spirito Santo*, 181.

the unpredictable mystery of God, who is present with his incommensurable love in the "today" of our history. It was, finally, a "Yes" that gave forth an extraordinary light and is the most important feature in the spiritual portrait of Mary and the heart of her greatness and of the entire mystery that surrounds her.

Among the evangelists Luke in particular (whom tradition has, not by chance, imagined to have been a painter) has depicted for us the theological and spiritual face of the Virgin of Nazareth. From his work the Fathers and theologians generally have derived a valuable starting point for the development of a Marian pneumatology, as well as a sufficient textual basis for asserting that God's work in Mary began before she became Mother of God.

If we read it carefully, the Virgin's answer to the angelic messenger (Lk 1:38) expressed a longstanding attitude, so that the angel could say to her even before she spoke: "Do not be afraid, Mary, for you have found favor with God" (Lk 1:30). At that moment, the angel's gaze penetrated to the depths of Mary's mind and moved back to the beginning of her life. First, to the moment of her birth, when she received a name meaning "Beloved of God," but then, even before her birth to the first instant of her existence, because she had been recipient of this exceptional divine love from the first moment of her conception.

At the very beginning of the great message the angel addressed Mary as "full of grace" (see Lk 1:28). The Greek text of Luke's gospel uses the term *kecharitomene* ("you who have been, and remain, filled with the divine favor"); it is as if the angel were saying: "you who are especially loved by God, utterly pervaded by his love, completely established in it as though you were formed entirely by it." This Greek word — this new name — so full of meaning, with which the angel addresses Mary, "shows clearly, and not merely in a more or less implicit way" that this young girl of Nazareth "was already fully justified at the moment when the angel greeted her. She did not become holy at that moment but was already holy and in an outstanding way."[21]

The question Mary asks of the angel: "How can this be, since I have no relations with a man?" (Lk 1:34) is another basis for concluding that Mary had always and wholly belonged to the Lord and had always had this intense and ineffable experience. The very question lets us know that she had chosen the way of virginity. St. Augustine speaks even of a vow of virginity, a fundamental, indeed radical choice of God on Mary's part (see *Sermons* 215, 2 and 291, 5). If she renounced being possessed by a man, the reason was that God had long since entered her life and that she wished to know him alone.

In fact, at Nazareth we find ourselves in the presence of a young woman whose guileless response of complete commitment to God (Lk 1:38) does not offer him anything outside herself, nor does she offer only part of her possessions to the Lord as devout Israelites used to do in the temple during the annual feasts. Rather she gives the whole of herself, consecrates herself unconditionally to her creator, and places at his disposal the first fruits of her virginal femininity: her chaste love, the life she might have transmitted to others, her sensibilities as a woman, her limitless capacity for self-surrender.

Well-known in this context are the descriptions given by Athanasius and Ambrose as they recount the details of Mary's life, narrate its external aspects, her actions, and her behavior, while also reading the inner life of her soul. They portray a Christian virgin who is totally committed to a life of perfect love of God and neighbor. Ambrose's conclusion: that is how the evangelist describes her, that is what the angel

---

21. M. Jugie, cited in Jean Galot, *Maria, la donna*, 193.

found her to be, that is what the Holy Spirit chose her to be.[22] Origen, too, commenting on the words "looked upon the humility," paints a picture of Mary's interior life: it was one marked by such acquired virtue that it persuaded God to fix his gaze on her (*Homilies on Luke* VIII, 4–5; GCS 49).

This extraordinary and unequaled openness of the Virgin to God leads us back to the wellspring of life. In the abyss of the trinitarian mystery we discern the radical docility with which from all eternity the Holy Spirit allows himself to respond to the impulse of the love of the Father and the Son. The lovableness of the Madonna is but a created reflection of the infinite lovableness of the Spirit of God.

B. The Annunciation
(The High Point of the Spirit's Action and Life)

1. Introductory Remarks

> From eternity Mary was thought, loved, and
> created for this unique moment in history.
>
> (Leonardo Boff)

The scene of the Annunciation has been an almost unbelievable favorite of all generations of Christians. Our approach has barely touched on some of its inexhaustible riches.

The Annunciation is the crown upon all that preceded and the foundation of all that follows; it marks the central and determining moment of the entire mystery of Mary and it is the basic event in the hidden relationship between the Holy Spirit and Mary. Everything leads up to and has its beginning here, in this moment in which the Holy Spirit — the Power of God, and the Lord and Giver of life — descends upon Mary and raises her up to be a partner in a humanly impossible work: the virginal conception of the

---

22. See Athanasius, *De virginitate* (CSCO 151), 58–64; Ambrose, *De virginibus* 2, 2–6.

Son of God (Lk 1:31–35). This is the supreme work, the miracle of miracles of God "who so loved the world that he gave his only Son" (Jn 3:16).

Covered by the ineffable shadow of the Holy Spirit, Mary, already full of grace, is now filled to overflowing with it. After having prepared a dwelling, the Spirit now makes it fruitful and inhabited. In him and by means of him the Father entrusts to the Virgin his own Son and through her gives him to the world. The Spirit acts as mediator between the Father who gives his Son and Mary who receives him. This mediation takes place in an atmosphere of love, of unreserved self-giving, and of life. Mary is involved in it. The fruitful love that makes her a mother is taken and received from its very Source: directly, with supreme purity, and with ineffable joy.

As someone has observed, between the Virgin of Nazareth and the child she is about to conceive there is a measureless abyss. The Holy Spirit, who is love and fulfillment, is sent to annihilate this infinite distance and place the Virgin in direct contact with the mystery of God. In uniting the Virgin to himself, God embraces her and fills her whole being, not only spiritually but physically; he consecrates her mind and body, her entire being, her whole person, and all her powers, and raises her to dizzying heights,[23] where she can appropriately receive into her womb him by whom all things have been made.

In order that no problem might arise from the frailty of the human body, the Power of the Most High overshadowed the Virgin, sanctifying the very depths of her being, so that she might give the Holy One a human origin. He strengthened her native creaturely weakness so that she might receive the invading power of the Holy Spirit and become the source of

---

23. See A. Amato, "Lo Spirito Santo e Maria. Elementi della Tradizione Patristico-Teologica," in *NDM*, 1336–37.

Christ's corporeal life. In this context I may cite, among others, St. Hilary of Poitiers, who writes: "Coming from on high the Holy Spirit sanctified the Virgin's womb and, by breathing into it, blended with the nature of human flesh; that which was different from himself he took over by his own power" (*NDM*, 1069–70). And Cyrillonas in one his poems writes: "The fire of the Spirit descended / in tongues of flesh, and there took place / a divine conception / in the fleshly womb of a daughter of man" (*Carmen* 3, 191–202).

The Annunciation was a true and proper Pentecost, as Mary's entire being received a personal fullness of the Holy Spirit and grace; this fullness was not simply prophetic and momentary but sanctifying and lasting. Origen writes: "Mary was filled with the Holy Spirit at the moment in which she began to have the Savior dwelling in her womb. As soon as she received the Holy Spirit as shaper of the Lord's body, as soon as the Son of God entered her womb, she was also filled with the Holy Spirit" (*Homilies on Luke* VII, 3; GCS 49).

The Spirit touched the chords of her heart and set her vibrating interiorly; she remained wholly pervaded by his light, even in the most secret fibers of her being, like a transparent crystal flooded by the sun. When the Holy Spirit descended on Mary, he found her ready; he filled her with vigorous life, far more so than he had filled the charismatic individuals of the past, and he enabled her to act as a perfect woman and as a mother.[24] Being made transparent by and in the Spirit, she became true mother of the Word: "One who is wholly pure offers God her spotless flesh as holy temple of the divinity" (Cyril of Jerusalem).

All this, once again, extols God's generosity toward the Virgin. Not only did he predestine her for divine motherhood, but he also aided her continually by his abundant

---

24. See Alessio Martinelli, in *Maria Santissima e lo Spirito Santo*, 88–89.

charisms that enabled her to comply suitably with her exceptional vocation.

2. Salvation Comes Down from Heaven but Also Springs Up from the Earth

> Hail, most holy Mother of our Savior God,
> infinitely aromatic perfume of all the virtues!
> The Lord, drawn by your fragrance,
> has taken his rest within you;
> through you he has come to live among us
> and we with him.[25]

The scene of the Annunciation as described by Luke can be regarded as the narrative of Mary's cooperation in the work of salvation; it tells us that in saving us God chose a "method," that of working through creatures. Our rebirth comes, it is true, from the paschal mystery, but it begins in the virginal womb of Mary.

According to Archbishop Carli, the Holy Spirit and Mary ever-virgin, in different but conjoined ways, formed the "new man" par excellence, "the man who comes from heaven," that is, Jesus, who reconciles us and even more marvelously forms anew the wonderful plan for creation, now disfigured by sin.[26] He is the fruit of the divine power of love and of Mary's "Yes." If the mystery of the Incarnation brings heaven down to our level and makes earth bend its knee, it does so due to the power of Mary's "Yes."

Theologians, especially those of the East, while attending first of all to the greatness of the divine work accomplished in Mary, have not failed to emphasize the active role of the Virgin Mother in carrying out this work. They state explicitly that the miracle of the Incarnation is indeed the work of grace, but also that the reliable collaboration of Mary is a bottomless

---

25. From the Fathers of the Church, in *LM*, 92 and *TMPM* II, 646.
26. Archbishop Luigi Maria Carli, in *Marianum* 38 (1976) 470.

abyss. At the Annunciation we encounter a creature who, far from being a passive instrument in the hands of God (*LG* 53), opens herself to receive God in a way that displays a complete physical and spiritual balance. Her pure heart, already given wholly to God since her infancy, here widens, as it were, to utter the generous, unconditional "Yes" with which she agrees to become the Mother of the Messiah.

God willed to tie the destiny of the historical world to this spousal "Yes" that is permeated with infinity, light, and salvation for every human being ever born, to this "Yes" that burst forth on our earth and is the greatest thing our earth could have given. God did not decree that his Son should become a member of the human race solely as a result of his divine decision. No, the Incarnation was to result both from his supreme initiative and from the Virgin's free consent. "God was able to create all things from nothing, but after they had been ruined, he willed not to restore them without Mary's aid" (St. Anselm).

On this point Cabasilas writes: "The Incarnation of the Word was not solely the work of the Father, his power, and his Spirit, but also the work of the Virgin's will and faith. Just as this plan could not have been carried out without the former, it was also impossible for the plan to be activated apart from the will and faith of Mary most holy."[27]

We can say, therefore, that the history of Jesus begins with the faith and consent of Mary. St. Catherine of Siena, who felt all the fascination and enchantment of the Annunciation, speaks thus in a prayer:

> Mother, the eternal deity knocked at your gate, but if you had not opened the door of your will, God would not have taken flesh in you. The Son of God did not descend into your womb until you had given your

---

27. Nicholas Cabasilas, *On the Dormition* 12 (PO 19:508).

deliberate consent. He who desired to come into you waited at the door of your will for it to be opened to him; he would never have entered if you had not opened to him (*TMSM* IV, 568).

The Son willed to take flesh, but he also willed that his mother should give birth to him freely and with full consent (Cabasilas). The Father's infinite love is pleased only with what is spontaneously offered to him out of love; everything else is tasteless to him. For this reason, it was only when Mary said: "Behold ... may it be done to me according to your word" (Lk 1:38) — only then was the mystery of Christ's coming accomplished. We are not dealing here with words of God spoken through the prophets; at Mary's reply, the Word really became flesh. Mary believed, and in her that which she believed took place (St. Augustine); through her pure faith and virginal womb the Son of God entered into human history.

After giving God this answer and freely offering her fruitfulness to the Spirit, Mary received this same Spirit, who took from her a flesh wholly permeated by divinity. Indeed we must agree with Cantalamessa: "The great thing that happened in Nazareth after the angel's greeting was that Mary believed." By her belief she determined the accomplishment of the mystery on its human side. "Never in the history of humanity did so much depend on the consent of a human creature" (John Paul II). "Never would a human being rise to become an active protagonist in a more glorious event; never would a human being exercise a more decisive influence or role even in the history of the world and on the destiny of the entire human race."[28]

---

28. Jean Galot, "Maria immagine della donna," *La Civiltà Cattolica*, May 4, 1974, 219f.

Through you, immaculate Virgin,
we have regained life,
for you conceived by the action
of the Holy Spirit, and from you
the world received its Savior (Liturgy)
To you, "lampstand of divine light,"
belong all our love, our praise,
and our undying gratitude.

3. Holy Dwelling of God

Exalting thy childbearing
we all glorify thee, too,
as a living temple, O Mother of God

(The Akathistos Hymn, stanza 23)

The bright cloud that embraced and covered the Tent of Meeting with its shadow signified that the interior of the dwelling was filled with the glory of Yahweh (see Ex 40:35). So, too, the power of the Spirit, which came down and over-shadowed Mary, caused her womb to be filled with the incarnate presence of the Holy One, the Son of God (see Lk 1:35). The point of this parallel is obvious: the evangelist meant to emphasize the fact that Mary is the new Tent of Meeting, the new dwelling of the Glory, the new temple of God, the place where Yahweh permanently visits his people.

In his Spirit God descended in the form of a cloud to dwell on Mount Sinai, then in the Ark, and then in the temple. In these last times he found his resting place in the womb of a woman, Mary of Nazareth. "He set up his tent in her womb as in a light-filled heaven" (Sophronius of Jerusalem). In her the great eschatological longing of the Old Testament was satisfied, namely, that God should dwell "in the bosom" of his people (see Is 12:6; Ps 44:6; Hos 11:9; Mi 3:11). In her the words of Scripture were accomplished for the first time and in an entirely extraordinary way: "He who created me has rested in my tent" (Sir 24:8; author's translation).

From her early childhood Mary had learned to venerate this divine presence in a single place on earth, there where the high priest entered by himself, and only once a year, on the great day of atonement. Now the angel Gabriel teaches her that henceforth she is to adore that presence within herself. The Fathers of the Church celebrated with deep feeling the greatness of this woman who was the first tabernacle; in doing so they used an original and entirely fitting image: "Mary is the *loom* or *workroom* in which the Holy Spirit wove the human garment of the Word."[29] She is the *workshop*[30] of the divine economy, the *receptacle* of what cannot be contained, the holy virginal womb in which she contained the Uncontainable.[31]

4. Temple of the Holy Spirit

> I greet you, indescribable dwelling
>   of the Holy Spirit!
>
> (John Geometres)

As we saw, the coming of the Holy Spirit at the Annunciation caused the Son of God to dwell in the womb of the Virgin. Because her virginal body was thus privileged, Mary became the temple of the Word made flesh and thus in a unique way a temple of God. It is chiefly on this account that the title "temple of a divine Person" is to be given to her, and on this account, too, we must say with St. Irenaeus that in an extraordinary way "Mary carried God" (*Against the Heresies* 5, 19, 1). Put more succinctly, Mary deserves the description of "temple" in an exceptional way because she is "Mother of God."

---

29. St. Basil, *Homily on the Holy Birth of Christ*, 3 (PG 31:1464).
30. "Workshop" (*ergasterion*): a very evocative and poetic term which many of the Fathers applied to Mary.
31. See *TMPM* I, 490–91; II, 825, 419; IV, 937.

In the order of grace Mary is to be called not only "Temple of the Son" but also "Temple of the Holy Spirit." This description, like its synonyms (tabernacle, sanctuary, dwelling of the Spirit) which were widely used by the Fathers, describes the indwelling of the Holy Spirit in Mary, this inhabitation being understood as quite special and as superior to the indwelling in other Christians. But the position of the Virgin here is unique and exceptional only because of the completeness of her consecration; fundamentally, she is a temple in the way in which all Christians are called to be temples. In virtue of her privileged holiness and of the fullness of grace and love with which she was blessed, "Mary is [a temple] in a more perfect way, but she is such as a model of what ought to be true of all who receive the life of grace" (Jean Galot).

"Do you not know that you are the temple of God, and that the Spirit of God dwells in you?" (1 Cor 3:16). The word of God tells us that the entire being of Christians belongs to God and that their entire person is the temple in which the Holy Spirit dwells with a sanctifying presence that draws the other two Persons. The temple that was Mary never experienced anything opposed to this fundamental consecration. The life of grace developed in her without meeting any obstacle. From the first instant of her existence the Holy Spirit took complete possession of her being and made her his permanent dwelling. He found in her a temple in which it pleased him to dwell as an always-welcome guest; he found her to be, like no other creature, his temple par excellence and his ideal sanctuary.

These sublime harmonies make Mary the exemplary sanctuary of the Holy Spirit, and Christians are urged to contemplate her in order that they may be able to imitate her.

5. *Spouse of the Holy Spirit*

Because the third Person of the Trinity, with the cooperation of Mary, effected the virginal conception of the Word,
the title "spouse" has in recent times passed from the Father
to the Holy Spirit. Mary is most appropriately called spouse
of the Holy Spirit. Jean Galot, an outstanding theologian
explains:

> The personal action of the Holy Spirit has for its effect
> the formation of the infant in Mary's womb and is
> therefore to be described as that of a spouse who acts
> spiritually in bringing about a corporeal procreation.
> The spiritual character of his activity does not exclude
> its effect from being a corporeal fertilization.
>
> If we want to bring out the proper relationships of
> Mary with the divine Persons, we must describe her as
> being by singular title the spouse of the Holy Spirit and
> the temple of the incarnate Word. These relationships
> are hers in the mystery of the Incarnation and describe
> an extraordinary and indeed unique situation.
>
> In the Old Testament the transcendence of Yahweh
> did not keep the people from being called his spouse.
> Similarly, the transcendence of the Holy Spirit could
> not keep Mary from receiving that same name on quite
> special grounds. She was called to become Mother of
> the promised Messiah; it was therefore fitting that she
> should be elevated to the rank of spouse of the Holy
> Spirit. Mary could here see emerging the characteris-
> tics of a divine spouse, because Israelite religion had
> told her of the covenant which God had established
> with his people.[32]

---

32. Galot, *Maria: itinerario*, 54–57 and 61.

It was the task of the Holy Spirit to turn God's covenant with Israel into a reality, that is, into the definitive covenant for which Mary had been hoping and which she now saw coming to pass. It was to her that God offered the conjugal love which he had promised to his people, and it was in her womb that his union with humanity was accomplished. It was there that Jesus Christ drew human nature to himself in order to espouse it and to unite himself with it in a genuine marriage, thereby restoring humanity's ancient splendor and bestowing on it for ever its extraordinary dignity. It was in the Virgin's inviolable womb that Bridegroom and bride, Word and flesh, Creator and creature were united.

The title "spouse" had been simply an image in the language of the prophets, but here it takes on its full concrete meaning. "The Holy Spirit will come upon you, and the power of the Most High will overshadow you" (Lk 1:34–35). This answer of the angel to the young girl of Nazareth when she had expressed her desire to remain a virgin quite justifies the title, given to Mary, of "spouse" of the Holy Spirit. Her divine maternity is not part of the ordinary system of grace but is due to the extraordinary action of the Holy Spirit, an exceptional use of his power.

The situation here implies that the Holy Spirit substitutes for a human husband in a childbearing that does not derive from a physical union and that he thus acts as an authentic divine spouse. While maintaining his transcendence he comes to Mary and enters into an intimate contact with her that has all the appearances of a nuptial relationship: a sublime marriage that is fulfilled not by a physical embrace but by a chaste response of faith. St. Cyril of Jerusalem declares: "What kind of marriage will the Virgin, the holy spouse, have? Listen, 'I will espouse you to me in faith!' " (*Catecheses* 12, 24). And in fact, when she is told of the proposed coming of the Holy Spirit to form the messianic child, she responds with a faith-inspired complete surrender of herself.

It is true that her "Yes" was essentially a "Yes" to the birth of the Savior, but at the same time it was a "Yes" to the coming of the Holy Spirit. It was the "Yes" of a virgin who docilely made herself available to the action of the divine transcendent Spouse, the "Yes" of a bride who was fully receptive to the love of the divine Bridegroom which sought her motherhood.

It needs to be made clear that the absence of any physical union between Mary and the Holy Spirit does not imply a lesser love or even a less intense spiritual union. The moment of the Annunciation, when the divine spouse approached the Virgin of Nazareth, was a culmination of love and union: "a completely interior union … of Mary's being with the being of the Holy Spirit, but in a way incomparably more perfect than what the word 'spouse' can express among human beings."[33] This was the same transcendent divine being who desired to establish the deepest relationship of intimacy with his creatures and who now presented himself to them as a spouse who asks that his partner too have the heart of a spouse.

The angel did not approach Mary as though she were simply an instrument or a field of activity in which God was to work. She was more than an instrument, more than a field of activity: she was a human being with whom he willed to establish a covenant. God never treats human beings merely as places or as tools; he treats them as what he created them to be: as persons and therefore as his collaborators and partners in dialogue. God proposes but

---

33. St. Maximilian Kolbe, in *Meditazioni mariane*, 157–58.

does not impose: he created his children as free and he respects their freedom.

Some scholars say that the title "spouse of the Spirit" claims not too much but rather too little: "The Holy Spirit permeates Mary in such an ineffable way that the definition 'spouse of the Holy Spirit' is a very inadequate image for expressing the life of the Holy Spirit in her and through her."[34] But Theophanes of Nicea said: "The close union of the Paraclete with the most holy Virgin is of such a nature and so extensive that no words can express it and no intellect is capable of grasping it."[35]

The title "spouse of the Holy Spirit" as given to Mary must indeed be understood as analogous, but at the same time it is not to be interpreted as simply poetic or lyrical. No, it has a doctrinal value and expresses a real though spiritual spousal relationship with the Holy Spirit. On the other hand, it is not lacking in a poetic quality: "Has there ever been a love poetry more intense than that in which a divine person comes to the Virgin of Nazareth in order to make her Mother of the Son of God and irrevocably to combine divine love with a human destiny?"[36]

6. Mary: Complete Charismatic

If we understand "charism" as Paul does, that is, as "the manifestation of the Spirit ... given for some benefit" (1 Cor 12:7), we must ask: Has any manifestation of the Spirit contributed more to the common good than the divine maternity or the Incarnation, which was "a culminating moment of the Spirit's action in the history of salvation" (*MC* 26)?

---

34. Idem, *Chi sei, o Immacolata?*, 29.
35. Cited in Roschini, *Il Tuttosanto e la Tuttasanta*, 139–40.
36. Galot, *Maria: itinerario*, 62.

At the coming of the Holy Spirit in the Annunciation Mary opened like the petals of a flower in order to receive the divine content. She is the chaste Virgin of whom the *Odes of Solomon* speak, who takes possession of the milk of the Father and his Word in order then to offer it as a drink to the world (*Odes of Solomon* 19). Or, as we read in the *Abercius Inscription*, she catches the great, pure fish in the fountain of the divinity and gives it to her friends as a perpetual food (text in *DALI*, 83).

Mary of Nazareth is, then, the supreme charismatic in the history of salvation. This does not mean that she had the greatest number of charisms; on the contrary, she appears outwardly poor in charisms. What miracles did she perform? Of the apostles it is said that even their shadow cured the sick (see Acts 5:15). We do not know of any miracle or any marvelous or sensational action that she accomplished in her lifetime. The reason why she is the greatest of the charismatics is that in her the Holy Spirit performed the greatest of his wonders: he gave Mary not the gifts of governing or prophesying or having visions or dreams or words of wisdom, but the gift of giving life to the Messiah.

Through the Virgin Mother we have been given the supreme grace: Jesus. Through this miracle of grace and salvation which places "Mary on the pinnacle of grace and merit, she rises above all creatures except the incarnate Word. We can say that as all rivers flow into the sea, so all the charisms of the saints find their place in her" (see *NDM*, 1347).

The Fathers, having in mind chiefly the Magnificat, sometimes call Mary a prophetess. But if she is a prophetess, she is one in a new and sublime way, in the sense that she "spoke forth" in silence the one "Word" of God; she gave him birth. The Word of God "came" upon the prophets, including John the Baptist: "the word of God came to

John" (Lk 3:2), that is, the word became an active reality in them. But thanks to an extraordinary intervention of the Spirit, the Word did not come to Mary just for a moment but took up his dwelling in her; he did not become simply an "active reality" but became flesh. No longer did the Word of the Lord simply "come," but "the Word was made flesh" (Jn 1:14).

A prophet is one who "eats" the scroll that contains God's word and fills him interiorly (see Jer 15:16; Ez 3:1–2; Rev 10:8–9). But what is that when compared with what took place in Mary? Her body was filled by the Word, not only metaphorically but really. The word found complete acceptance in her, not only in her hearing, her mind, and her heart, but also in her maternal womb.

Her charism, then, was unique and the greatest, never given to another human creature or, for that matter, to an angelic creature. It transcends even that of the sacred writers who were inspired, or moved by the Spirit, to speak on behalf of God (see 2 Pt 1:21).

7. Sign of the Perennial Fruitfulness of the Spirit
(The Work of the Holy Spirit in Mary Is the Source of Birth and Salvation for All Human Beings)

> The power from on high …
> converted her fruitless womb
> into a meadow sweet for all men.

> (*The Akathistos Hymn*, stanza 4)

With the stroke of a pen that is driven by an artist's holy inspiration, this wonderful ancient hymn is a summary of Marian doctrine and it springs more from the heart of the original undivided Church than from the mind of a single scholar. It celebrates the Mother of Jesus as the supreme manifestation of the fruitfulness of the Holy Spirit, for her virginal womb, made fruitful by the divine Spirit, became a perennial source of spiritual plenitude for those who accept God's gift. Everything in this hymn provides the substance of the thoughts we shall be developing here.

The tradition has been quite familiar with the idea that the divine Spirit endows virgins with a spiritual fruitfulness. All the more, therefore, must we emphasize the unique spiritual fruitfulness given to Mary by the action of the Holy Spirit.

Montfort makes the point that no further divine person proceeds from the Holy Spirit; rather the Spirit closes the trinitarian circle. But he does become fruitful through Mary, his spouse. With her, in her, and from her he formed his masterpiece, God-made-man, and until the end of the world will constantly form those who are the predestined members of the body of this adorable Head (*DV*, 20). St. Maximilian Kolbe seems to be echoing Montfort when he writes: "It is in the womb of Mary, his spouse, that the Holy Spirit conceives within time the divine life of the God-man, and in her womb human beings will always be able to be incorporated into Christ, that is, be reborn to new life."[37]

A medieval writer says: "The holy Virgin unceasingly gives birth and rebirth to Christ in us, until he shall have reached his perfect stature in us.... Her womb was made fruitful only once, yet it never ceases to be fruitful," because at all times she continues to form Christ in all those who conceived him. It can be said that "the blessed fruit of her womb always dwells in her yet also emerges from her. And this wellspring overflows and floods souls around Mary."[38]

The action of the Holy Spirit in Mary takes the form of concentric circles, as it were, in the sense that it does not end

37. Cited by Ernesto M. Piacentini, *Maria nel pensiero di san Massimiliano M. Kolbe*, 20–78.
38. Guerric of Igny, in *Marianum* 54 (1992) 249.

with the mystery of the Incarnation, but spreads its effects abroad through space and time, inasmuch as in every age and in every place the working of the Holy Spirit in the Virgin of Nazareth will be the source of birth and salvation for all human beings. "Mary exists to be the Mother of Jesus; this is her calling and her predestined role. The purpose of her life is to give flesh to Jesus and to be his Mother. But this purpose could not and did not end with the Incarnation."[39] From the womb of the Virgin Mother the creative action of the Holy Spirit reaches out at the same time from the humanity of Christ to the new people of God, the people made up of the redeemed and inseparable from him who came to save it.

Thus the new world that is the object of biblical hope is born from the womb of a woman,[40] Mary, the new Zion of messianic times. It is in her womb that the seed of eternal life for a new humanity began to sprout. It is there that the New Adam and with him the renewed human race acquired their life. The supernatural action of the Holy Spirit by which he formed a new human being in Mary's womb, forecast the birth of a new human being, that is, the birth of a supernatural order that will be brought about in the human race by the same Spirit. Thus the virginal birth of Jesus became the source of a new birth for Christians. It is this universal significance of the virginal conception that the Fathers bring out when they say that in Mary the entire human race began to be reborn along with Jesus.

The collaboration of Mary with the Holy Spirit in the formation of "new life" for Christians is a permanent reality, as is grace itself. This special aspect of the mystery of the Mother of Christ is also a recurrent theme that appears strongly and clearly in the writings of not a few notable

---

39. Roberto Masi, in *Lo Spirito Santo e Maria Santissima*, 116–17.
40. See Choan Song Song, *Third-Eye Theology. Theology in Formation in Asian Settings* (Maryknoll, NY: Orbis, 1979).

exegetes and theologians of our time, as well as in the authoritative ordinary magisterium of the Church. Thus Archbishop Carli teaches: "The new life of Christians is formed, nourished, and strengthened by the power of the Holy Spirit, but not without the subordinate cooperation of Mary that begins with baptism and continues until the human being reaches full stature." [41]

The Holy Spirit, who with the aid of Mary formed the child Jesus at the Incarnation, continues to ask her aid in the development of Christ's life in other men and women (Jean Galot). Just as the Incarnation is the result of the Holy Spirit's work in collaboration with Mary, so is the continuation of the Incarnation through baptism. Therefore the "new life" given to every baptized person is trinitarian, ecclesial, and Marian. The fruits of the redemption accomplished by Christ and those flowing from the life and holiness given by the Spirit will forever bear the mark of the powerful, maternal intervention of Mary. [42]

The Mother of the Church, who gave human life to its Head, continues to give rebirth to his members through the sacraments that bestow light and grace. These members spring from her womb and her heart. In a sense, she carried in her maternal womb not only the humanity of the Son but us as well; with unwearying love she also continues to give us rebirth until his life breaks through with power into ours and we become once again little children at the knee of this most loving Mother.

The Holy Spirit is active in Mary, and through her pours himself out into hearts. He is in Mary as one sent by the Father and the Son, instilling in her not only the spirit of adoption as God's child (as he does in the other faithful)

---

41. Archbishop Luigi Maria Carli, in *Marianum* 38 (1976) 474.
42. See Agnoletti, *Maria Sacramento di Dio*, 180.

but also a spirit of motherhood, as a result of which the Virgin is "in labor until Christ be formed" in us (Gal 4:19).

As a creature taken over by the Spirit for the carrying out of God's plan, Mary received, in a sense, the power to draw the Spirit into the hearts of her children. She does this in a way peculiar to herself, one that is completely maternal and in accordance with the requirements of her mission. It can be said of her that in the divine plan "she is precisely one of the privileged means by which the Holy Spirit is able to guide souls and lead them to likeness with Christ."[43] Among others convinced of this truth was Ildephonsus of Toledo, who "in a prayer of supplication, amazing in its doctrine and powerful prayer" (*MC*, 26), asks the Virgin to intercede for him that he may receive from the Holy Spirit the ability to give birth to Christ in his own soul. "Holy Virgin, I pray you, I pray you that I may receive Jesus from the same Spirit by whose power you yourself gave birth to him. May my soul receive Jesus by the working of the same Spirit through whom your flesh conceived that same Jesus.… Let me love Jesus in that same Spirit in whom you adored him as Lord and contemplated him as Son." [44]

St. Louis Grignion de Montfort, in his valuable treatise on true devotion to Mary, sets down this principle: "The more He [the Holy Spirit,] finds Mary, His dear and inseparable Spouse, in any soul, the more active and mighty He becomes in producing Jesus Christ in that soul, and that soul in Jesus Christ.… One of the great reasons why the Holy Spirit does not now do startling wonders in our souls is because He does not find there a sufficiently great union with His faithful and inseparable Spouse" (*True Devotion*, 20 and 36). As though to complete this thought, in a sentence rich in enthusiasm no less than in theological truth, Montfort assures us:

43. Cantalamessa, *Maria uno specchio per la Chiesa*, 160.
44. *De virginitate perpetua sanctae Mariae*, ch. 12 (PL 96:106).

"Wonderful things will come to pass in this wretched world when the Holy Spirit, finding his beloved spouse reproduced as it were in souls, descends with abundance into them and fills them with his gifts, especially the gift of wisdom, so that they will perform marvels of grace."[45]

In this context some concluding thoughts are in place. First and foremost we must not forget that what Mary accomplishes she accomplishes under the action of the Holy Spirit and in dependence on him. Everything great, beautiful, and holy in her, everything she accomplishes as Mother of Christ and of the Church, is only a participation in the principal causality of the Holy Spirit, whose very humble and faithful instrument she is.

Furthermore, Mary's maternal activity on behalf of the redeemed does not rival or detract in any way from the omnipotent and universal action of the Holy Spirit. Rather she prays and prepares for that action not only by her intercessory prayer but also by the direct influence of her example, including the very important one of utmost docility to the desires of the divine Spirit.[46] There is no basis, then, for the objection of some eastern writers who see in western Catholic Mariology a tendency to substitute the action of Mary for that of the Holy Spirit.

Reflection on the Holy Spirit and reflection on Mary are not two mutually exclusive areas of theology, but two areas that complete, strengthen, and illumine one another. "There should, then, be no fear that veneration of the Virgin may usurp the place belonging to the Holy Spirit. Is not Mary the supreme living testimony and most luminous epiphany of the person and work of the Holy Spirit, whose infinite virtualities she manifests?" (Paul VI).

---

45. As cited by Francesco Franzi in *Maria Santissima e lo Spirito Santo*, 133.
46. See Paul VI, *Letter to Cardinal L. J. Suenens*, May 13, 1975 (AAS 67 [1975] 354–59).

According to the lovely and inspired words of Kolbe, which are permanently valid and very relevant, especially in ecumenical dialogue: "Our Lady exists in order that the Holy Spirit may be better known" (*Conference*, September 15, 1937).

C. After the Annunciation
(New Key Moments in the Life of the Spirit)

From the Immaculate Conception to the Assumption into heaven, Mary with her openness to divine Love showed herself increasingly to be a true "harp of the Holy Spirit," from which the divine Master drew the most beautiful and sublime harmonies. As the beneficiary of the proto-Pentecost (see Lk 1:35), which had given her life a strong vital impulse and an extraordinary turn, the Virgin of Nazareth would experience new secret relationships with the Holy Spirit, while at the same time being raised up to an ever-greater conformity to Christ and his saving work.

During the earthly life she lived with the Savior her spiritual dispositions were those of a spouse. The powerful maternal love which the Spirit's coming aroused in Mary only increased her virginal love for him. It is normal, of course, that a mother becomes more fully a spouse as a result of her motherhood and that the child becomes a further bond of union with her husband. Far from being opposed, then, conjugal love and maternal love strengthen each other. The mother rejoices to see the features of her husband in the child, and her maternal admiration deepens his affection for her. Thus the love which the Virgin devoted to Jesus strengthened the spousal love that joined her to the Holy Spirit. Meanwhile, "the years passed, grace increased, and in this order of grace, Mary grew from day to day, until she

reached wonderful heights" (Berulle). This growth was
aided by new events and new profound experiences in the
life of the Spirit.

Scholars see the Spirit's extraordinary action in Mary
during the post-Annunciation period in Luke's passage
on the Visitation (1:39–56), at Pentecost (Acts 1:14;
2:1–4), and at the Assumption.

1. *The Visitation*

The coming of the Holy Spirit for the Incarnation of the
Word had filled the Virgin of Nazareth with a great enthusiasm. She thought with tender love about this divine
spouse who had deigned to come to her and to whom she
felt forever bound in an extraordinary union. If we want
to gain some idea of the eagerness that had taken hold of
her, we need only to look at her as she travels the road
through the mountains of Judah, shortly after receiving
her good news. The evangelist himself paints for us a picture that has a by no means secondary importance for exegetes: "During those days Mary set out and traveled to the
hill country in haste to a town of Judah" (Lk 1:39).

As traditionally read, this hasty journey of the Mother of
God into the hills has been interpreted as a symbol; that is, it
tells us of an individual action of a Mary wholly bent on lis-
tening to the words of the Spirit and putting them into practice, a woman wholly devoted especially to discovering, in
the person of her Son, the Word of the Father, the words that
give life.

This was the line of interpretation adopted by Origen,
who would thereby establish the path to be followed by the
subsequent eastern and western traditions. He writes: "The
hasty ascent into the hills is a kind of outward veil hiding
Mary's rapid interior ascent to the heights of perfection."
That is, the fullness of the Spirit that wells up in her from the

Incarnate Word as from a fountain becomes a demand impelling her to traverse quickly the paths of perfection. It also arouses in her a need to communicate to others the grace she has received and thereby to serve the brethren. "Thus her love expands horizontally in order to communicate to others the Lord who fills her. Her voice becomes a voice of the Word and an eruption of the Holy Spirit" (*Homilies on Luke*, 7–9).

But Mary reminds us that the value of human beings is measured by the degree of their love for God and neighbor, and by nothing else. "The ineffable vision which she contemplated within herself never lessened her love for others, because contemplation is not solely praise and enjoyment of God but also a spur to love other human beings."[47] Thus in the days following her conversation with the angel, Mary rose up and set out in haste into the hills to reach the village of Judah where her cousin Elizabeth lived (Lk 1:39–40). She hastened because she was urged on by the interior power of the Spirit.

One of the most important aspects of the story of the Visitation is the infectious joy that radiated from the Mother of God: her very presence spread joy and a messianic exultation in the Holy Spirit. Indeed, her entrance into the home of her cousin Elizabeth was marked by a little Pentecost. Hardly had Elizabeth heard Mary's voice when she herself was "filled with the Holy Spirit" and "the infant leaped in her womb" (Lk 1:41, 44). The Holy Spirit gave himself to Elizabeth and her son through the Virgin, for Mary was living the life of the Spirit so intensely that her greeting sounded in Elizabeth's ears like a voice from God. Her voice was that not of an

---

47. Elizabeth of the Trinity, cited in M. Philipon, *En presence de Dieu*.

ordinary creature but of a creature in whom the Eternal
One was dwelling.

The way in which Luke's narrative advances has led
many exegetes to see in it analogies with the account of the
transfer of the Ark of the Covenant from Baala of Judah to
Jerusalem (see 2 Sm 6:1–23).[48] Just as the transfer of the ark,
the place of God's presence, aroused the excitement of the
people and manifestations of joy by David, who danced
before Yahweh, so Mary's arrival in Ain Karim caused Elizabeth to exult and John the Baptist to leap for joy in his
mother's womb (Lk 1:41, 44). It is significant that Luke's
verb *skirtao* ("leap") calls to mind the leaping for joy that in
the Old Testament accompanied the coming of the Lord (see
Mal 3:20; Ps 114:4, 6; Ws 19:9; etc.). In Luke's setting
these manifestations of joy acquire wide-ranging liturgical
echoes: When Mary's greeting reaches Elizabeth, the latter
utters a joyous shout, that is, she thanks and praises God and
him alone. She sees in Mary one who carries the "Holy Presence" and therefore cannot restrain the great ecstatic shout
that greeted the appearance of the ark (see Lk 1:42–43).

The humble mother of the Precursor, who has experienced in an extraordinary way the power of God for whom
"nothing will be impossible" (Lk 1:37), is herself now an
agent of the Spirit. She reveals the mystery of Christ born of
the Virgin and urges all to accept it by faith. Her voice
echoes through the house of Zechariah, but it is so powerful
that it reaches Luke's entire community and later on the
believers of every age. The mystery of the divine maternity
had remained hidden in the heart of the young girl of Nazareth; now it is officially revealed. Silence becomes impossi-

---

48. There is a noteworthy number of exegetes, especially of the French school, who
have remarked on the similarity between the two scenes. The parallelism is indeed
obvious, if we include the fact that before being transferred to the City of David the
ark remained for three months in the house of Obededom the Gittite, just as "Mary
remained with her [Elizabeth] for about three months" (Lk 1:56).

ble in the presence of Yahweh's wonders; it turns into exultant adoration. Here, in Ain Karim, we learn that the deeper truth of Mary comes from the Holy Spirit, in the form of prophecy and poetry. It is a poetry of interior realities that with its beauty pervades the human spirit and fills the human heart with song.

It is under the movement of the Holy Spirit that Elizabeth grasps the inestimable gift of grace which Mary carries. It is under this impulse that Elizabeth, beginning with a superlative in the Hebrew manner, utters her well-known prophetic cry: "Most blessed are you among women, and blessed is the fruit of your womb. And how does this happen to me, that the mother of my Lord should come to me?" (Lk 1:42–43).

In response to this warm greeting, a wave produced, as it were, by the wings of the Spirit, passes into and pervades the Virgin herself. Like a real Pentecost, it transforms her, far more than the sister of Moses or Judith or the mother of Samuel or even David himself, into a prophetess and poetess. She reveals herself and the mystery she carries, and sings of the works which God has accomplished through her, his humble servant.

Thus, from the depths of Mary's heart and of her entire being and from her exuberant, charismatic joy in the Spirit, there springs forth an exultant canticle, the Magnificat (Lk 1:46–55). This is the most sublime hymn in Sacred Scripture and perhaps the most beautiful in all of human literature. It is the hymn par excellence of praise and gratitude to the Most High, a jewel jealously kept in the hearts of the faithful, and a liturgical masterpiece of immense importance to the Church, one that has all the characteristics of the promised marriage between God and his people. The words that pour from Mary in this canticle seem to express all the exultation of a mother's heart. In it she uses a wealth of biblical reminiscences to tell the story of salvation to her children and to give voice to a humiliated human race that has been surprised by the down-to-earth tender love of God, to a poor and suffering human race that listens attentively to what God is doing in her.

There is a sweet harmony between the hymns of these two privileged mothers: "Most blessed are you among women, and blessed is the fruit of your womb" (Lk 1:42), and "My soul proclaims the greatness of the Lord.... The Mighty One has done great things for me, and holy is his name" (Lk 1:46, 49).

In the house of Zechariah everything sings and shouts for joy, and everything seems to exult as John does in the womb of Elizabeth. Yet we realize that the language here is meant solely to praise and bless him who with both power and sweetness, both justice and love, directs the course of human history.

> Holy Mary, mother tender and strong,
> our fellow journeyer on the roads of life,
> whenever we contemplate
> the great things the Almighty has done in you,
> we experience such a deep sadness at our slack-
> ness that we feel the need of lengthening our
>   steps
> in order to journey close to you.
> Comply, then, with our longing to take your
> hand; hasten our wearied strides along the road.
> Once we too have become pilgrims in the faith,
> not only shall we seek the face of the Lord, but,
> contemplating you as the image of human con-
> cern for those in need,
> we shall reach the "city" in haste
> and gather there the same joyous fruits
> you once brought to distant Elizabeth.[49]

---

49. Antonino Bello, *Maria, donna dei nostri giorni.*

2. Pentecost

A special day, the fiftieth after the resurrection, brought Pentecost, when the visible mission of the Holy Spirit to the Virgin and the others in the upper room took place. This mission meant "an increase of grace (and charisms) in Mary, an increase of the synergy of the Holy Spirit in her. Mary becomes the increasingly visible *sign* of the Holy Spirit who is acting in her and leading her; she becomes an ever more sacred temple because of the presence in her of the sanctifying and life-giving Spirit."[50]

We may say that Pentecost brought to maturity the way of availability and faith which Mary had been following in her dialogue with the Spirit of God. Due to the outpouring of the Holy Spirit sent by the risen Jesus, Mary shared, within the circle of the apostles, in the fulfillment of the great promise (see especially Jn 15:26; 16:6ff.; and Lk 24:49) and in the exuberant flowering of the first Christian community. "Now was the time of the harvest that crowned her earthly existence."[51]

Under the movement of the Spirit of Pentecost Mary found herself connected no longer with her Son alone but also with his mystical body, the Church. For in Luke's view, the Church is built not only on the foundation of the apostles and prophets but also on the foundation of the entire Christian Pentecostal community in which Mary has a pre-eminent role. In Luke 1:35 the Holy Spirit descends upon the Virgin in order to accomplish the mystery of the Incarnation; now in Acts 2:1–4 he comes upon the apostles in order to bring into being the mystery of the Church, at whose foundation the presence of Mary points

---

50. Bertetto, "La sinergia dello Spirito Santo con Maria," in *Maria e lo Spirito Santo*, 301.

51. Merk, *La figura di Maria nel Nuovo Testamento*, 80.

to the unbreakable bond of the Mother of God with the
Spirit and, through the Spirit, with Christ and the Church.
The same Spirit who had acted in Mary at the Incarnation
in order to make her the Mother of Christ, the head of the
Church, now confirms her as Mother of the Whole Christ.

3. The Assumption

> The icon of the Spirit, which Mary all-holy is,
> is completed by her becoming Queen of
> Heaven.

Also attributed to the Holy Spirit is the freedom of the
Virgin's body from corruption and our knowledge, developed in the course of time, of her glorious Assumption.
Mary is "the temple of the Holy Spirit" that could not col-
lapse (St. Robert Bellarmine).

The Assumption, that splendid crown upon her earthly
life, ended her pilgrimage of faith. At the same time, the
growing power of her synergy with the Spirit brought her to
the exalted place due to her as both Mother and dear companion of Jesus the Redeemer. After preparing her here on
earth for the supreme encounter with God, the Spirit of holiness brought the Virgin, the ideal woman and Mother of the
Word Incarnate, into the glory of heaven; there, embracing
her with his divine power, he drew her permanently into
direct communion with God. Thus, plunged into the eternal
beatific mystery, Mary participates, as no other mere creature does, in the life of the Father and the Son, in their ecsta-
sies of love, in their reciprocal self-donation, and in their
endless happiness.

In the Madonna assumed into heaven, in this living
temple of the Holy Spirit, "the Father and the Son meet,
exchange their love, and communicate to each other their
own good will and joy. God the Father, who at the end
will be 'all in all' (1 Cor 15:28), is already present in a

perfect way in the glorified Virgin. The Son, too, reigns in his Mother, now raised to heavenly glory; he freely devotes himself to her and dwells in her with all the fullness of his love."[52] The Spirit, for his part, develops to their utmost degree the potentialities for union that bind the Mother to the Son, so much so that she has no other will but that of Christ (see Phil 2:5). And she, immersed as she is in Christ, ardently desires that the fire of divine Love (which is, in effect, the Spirit of God) would create a new heart in all human beings (see Ez 36:26–27; Ps 50:12; Lk 12:49).[53]

In the "new creation" (see Mt 19:28) Mary, the archetype and sign of the communion of love between the elect and Christ, rejoices among the redeemed, whom she embraces with maternal love. In the Assumption the kingdom of God, which began in Mary at the first moment of her conception, achieves its full form in her due to the final action of the Holy Spirit. Mary is now wholly open to receiving the Spirit within her, even in the most hidden fibers of her being. The Magnificat which she had sung on the day of her visit to Elizabeth, she now sings in the full light of glory, for the One and Triune God dwells in her as in his holiest creature, the one who on earth had been always and completely his.

In the Assumption the eye of faith can contemplate in its completeness "the dynamism at work in the indwelling of God in human beings: encounter, communion, and mutual possession.... And all these exchanges of life and love, these forms of reciprocal belonging, this dwelling and cohabitation, take place in the Holy Spirit. If Mary is the ideal dwelling of God among human beings, if the Father and the Son

---

52. A. Martinelli, *La Vergine Maria, Dim. Esc. di Dio ad opera dello Spirito Santo*, 99–103.

53. See the interesting article by A. Serra, "Regina," in *NDM*, 1189–1296.

dwell in her with utmost delight, it is because their common Spirit reigns supreme in her."[54]

At this point there is nothing left for us to do but to contemplate and adore the unfathomable mystery of the active presence of the Holy Spirit in his spotless sanctuary and to draw from it reasons for a renewed love and a renewed devotion to the Holy Spirit and to Mary.

D. Perfect Icon of the Divine Beauty
(A Beauty Named Mary)

Mary, focal point of beauty,
in whom humble but pure rays from earth
encounter supreme but accessible rays
from heaven (Paul VI).
The beauty of the divine being
is movingly reflected in her (John Paul II).

1. Overview

At the end of our exciting but not easy journey on the wings of the Holy Spirit, it is both interesting and important to turn to an aspect of the Virgin Mother that has never ceased to astonish and delight our gaze: her heavenly beauty. This is a sacred space like a river bed in which the abundant supernatural riches poured out by God upon this lofty creature join together harmoniously and with crystalline clarity. It is a dimension of Mary that reflects in a marvelous way the light radiating from the Holy Spirit, the splendor of intangible beauty wrought in her by the divine craftsman through a miracle of his omnipotence.

The picture of Mary given to us in Revelation has, in fact, an intense and even incomparable esthetic quality that is the effect and pure echo of the presence of the Holy

---

54. Martinelli, *La Vergine Maria*, 99–101.

Spirit acting in her. The latter is the secret of Mary's extraordinary beauty, her spiritual beauty that has been brought out, in a vigorous style and a wealth of details, especially by the enthusiastic pen of Paul VI. Few persons of his time have been so successful in awakening in modern men and women the thrill and wonder of the mystery:

Mary is the woman full of grace, the creature bathed in the Holy Spirit ... the creature who carries the Holy Spirit within her. As a result of her unique position, she reaches the pinnacle of beauty, not only spiritual but human as well; light, intelligence, profound love — in a word, beauty — are to be seen in her bright and innocent face. As an indescribable mirror of a concept of divine perfection, an idea, a divine dream, she is truly a joy for the world, a masterpiece of humanity,[55] which God, the supreme maker of the beautiful, produced. After the humanity of Christ, Mary is God's most beautiful work, the masterpiece of his grace. Permeated in an entirely personal and singular way by the life-giving power of this grace and by the holiness of God, "the light of the Holy Spirit shines out from her with an incomparable splendor" (John Paul II). "The Guest who dwells in her, and a beauty that does not pass away," shine forth from her.[56]

Mary's beauty, then, is unmatched for brilliance and has been a source of inspiration for talented artists, who in every age have delighted to represent her in their works. It is a beauty that has given rise to some of the noblest examples of architecture, some of the world's most beautiful paintings, and some of its most moving poetry.

---

55. Paul VI, *Insegnamenti* 14 (1976) 643. See also *NDM,* 228, and *L'Osservatore Romano*, December 10–11, 1973.

56. Elizabeth of the Trinity, in *Meditazioni mariane*, 290.

Everything in you is beautiful....
You are pleasing in every way ...
everything about you is beautiful.
You are beautiful by nature,
more beautiful through grace,
most beautiful in glory.[57]

Gonzalo de Berceo extols the beauty of the Mother of God as though he were a lover:

Sweet is your name and everything about you,
your beauty outshines all the flowers,
sweet to the spirit is your word:
Mother, God made you full of grace
(*NDM*, 740).

In the atmosphere created by this and other lyrical outbursts poets have sung with fresh inspiration of the superhuman beauty of the Mother of God and the powerful splendor that radiates from her like a pure fragrance of the Holy Spirit. Outstanding in this realm is what Carducci has called "the most beautiful poetry addressed to the Madonna by a Catholic heart," namely, Petrarch's *Prayer to the Virgin*:

Beautiful Virgin ... clothed in the sun ...
it pleased the supreme Sun
to light his lamp in you....
You alone in the world, without a parallel,
enamored heaven with your beauty.

All these are but brief fragments from among the many that might be cited. In them we hear echoes of the very attractive and theologically rich expressions and crystalline images of the liturgy. For the latter never wearies of saying to the Mother of God, "you are all beautiful," "beautiful as the moon," "brightly shining as the sun." The Church has in fact always contemplated the mystery of Mary's heavenly

---

57. Richard of St. Victor, *Sermon 9 on the Conception of Mary* (PL 177:918).

beauty, of that divinely radiant beauty that ravishes the heart of the One who delights in the beauty of souls, ravishes the very heart of God:

> You have ravished my heart,
>   my sister, my bride,
> you have ravished my heart
>   with one glance of your eyes (Sg 4:9).

An enraptured Pius XII exclaimed:

> How beautiful the Virgin must be! How often we are struck by the beauty of an angelic face, by a baby's enchanting smile, by the attractiveness of an innocent glance! Certainly, then, God has adorned the face of his own Mother with all the splendors available to his divine art.... He has endowed her gaze with something of his own suprahuman and divine dignity. A ray of God's own beauty shines in the eyes of his Mother.
>
> Mary's gaze! Mary's smile! Mary's sweetness! The majesty of Mary as queen of heaven and earth! As the moon shines in the dark sky, so her beauty stands out from all other beauties, which seem to be but shadows compared with her (Address to Catholic Youth, December 8, 1953).

Indeed, "who could be more splendid than the woman chosen by Splendor itself?" (St. Ambrose). Who could be more filled with light than the woman who gave flesh to the "splendor of eternal light," to Brightness without stain, to the one who is "fairer in beauty … than the sons of men" (Ps 45:3). In Mary, "mirror of divine beauty" (Paul VI), we see the first reflection of the splendor of the New Adam whom she carried in her womb. In her, next only to Christ, is concentrated all the splendor of the new creature formed by the creative Spirit of God. As a result, humanity — every human being — learns once again that it too can become transparent to the divine.

2. Some Particulars

a) An Interior Beauty
That Is Reflected in Mary's Whole Person

> In the Virgin Mary "are found all supernatural beauties" (John Geometres).

> "Her outward adornments were abundant and competed, as it were, with her interior riches" (Severus of Antioch).

The Virgin Mary shows us "the whole beauty of the image of God as seen on a human face never disfigured by sin" (Paul VI). We may say that she is God made transparent; the divine shows itself in all of her life. That is how A. Bello thinks of her when he writes: "Her soul was so limpid that God saw himself mirrored in her, just as the everlasting Alps are reflected in the motionless clarity of the lakes" (*Maria donna dei nostri giorni* 108). St. Ambrose rightly remarked that "beauty befitted Mary, for the beauty of her body was the mirror of her soul."

The "virgin" whom Luke shows us at the Annunciation was not just any virgin or even just the virgin foretold by Isaiah. She was the Virgin of virgins, the one chosen from among all others for her interior beauty. It was this beauty that Gabriel admired when he approached Mary and addressed her by a new name: "Full of grace." It is a name that has its equivalent in the superlative "most beautiful" that is used in the Old Testament to describe a woman endowed with physical grace, bodily beauty, attractiveness, and loveableness.

All this shines through in Luke's description of Mary, but as the outward effect of an internal splendor. The angel's greeting refers to beauty as an interior quality of Mary: a quality belonging to the Virgin's being, a beauty in God's eyes.

When the expression "full of grace" is used in the Old Testament to emphasize a person's moral stature, it might be translated as "a perfect individual." In Luke we are confronted with a "perfect woman" in whom divine grace has woven all its virtualities and all its spiritual attractiveness, this for the sake of her becoming mother of the Messiah. Mary appears to us as "the feminine universe sublimated by God."[58]

b) An Intrinsic Beauty

> Mary's beauty is human and not only esthetic
> but essential, ontological, the result of a
> conjunction with divine love (Paul VI).

Beauty has its foundation in the very structure and dynamics of being. The ontological condition for its existence is integrity. But it is evident that our Lady is the supreme ideal of perfection and the embodiment of an "altogether divine purity, which never has had, and never can have, its equal under heaven" (*True Devotion*, 260). This beauty is indeed intrinsic: intrinsic to the splendor of her soul in which everything is light and harmony, and intrinsic to the incorruptibility and glorification of her body.

From Mary there shines forth this intrinsic pneumatico-substantial beauty. She embodies a sublime divine-human synthesis in which the purest rays of human beauty join with the sovereign, yet accessible, rays of supernatural beauty. In both dimensions of her being, the spiritual and the corporeal, we find the intrinsic beauty which God in his original plan had in mind for humanity (Paul VI).

---

58. Mario Luzi, interview in *Il Popolo*, January 22, 1988.

Desiring to create an image of absolute purity and to demonstrate to the angels and human beings the power of his art, God made Mary to be truly all-beautiful. He made her to be a synthesis of all the divine, angelic, and human perfections and gave her a sublime beauty that embellishes the two worlds, rises from earth to heaven, and even transcends heaven itself (Gregory Palamas).

c) Beauty, Like Goodness and Truth, Expresses the Glory of God

In the Bible, beauty is the verifiable effect of an interior wealth of power and life. In this wealth human and religious values come first, for without them "charm is deceptive and beauty fleeting" (Prv 31:30). "We, unpretentious but loving disciples of Christian wisdom, must remember that true beauty is inseparable from goodness" (Paul VI). The truly beautiful cannot be separated from the good, for beauty as such is always combined with goodness and is identical with it.

The pope's teaching spontaneously confirms for us the validity of the "theology of beauty" approach taken by Hans Urs von Balthasar. Indeed, the latter is rightly credited with having recovered and validated the category of beauty in the interpretation of the Christian message.[59] His thought takes wing as he turns from beauty as simply a philosophico-esthetic concept to beauty as a subject of religious study, thereby restoring its true characteristic features. In this fresh approach he emphasizes Mary's beauty even on the natural level. His theological thinking stresses the identity, in Greek, of the ideas of "beautiful" and "good": beautiful because holy.

---

59. See especially the powerful work titled *The Glory of the Lord. A Theological Aesthetic I. Seeing the Form*, trans. by Erasmo Leiva-Merikakis (San Francisco: Ignatius Press/New York: Crossroad Publications, 1982).

Socrates used to say, long ago: "Allow me to become beautiful interiorly." This signifies that beauty is an exemplary idea. For Plato, the beautiful is the "dominant idea" governing the world and life, a idea that is one with the divine. It would therefore be very wrong to separate the reality of the good from the reality of the beautiful, for every good is beautiful.

The subject matter of the theology of beauty is "glory" (in the biblical meaning of the term). "Glory" is the sign behind which God, the source and author of all beauty (see Ws 13:3), decided to conceal himself when manifesting his presence among human beings and revealing to them the beauty of his mystery and his trinitarian love.

In this context there emerges a sublime reality that challenges all of us: "The glory of God is [first and foremost] the living human being" (St. Irenaeus), who was to be "the spokesman for all creatures" (from the liturgy). Human beings are specially marked by God: from among all created beings they are destined in a special way to let God shine forth in their lives, so that he may be contemplated and loved in them.

As everyone knows, the most resplendent fulfillment of this ineffable plan of love, is Mary of Nazareth, "a work of art that praises its lofty craftsman" (Venantius Fortunatus). Beyond every other human being, she is one of those radiant signs on which the divine beauty leaves its imprint. Gouhier remarks that the Virgin possesses an esthetico-theological identity never before known, for she is a woman of radiant human splendor who has been established as foundress of a human race that has been promised the grandeur emanating from the Messiah (*NDM*, 229). In her the reflection of God's glory that is innate in every creature attains its true maximum.

In keeping with what the Book of Wisdom asserts (13:5), the beauty of Mary lifts us up to a recognition of the very source of all beauty. With justice Montfort could say to Jesus: "If we knew the glory and the love which Thou receivest in this admirable creature, we should have very different thoughts of both Thee and her from what we have now" (*True Devotion*, 63).

d) Mary's Beauty: Object of Contemplation and Way to God

> Resplendent beauty, which is, above all,
> the beauty of a loving heart, anticipates
> eternity; it is the totality of the fragment.
>
> (Bruno Forte)

> She is a lamp that is never extinguished
> and gives meaning and beauty
> even to the present life.

Life in the Spirit is a beautiful poem to be lived out with God: the state of grace is a state of beauty. When human beings enter this realm, their words, their actions, their works, the whole world of their life embodies the mysterious and ineffable journey and becomes a sign revealing God. With penetrating insight the Fathers of the Church gave this spiritual journey the name "Philokalia," that is, "love of the divine beauty," which is itself a shining forth of the divine goodness. On these pathways of the Spirit human beings do not simply testify to the personal perfection they have reached, but are also naturally ordered to others and draw them, because beauty is a prerequisite for love. It is along these lines that we should speak of the Virgin's extraordinary contribution to beauty.

C. Tullio Altan has written that the thirst for marvels is widespread in contemporary society, but the phenomenon has had distant roots in cultures ever since ancient Greece (see our earlier reference to the Greeks). It is an ancient hunger, therefore, a constant aspect of the restless human heart, a subterranean refrain that winds its way through the labyrinths of history. Since the time of Diogenes human beings have sought a peaceful face for themselves, the features of an identity that accepts its desires and satisfies its expectations. And, in a ceaseless pilgrimage of their souls to scenes that fascinate and enchant, they walk the paths of art and poetry, as though led on by an obscure and vague recollection of a lost treasure and a promised land. Today as in the past they sense its taste, its perfume, its traces.[60]

"Recollection ... taste, perfume, traces of a lost treasure and a promised land." For us, all these things have a name: God, the Eternal Beauty, which Mary allowed to dwell in her. She is a true image and likeness of the original beauty, the "Beauty so ancient and so new."[61] On her pure and radiant face human beings discover the signs of a lost divine beauty, an undiminished beauty that provides each of us with an unsurpassable ideal of perfection, a model and inspiration, a hope and consolation, and a source of joy.

Paul VI, who taught so much about exemplarity, laid a very timely emphasis on this point in words that make us really reflect and can waken echoes in our souls. By introducing Mary into the web of contemporary expectations he points out a way to be followed in our day.

In his memorable discourse to the participants in the International Mariological Congress (May 17–21, 1975) the pope presents two intellectual ways of approaching Mary: "the way of truth" (typical of biblical, historical, and theological thinking) and, in harmony with this, "the way of beauty" (*via*

---

60. See Pifano, *Tra Teologia e letteratura*, 275.
61. St. Augustine, *Confessions* 10, 27, 38, trans. Maria Boulding, O.S.B. (The Works of Saint Augustine: A Translation for the 21st Century; Hyde Park, NY: New City Press, 1997) I/1, 262.

pulchritudinis). This last is a new way that is accessible to all, even the most untutored souls.

> In every age Mary is and remains the supreme ideal, the most sublime representative of the longing of human beings for goodness and beauty, a longing which they carry within them, like a divine seed, in the recesses of their hearts.

> In every age we shall always have this beauty, the innocent beauty, of Mary with us to enlighten and inspire. It is a human beauty in which all can recognize the familiar and idealized faces of their own mothers. It is a heavenly beauty in which the angelic and immediately evident splendor of that sweet face enchants the gaze and rescues it from any impression made by a false and inferior beauty; it urges the visual power of the spirit to an ecstatic, transcending leap of ineffable joy. It is a fascinating beauty which saints and artists have tried to capture in famous and widely loved images and which the faithful claim as their own treasure, for these images reflect their innate dream of a sublime archetypal form.

> In our day, when women are forging ahead in the life of society, nothing can be more beneficial and more inspiring than the example of the Virgin Mother ... whose beauty recapitulates and embodies authentic spiritual values.... What noble sentiments, what a yearning for purity, what a renewing spirituality can come from contemplation of such sublime beauty! Our Lady urges us to model our weak and transient lives on the perfection of her life and to enrich our impoverished lives with the sense of beauty and with the taste and longing for it.

> Yes, we need to gaze on Mary and keep hold of her unsullied beauty, because our eyes are too often

> hurt and blinded, as it were, by this world's deceitful images of beauty. We need her beauty in order to restore within us, in our minds, and outwardly as well, in our habits, the idea of the truly beautiful and the joy it brings.
>
> Mary, beautiful and perfect, elicits in us thoughts that are good, pure, magnanimous, heroic, and very humane, because they are also full of divinity. If we approach her with faith and tender love, we shall find the rays of her beauty and holiness pouring out upon us.[62]

It is also true that "this exceptional beauty," radiant with divinity, is laden with mystery, because "it is fully known to God alone but ... at the same time says so much to human beings" (John Paul II). Any commentary on Paul VI's words would only detract from their freshness and driving power. They seem to be almost a paraphrase of von Balthasar's pithy statement: "Mary provides and communicates a salvific value to the cult of beauty. Because of her we may really believe that 'beauty will save the world' " (*NDM*, 1377).[63] Like von Balthasar, Solzhenitsyn cites the famous sentence of Dostoievsky in his address for the reception of the Nobel Prize. He interprets it as meaning that "every authentic masterpiece [such as the Blessed Virgin] has an absolutely irresistible power to convince and ends by conquering rebellious hearts."[64]

---

62. The thought of Mary's innocent, attractive and healing beauty occurs frequently in the addresses of Paul VI. From his abundant writings I shall refer only to *Insegnamenti* II (1964) 1146; XI (1973) 787 and 788; XIII (1975) 1494; XIV (1976) 644; XV (1977) 765.

63. Dostoievsky uses the cited words (in *The Idiot*) in a problematic context in which he admits that "beauty is enigmatic" and therefore needs to be properly understood: "What kind of beauty will save the world?"

64. The address was never delivered. See A. Martin, *Solzenicyn il credente. Lettere, discorsi, testimonianze* (Bari: Ed. Paoline, 1974) 94–95.

To the extent that the Church is an interior image of Mary, it too becomes an exemplar of spiritual beauty and is able to attract and convince.

We must therefore, as Paul VI asks and hopes, enter upon the "way of beauty" represented by the Virgin Mary, for it is "a very sure way of reaching God and the mystery of things."[65] "We must fix our intoxicated and searching gaze on her humble and modest face" (Paul VI). Luther himself said of Mary: "No image of a woman elicits such pure thoughts in men as does the image of this virgin."[66]

Even on the natural level, the image of Mary is beyond criticism: even for unbelievers it suggests an intangible beauty, when they think of it not as an image of faith but simply as a venerable symbol conveying a merely human value.

Beauty is to be contemplated, not defined. Silence rather than words is the proper response to its presence (Turoldo), but an embracing silence that can be receptive to the wealth of values and the vast range of meanings contained in the divine innocence of the immaculate Virgin; a silence that allows one to be drawn and transported by her suprahuman beauty, so that one becomes what one contemplates. The call to make one's own Mary's experience of full acceptance of God by a human person in both spirit and body; the call to grasp the beauty of Mary, to contemplate it, and to be challenged, in a selfless and disinterested way, by its fascination: these are, in substance, the calls issued by the theology of beauty. In this context, the Pauline wish that we might have the mind of God means to have a sense of beauty and a desire for it.

Mary, pearl of the cosmos, a poem of authentic beauty "from which the Spirit drew inspiration in completing the

---

65. D. M. Turoldo, "Il mistero della bellezza," in *NDM*, 223–24.
66. Luther, *Kirchenpostille*, Weimar ed. 10/1, 68.

harmony of the universe" (von Balthasar), proclaims to all that there is a creature whose sole meaning is to be a reflection of the eternal splendor of God.[67]

The removal of this beauty named "Mary" from the world would help only to impoverish it. In contrast, to make her known in a way that is theological and is purified of misunderstandings is to derive from within the historical human community a marvelous reason for praising and glorifying the God of the covenant, who has done such great things in his humble servant, Mary.[68]

---

67. See Gertrude von Le Fort, *La donna eterna* (Milan, 1942) 48.
68. See *NDM*, 914.

Chapter Six
Supplementary and Concluding Remarks

A. Mary, Our First-Fruits

1. Image and First-Fruits of the New Israel

Mary is both image and full revelation
of what every human being and the entire
Church are called to become:
"In her the Father has established the beginning
of the Church, the Spouse of Christ
that is without spot or wrinkle, resplendent
with beauty" (Liturgy).

The Church is nothing else but the dwelling of God in the midst of humanity. The stones that constitute it are the unconditional "Yeses" spoken to him, and Mary, the purest and fullest embodiment of the mystery of the Church, is its first living stone. As a creation of the Word of God, she is associated with the whole ecclesial body that is sustained, fed, and guided by the Word. She is the First-Fruits of the new Israel, which is the Church of Christ.

Given the profound likeness that binds them, we cannot speak of the Church, its motherhood, humanity, faith, and joy without seeing Mary as its image, its archetype, and its first embodiment: Mary-Church. As Mother of the Messiah, she truly carried in her individual person the destiny of the chosen people; in accordance with the proclamations of the prophets, in her it is the messianic community that gives birth to the Messiah.

Rahner finds that the Fathers already had the idea that Mary is a type of the Church, that is, the exemplar, substance, and compendium of everything that would emerge regarding the nature and destiny of the Church, especially its motherhood and virginity. When we call Mary a "type of the Church," we are seeing in her the perfect beginning of the Church in the latter's theological essence, that is, in its state of virginity (understood as the completeness of its faith, hope, and charity; this takes the form, in the final analysis, of fidelity to its Spouse) and of motherhood (giving rebirth to the children of God by the power of the Holy Spirit).

It is characteristic that Mary, according to the testimony of John's Gospel, stood beneath the cross of her Son when she received the First-Fruits of the Spirit (Jn 19:25). This was the Spirit whom the dying Christ was giving as spouse to his Church, which was being born of the one, definitive sacrifice of the Messiah and Lord. All this shows clearly that Mary is truly the first-born, the first sublime embodiment of the new people made up of the children of God. With her, after the long expectation created by the promises, the age of the Jewish Church was completed, and the age of the new salvific economy of the Church of Christ began that would be marked by the fullness of the grace of the Holy Spirit.

Theologians and exegetes teach that from the moment of the Incarnation Mary was already the Church in seed, the Church in its first member. She was already one body and one spirit with Christ the head, in a way even deeper than the Church would later be.

As Archbishop Carli explains, the mystical body began in Mary and through her when and because she, a woman "full of grace" (Lk 1:28), conceived its Head by the power of the Holy Spirit.[1] It can be said that

> during the earthly life of Jesus the Church was as it were concentrated in and hidden in Mary.... In her it already possessed its main characteristics: it was

---

1. Archbishop Luigi Maria Carli, *DME* in *Marianum* 38 (1976) 472.

perfectly one, holy, and fundamentally catholic, since Mary was the most universal of mere creatures and, as it were, the synthesis of all the good found in the human race. It was indeed still a Church without sacraments, because the source of grace was still present; without hierarchy or priesthood, because the great king and high priest had not yet established them; an ideal Church, without imperfections or ugliness.[2]

In the Church the Virgin has always represented the ideal type of Christian newness. She is its most outstanding member, "a member who surpasses all in dignity" (St. Augustine) and is capable of being the Church as no other will ever be here below. She is therefore "hailed as pre-eminent and as a wholly unique member of the Church" (*LG* 53), which in her attains to its highest self. The Church is theandric, Christic, spiritual, and holy, but it is the Virgin Mary, the supreme and choicest part of the ecclesial universe, who possesses these characteristics in the highest degree. In V. Lossky's summation, Mary all-holy concentrates in herself the holiness of the Church, all the holiness possible for a created being; she is and will always be the ultimate ideal, the final goal, toward which the "new people of God" is moving in its work of growth and completion.

As we contemplate Mary's lofty, resplendent holiness, we must not think that she "eclipses the glory of all the saints, as the sun at its rising makes all the stars disappear."[3] On the contrary, in her uniqueness the Blessed Virgin surpasses but at the same time "adorns all the members of the Church," both on earth and in heaven.[4]

---

2. D. Bertetto, *Maria e la Chiesa* (Naples, 1963) 11.

3. H. de Lubac, *Meditazioni sulla Chiesa*, 462, where the author cites the well-known lament of St. Therese of Lisieux in her *Novissima verba*, 156–57.

4. St. Bonaventure, *Sermons on the Nativity of the Blessed Virgin Mary* 3 (Quaracchi ed.: IX, 712).

2. First-Fruits of Faith
(The First Evangelical Beatitude Belongs to Mary)

Hail, First-Fruits of our joy!

(*Typikon, Ode VII*)

Attachment to Christ means first of all an adherence by faith, something that Mary had from the beginning when she consented to the will of the Father. She believed in Christ even before he existed as her Son, and she was urged to believe in him in order that he might thus exist. She is the only person who believed in Jesus before he existed as Jesus; others would be called to faith after his coming on earth. Mary's faith is at the source of our faith, because it was in her soul that the Church's faith in the divinity of Jesus Christ began to be formed and lived. Thus, by inaugurating the new relationship that was to unite human beings with Christ, she headed the Church's pilgrim journey through the ages and generations.

As Jean Galot explains, Mary was the first to believe in the Savior because she was the first creature to whom God made known the coming of his Son into the world. In order to accept the angel's proposal, the Virgin of Nazareth had to believe him. She had to make this act of confidence in God that finds expression in faith. By believing, she traced out the path of faith[5] and opened up the way of faith in Christ. As we just said, her faith preceded the coming of the Savior; it was an immense faith, a faith deeply felt and blessed, the faith of those "who have not seen and have believed" (Jn 20:29).

It is Luke the evangelist, and he alone, who draws attention to the first act of faith. In the account of the Annunciation he describes Mary's humble and docile attitude when she hears the angel's message, and in the account of the Visitation he gives a first interpretation of this attitude: Mary is said to be blessed because she has believed: "Blessed are you who

---

5. Cited in *Meditazioni mariane*, 110–11.

believed that what was spoken to you by the Lord would be fulfilled" (Lk 1:45). After celebrating Mary's motherhood (v. 42), Elizabeth recognizes her unique dignity (v. 43) and makes known its mysterious foundation: her faith (v. 45). In response to this faith, she is blessed because, like Abraham, she has experienced God's fidelity to his promises. Faith is the final word both in the Annunciation and in Elizabeth's words at the Visitation. "Through space and time, and even more through the history of souls ... Mary is present, as the one who is 'blessed because she believed' " (*RM* 25).

Believing brings a happiness of its own, not simply the spontaneous joy that accompanies the movement of faith, but the deeper joy that comes from God. Mary experienced to the full this happiness of faith; the reason for the happiness is to be seen in her carrying out of the message in which she believed: "May it be done to me according to your word" (Lk 1:38). We may truthfully say, with Guardini, "If there is anything that reveals Mary's greatness, it is Elizabeth's exclamation: 'Blessed are you who believed.' "[6]

In these vibrant words of praise, inspired from on high, "we can ... rightly find a kind of 'key' which unlocks for us the innermost reality of Mary" (*RM* 19). She was the first and incomparable believer, so much so that she merited the first praise, the first evangelical beatitude: the blessedness of faith. To the privileges she had been given, the Virgin added the personal virtue of a pure and deep faith that took hold of her entire being: neither her life, even her simple human life, nor her activity would be understandable apart from faith. Mary merited first place in the beatitudes (Jean Galot).

The praise of Mary's authentic faith that is voiced by her cousin Elizabeth harmonizes wonderfully with what Jesus would say during his public life when he alludes to faith, without expressly mentioning it, and asserts the blessedness

6. Romano Guardini, *The Lord* (Chicago, 1954).

of those who hear the word of God and put it into practice (see Lk 8:20–21; 11:28; Mk 3:34; Mt 12:49). For example, when an unnamed woman praises him by declaring "blessed" the womb that carried him and the breasts that nourished him, he replies: "Rather, blessed are those who hear the word of God and observe it" (Lk 11:27–28). In saying this, he was proclaiming the blessedness first and foremost of his Mother who had always heard the word and put it into practice. By his reply, he lets us see that the basic reason for his Mother's blessedness was not the simple fact of her divine motherhood but her deep faith in God's word: the happiness is due to faith. To possess this blessedness, it would not have been enough for Mary to be the Mother of Jesus, although this would indeed have brought with it a natural happiness. True happiness, however, is to be found on a higher level, the supernatural.

As the Fathers of the Church remind us, "being a disciple of Christ was a higher dignity and brought greater happiness than being the Mother of Christ."[7] The highest human status, that of being mother of the Messiah (a position so many other women might have envied), could not fulfill Mary's being. Only faith exercised in the acceptance of God's word can make the heart radically happy.

It is in the light of Jesus' response to the anonymous woman that the first act of faith offered to God at the Annunciation reveals its full value. It marks the beginning of a new happiness for the race, a happiness that transcends all human joys. Mary was certainly the first to have tasted this happiness, but all human beings are invited to taste it in their turn by following the same path: the path of faith. By extending blessedness beyond the bonds of blood, Jesus includes all those who, like his Mother, are able to accept the word of God and keep it in their hearts (Lk 8:20–21). The Mother's

7. See St. Augustine, *Sermon* 25, 7–8 (PL 46:937), and others.

truest, fullest happiness is found in a sphere accessible to all who hear the word of God and put it into practice.

Thus, far from being a rejection of an earthly mother, the answer Jesus gives to the unnamed woman points out a new way of belonging to him, namely, by being his disciples. "Mary, the mother" is in harmony with and completed by "Mary, the disciple." In his encyclical *The Mother of the Redeemer* John Paul II writes: "Thus in a sense Mary as Mother [she who preceded all others in a fidelity to Christ alone through love] became the first disciple of her Son [the first Christian], the first to whom he seemed to say 'Follow me,' even before he addressed this call to the Apostles or to anyone else" (*RM* 20).

Indeed, the faith of the evangelists recognized in Mary the first disciple of the Lord, the person who comes before Christians as the perfect model of the authentic follower of Christ, because "in her earthly life she incarnated the evangelical beatitudes proclaimed by Jesus" (Paul VI). Lagrange, the philosopher, made the attractive and plausible suggestion that when Jesus on the mountain set forth the *magna carta*, the beatitudes, of the kingdom, he was thinking of his own Mother. Thus understood, each of the beatitudes can be regarded as contributing to a portrait of her spiritual face.[8]

The blessedness granted to Mary serves as a light helping us to pull away from the deceptive pursuit of exclusively earthly forms of happiness. As for the Virgin Mary, so for all of us, the basic key to happiness is to believe in Christ and to let ourselves be enlightened, permeated, and guided by his life-giving words.

---

8. Cited by Mariano Magrassi in *Meditazioni Mariane*, 63.

B. The History of Mary Is Inseparably Bound Up with the History of Every Person Saved

Hail, cloud of mercy
that carries the hopes of the entire world.

(James of Batna)

1. At the Center of the Divine Economy

When God has addressed himself to groups as he has to individuals, his purpose has always been to intervene for the salvation of the entire people. No personal history has ever been disconnected from the universal history of the race. It is in this realm that the unique history of the Virgin Mary is located. As the focal point of the entire economy of the Incarnation and of salvation, she is, after Christ, the greatest benefactress of humanity and a blessing that belongs to the entire Church and to all generations. Her holiness, her kindness, and her purity have benefited not only herself but all of us as well. In virtue of the unique service she provided in the divine plan, she retains a close relationship with redeemed humanity, which is reborn through faith in Christ. In the event that is the Incarnation, which is the fundamental messianic event in her life and her maternal function, Mary is an individual who makes history and is responsible for an important turning point in it.

Mühlen has pointed out, more specifically, that Mary of Nazareth occupies an important place in the economy of salvation not only by her personal, conscious, and free actions but also by her very existence itself, her ontological personhood, which exists beyond her free self-determination. It is this primordial being of hers that makes completely clear her special place in the history of salvation.[9]

---

9. See *NDM*, 1339–40.

As "workshop of ineffable wonders"[10] and Mother of him who will forever be the "light of the world" and "the way, the truth, and the life" (Jn 8:12; 14:6), Mary became the servant of the divine light that enlightens every human being, the only door that gives us access to salvation, and "the only way by which forgiven humanity may become 'God' " (*NDM*, 20). For this reason, the Virgin of Nazareth is at the center of the economy of our salvation and, by that very fact, the center of all our blessings and of all our joy and glory in God. She is an all-embracing, insuppressible mystery, which Christian faith and devotion have not failed to show forth:

> Rejoice also on our behalf, O Mary, Mother of God! Through you the Holy Trinity is glorified and adored; through you the priceless cross is celebrated and adored in every corner of the world. Because of you the heavens exult and the angels and archangels rejoice. By your means the demons are put to flight and the devil, the tempter, is cast down from heaven. By your means fallen creation is exalted to the heavens and the whole human race, enslaved to idolatry, has come to knowledge of the truth. Through you believers attain to the grace of baptism, churches are established throughout the world, and the nations are converted. Through you the Only-begotten Son of God shines forth as a light to those who are in darkness and in the shadow of death (Lk 1:79). It was through you that the prophets spoke their oracles, and through you that the apostles preached salvation to the nations. Through you the dead are raised to life.[11]

"Hail! by whom gladness will be enkindled; /hail! by whom the curse will be extinguished..../ Hail! thou by

---

10. *"Parakletike"* in *TMPM* II, 547.
11. *Synodal Homily VI* (attributed to Cyril of Alexandria), delivered at Ephesus against Nestorius (PG 77:991–96).

whom all creation is renewed; / Hail! thou through whom the Creator became a babe..../ Hail! by whom hell was despoiled; / hail! by whom we are clothed in glory..../hail! thou by whom was opened paradise" (*The Akathistos Hymn*, stanzas 1, 7, and 15).

"Through you God stooped to humanity. Through you humanity draws near to him with trust" (E. M. Toniolo).

"Through you, chaste Virgin and Mother ... peace was given to the desolated earth; you are the ship of riches on which the Father's treasure was sent to earth to enrich the wretched" (James of Batna).

"O blessed Virgin, in the blessing given to you every creature is blessed by its creator, and the creator is blessed by every creature" (St. Anselm). "O fullness of the graces bestowed by the Trinity; after the Trinity, queen of the universe, you are the triumph and divinization of our race" (John Geometres). "You carried the Power over the world; thanks to you all the ends of the earth won salvation; the whole world rejoices, as do the sea, its shores, and the heavens" (Venantius Fortunatus). "How shall we greet you? With what praises shall we crown your holy and glorious brow, O giver of gifts, dispenser of riches, ornament of the human race, boast of all creation, which through you is regarded as blessed indeed?" (John Damascene).

These are but a few of the many utterances that might be cited from the tradition, utterances that seek to grasp the vertiginous heights of the mediation exercised by the Mother of God. Due to that mediation the all-embracing inflow of the divine descends in floods into every fiber of the world. Truly the Virgin Mary, in her twofold function, both "personal" and "personological," is "one of the greatest symbols of Christianity. 'Symbol' here means a historical reality that because it embodies a set of ideal attitudes, cannot be captured in a chronicle of ephemeral things; that down through the generations continues its saving role in the economy of salvation;

and that can be ever better known, although the mystery it contains will be fully unveiled only at the end of time."[12]

2. *All Graces from Mary*
(Mary as Universal Mediatrix)

> Lady, you are so great and have such power
> that anyone who seeks a favor and does not turn
>   to you would have his desire fly
> up without wings.[13]

These well-known verses are from the greatest poem produced by Christian civilization and from its splendid theological *Prayer to the Virgin*. They echo the Mariology of that age, which from the idea of Mary's greatness as Mother of her own creator derived the fact of her universal mediation for the salvation of all human beings. Mary gave us Jesus and, with him, the very source of grace and all the implicit blessings of redemption.

St. Bonaventure teaches that because God was pleased to dwell in the womb of this holy virgin, she acquired a kind of jurisdiction over all graces. For when Jesus Christ came forth from her holy womb, there came forth with him, as from a heavenly ocean, all the floods of divine gifts. St. Bernardine of Siena says the same in even more explicit terms: "From the moment the Virgin Mother conceived the Divine Word in her womb, she acquired, as it were, a special claim over the gifts we receive from the Holy Spirit, so much so that no one has ever received any grace except through the hands of Mary."[14]

By agreeing to be Mother of God Mary contributed, with the Holy Spirit, to bringing the kingdom of God to birth in

---

12. *Fate quello che vi dirà. Riflessioni e proposte per la promozione della pietà mariana*, document issued by the 28th General Chapter of the Order of Servants of Mary (Rome: Curia Generalizia, 1983) 38 (no. 34).

13. Dante, *Paradiso* XXXIII, 13–15.

14. Cited in *The Glories of Mary* I, 99.

the world and in every soul. Therefore she will always be, in him and through him, a channel of mercy and grace for all the redeemed.

According to an ancient tradition, on Pentecost the Holy Spirit descended first of all on Mary, and did so in the form of a tongue of fire which then divided into twelve tongues that went to rest on the heads of the apostles. In this tradition the Mother of Jesus is seen as the distributor of all the graces and gifts of the Holy Spirit (*NDM*, 1347).

This is God's will, St. Bernard assures us, that we should receive everything through Mary. Everything passes through her hands ("God willed that we have nothing that has not passed through Mary's hands"). If then we have any hope, any grace, any gift, know that all of them come from her. Therefore, the saint concludes, whatever offering you are preparing to make to God, remember to entrust it to Mary in order that it may return to God, the giver of every grace, by the same channel through which grace reaches us.[15] It is Jesus himself who wills to use the services of his Mother as he did at Cana, at a moment filled with messianic overtones, when she with her simple and confident request obtained wine for the married couple.

We must admit that Mary's mediation is given in Scripture (Annunciation, Cana, Calvary) and is well founded in the tradition. It is a truth that has always been alive in the Church, grasped, experienced, and celebrated down the centuries by uninterrupted generations of believers. It has its fullest documentation in the writings of the major homilists of the eighth century.

Thus St. Germanus of Constantinople (d. 733), one of the greatest and most influential promotors of Marian devotion and a teacher of her mediation, maintains that the interces-

---

15. See St. Bernard, *On the Nativity of the Virgin* III, 10; *Sermon on the Nativity of the Blessed Virgin Mary: Mary as Aqueduct*, nos. 7 and 6.

sion and aid of Mary are indispensable for all, because no one receives grace from God except through her. During the present life and until the last judgment she helps and protects all in body and soul. "You are the Christian hope that does not deceive....Your gifts are countless because no one receives grace from God except through you, Most Holy Mary; no one is redeemed, no one attains to salvation, except through you, Mother of God" (*TMPM* II, 357).

St. John Damascene, Father, theologian, and liturgist, likewise regards Mary as a perpetual blessing for the human race, her shrines a source of grace and of healings both spiritual and bodily, and her intercession a sure anchor of hope for all.

Mediation, like co-redemption, has a single theological root: Mary's continual maternal cooperation in the saving work of Christ (from the Annunciation to the final coming of the Lord), and a single theological foundation: the interior union of the Mother with the Son in the carrying out of the divine plan. In the Catholic Church the title "universal mediatrix of all grace" clearly expresses Mary's mission in obtaining from God and distributing to all human beings every kind of favor, both temporal and those connected with eternal salvation; she is the most powerful petitioner and the most merciful distributor of all graces to all of humanity. Mary "is called Queen of mercy because she opens the abyss of the divine goodness."[16]

St. Bernard writes:

> It is God's very mercy that absorbs the Mother of the Savior into its infinite scope: the Love that for nine months rested corporeally in her womb filled her with mercy. This is the inexhaustible source of the mediation exercised by the Mother of God. If we hold an

---

16. Odo of Morimond, "Temi mariani nei discepoli di san Bernardo," *Marianum* 54 (1992) 253.

apple in our hand for a good while, doesn't it perfume
our fingers and doesn't its fragrance last for a long
time? What then shall we say of the chaste womb of
Mary in which Compassion in person rested for nine
months? This Compassion filled the mind and womb
of the Mother, and after she had given birth it did not
depart from her heart. Who, then, O blessed one, will
ever be able to probe the length and breadth, the height
and depth of your Mercy?

Even the eagle's gaze of this Marian teacher par excellence could not have penetrated farther. It is true, of course,
that the Church must turn to the Father through the Son, the
sole mediator between God and humankind, but this does
not mean that Mary's mediation is not powerful over the
Church on earth. Once again, the abbot of Clairvaux assures
us:

From the bosom of the Trinity, where she reigns glori-
ously for ever, the Blessed Virgin will always distrib-
ute gifts to humanity, and why should she not? She is
mercy itself; she is the Mother of the Only-begotten
Son of God; she is the "aqueduct" through which all
the riches of God flow down upon us, the channel that
conveys the wave of grace from its source, which is
Jesus, to us. This channel flows unceasingly: God did
not make use of it only once and for all. He is certainly
able to infuse any grace whatsoever into our souls,
even without the aqueduct; but in his infinite goodness
he willed to give us this means.[17]

In explaining Mary's role as mediatrix many writers, St.
Pius X among them, use the image of the "neck" that joins
the body to the head and through which the head conveys
strength and energy to the body. Mary serves as the "neck"

---

17. Citations in *Marianum* 54 (1992) 172 and 174–75.

for our spiritual head (Jesus); through it he transmits all spiritual gifts to his mystical body. An early Father explained: "The fullness of grace exists in Christ as in the head from which it descends, and in Mary as in the neck by which it is transmitted."

Another interesting illustrative image parallels the preceding: the image of the moon. According to St. Bonaventure, Mary is called a "moon," and "the reason ... is that just as the moon is a kind of intermediary between the sun and the earth and reflects upon the earth what it receives from the sun, so also does Mary act as an intermediary between God and ourselves. She pours out upon the world the heavenly graces she receives from the sun of justice."[18]

Nowadays, theologians prefer to use the image of the "heart," which exerts its influence on the members and the head and, at the same time, is influenced by the head; in addition, its action is hidden and silent. So too, through her motherhood Mary exerts a physical influence on the Head, from which in turn she receives spiritual life. At the same time, she influences the members of the mystical body by action that is not hierarchical and authoritative but maternal and therefore especially agreeable, silent, solicitous, and continual.

It is certain and beyond question that the source of all goodness, the wellspring from whose "fullness we have all received, grace in place of grace" (Jn 1:16), always is and will be Jesus, from whom our Lady herself receives all she has. No less true, however, is what theologians teach: eternal salvation is a grace (and gift of God) which reaches human beings through the Virgin Mary. "Every element of salvation (virtues, gifts, charisms, grace ...) comes from God, the Father, the Son, and the Holy Spirit, but it reaches us through the humanity of Christ and through our Lady to whom this

---

18. Cited in Liguori, *The Glories of Mary*, 99.

sacred humanity belongs."[19] Mary, who actively cooperated in the redemption wrought by Christ also cooperates in the communication of the spiritual blessings that originate in that redemptive work.

If, in fact, the Word of God works miracles and communicates grace to us through his humanity, the sacraments, and the saints, all the more can he use his most holy Mother's activity in distributing the fruits of redemption to us.

The Virgin Mother, "destined by the eternal God to bring to human beings the grace, the divine jewels of the Son, is here, close to us, and always waits in hope for us to become aware of her gaze and to accept her gift."[20]

C. Mary, Necessary Halting Place

1. In Religious Knowledge

> I greet you, Mary, delight of the Father,
> for through you the knowledge of God
> has spread to the farthest ends of the earth.
>
> (Terasius of Constantinople)

> God turned your womb into a book …
> and wrote in it with no ordinary ink
> but through the action of the Holy Spirit.
>
> (*Typikon, Ode VII*)

If we contemplate Mary, who is a "book" (as the Fathers liked to call her) in which all the mysteries are written and all the enigmas are explained, we can come to know the innermost movements of the history of salvation and perceive God manifesting himself in it. The Virgin, who silently makes the divine economy intelligible in her Son, becomes a shining reflection of the mystery and reveals the true face of

---

19. Cardinal Pietro Parente, in *Lo Spirito Santo e Maria Santissima*, 204.
20. Chiara Lubich, *Meditazioni* (Rome: Ed. Città Nuova, 1970) 117.

the tripersonal God. She is, therefore, "an indispensable stopping place for those who seek religious knowledge."[21]

The Virgin Mary has made legible the invisible Word, that Word which no human words can capture. This is the idea expressed by James of Batna when he wrote: "Mary is the letter in which the Father wrote down his secret, for through her flesh he showed himself to the world in order to renew the world.... She was a letter, and what was written in it was the Word; when it was read it shone brightly because of the news it brought to the world" (*LM*, 86).

Mary was the reality that made the heart of St. Catherine of Siena sing; she describes Mary in vivid and incisive images:

> O Mary, my sweet love, in you is written the Word from whom we have the teaching on true life. You are the book that gives us this teaching. If we do not read this book, we shall never learn the word of truth and life that is Jesus. You are the field in which bloomed the most beautiful flower in the world: sweet Jesus! If we do not go into this field, we shall never find this flower (*TMSM* IV, 568).

If we do not go to Mary, we will not find Jesus. This is the teaching of the saints and the great teachers of the faith. If we do not draw near to Mary the plant, we shall not gather Jesus, its fruit. No one is filled with knowledge of God except through Mary, who contains God[22] and whose service to human beings consists essentially in opening them to the gospel and teaching it to them.

In his usual figurative style Montfort writes: "Mary is a sacred magnet which, wherever it is, attracts eternal Wisdom with such power that the latter cannot resist. She is

---

21. See Vannucci, in *Libertà dello Spirito* (Sotto il Monte: Centro di Studi Ecumenici Giovanni XXIII, 1967) 134–36.
22. Germanus of Constantinople, in *TMPM* II, 357.

the magnet that draws this Wisdom to earth for the sake of all human beings and still draws it, every day and in every soul in which she dwells."[23] God has placed in her hands the salvation of all and the savior of all. It is, therefore, by turning to her that we must seek Jesus.

> Let us not forget, however, that in the evangelizing mission of the early Church the Virgin Mother had a very important role, being both the subject and the object of catechesis. The subject in the sense that she informed the community of the Nazarene's disciples about the grace-filled actions carried out by the very God of the covenant himself. The object, inasmuch as the Church in turn made known the "great things" (Lk 1:49) which the Lord had done in her for the good of his entire people.[24]

In fact, as Sacred Scripture points out, after those who made up the Church of Jerusalem (apostles, women, Mary, and the brothers of Jesus) had "all" been filled with the Spirit (Acts 2:1, 4a), they all became capable of bearing witness to the Lord Jesus, each of them in his or her proper degree.

On Pentecost, Mary, too, was fully enlightened by the Spirit about what Jesus had done and said. It is reasonable to think that from that point on she began to pour out on the Church the treasures she had until then kept locked in the jewel casket of her sapiential meditations. Thus the Virgin, too, became a witness to what had been seen and heard (see Lk 1:2). X. Pikasa comments that she bore witness to the birth of Jesus and to his childhood; the Church would not have received Jesus in the completeness of his humanity without the living testimony of the Mother who gave him

---

23. *Opere* I: *Scritti spirituali* (Rome: Ed. Monfortane, 1990) 109–238.
24. A. Serra, in the collective work *Il posto di Maria nella "nuova evangelizzazione"* (Rome: Centro di cultura Mariana "Madre della Chiesa," 1992) 53–74.

birth and raised him. Within the Church Mary is a part of Jesus, for she gave witness to things to which neither the apostles nor the women nor the brothers could have attested. It was up to Mary to entrust the Church with this unique and indispensable testimony. It is for this reason that she appears in Acts 1:14 (*NDM*, 273).

Only in heaven will we realize what the Church owes to Mary as far as understanding of the faith is concerned, and the simple will realize it even more than the prudent and the wise (Hans Urs von Balthasar).

If we approach Mary with simplicity and confidence and if we learn to consult her and listen to her on every subject, the Virgin will continue to be for us a presence that unveils and communicates the riches of our Christian faith. "Devotion to the Mother of the Lord becomes for the faithful an opportunity for growing in divine grace" (*MC*, 57), an enduring source of fruitful inspirations, and an incomparable teacher of the ways of God, but one who teaches within us without noisy words. Through her human beings will discover a new relationship with God and their supreme destiny and dignity. Through her we shall come to understand better the very mystery of the Church.

2. *On the Journey of Faith*

a) Mary Is Owed Proper Praise and Veneration

> O Mary, the Lord is with you!
> He willed that all creatures and even he himself
> should owe so much to you.
>
> (St. Anselm)

We have seen that in making Mary his Mother God placed every good within her for the sake of humanity. For this reason St. Bernard regards devotion to Mary not as an option but as a duty (see *Marianum* 54 [1992] 175).

The Mother of Jesus "excels in everything that deserves human praise."[25] All of us owe her constant gratitude and love: a sincere, authentic love that affects everything in us (mind, will, heart). We are reminded of this duty by, among others, the Dutch episcopate in a letter on Mary: "As a now living person, Mary asks Christians for a living response, a personal response, a response of mind and heart" (*NDM*, 849). To draw near to her is to approach not an indifferent object of study but a living person who desires to establish a bond of indescribable love with each of us.

Mary is understood by loving her, and by knowing her we love her all the more. St. Maximilian M. Kolbe used to say that we acquire knowledge of the Virgin primarily when we are on our knees, that is, through humble prayer. The saints have prayed without ceasing to obtain the gift of wisdom from the Holy Spirit; it is a gift that leads us to turn spontaneously and with receptive heart to the Virgin Mother.

It is to this truth that Paul VI appeals when he authoritatively exhorts us in words marked by an interior and not infrequently overwhelming fervor: "We must have great confidence in our Lady ... and bring all our needs to her. We must have a lack of constraint, a sense of freedom, in telling her of the ups and downs of our everyday life, our labors, our sufferings, and our hopes and in invoking her intercession, knowing that she will show a heart full of inexhaustible goodness and mercy."[26]

We must also be aware that "a special form of veneration is appropriate to the singular place which Mary occupies in [the divine]" (*MC*, Introd.). The mission of the Mother of the Savior and the lofty holiness reached by this servant of the Lord in her following are in fact the first and best reason for the attitude of reverence and devotion which Christian communities and individual disciples have toward the Virgin of

---

25. Eusebius Bruno, in *TMSM* III, 52.
26. *Insegnamenti* II (1964); XIV (1976) 644.

Nazareth. They also provide the basic reason why the recent Council "admonishes all the sons of the Church that the cult, especially the liturgical cult, of the Blessed Virgin be generously fostered, and that the practices and exercises of devotion towards her ... be highly esteemed" (*LG* 67).

"Praise the Lord in his saints," says the Psalmist (Ps 150:1 Vg). If our Lord is to be praised for those saints through whom he works miracles and wonders, how much more is he to be praised for her in whom he made his very self, which is a wonder beyond all wonders! (Blessed Aelred, abbot). During the Council of Ephesus a bishop in his homily addressed the assembled Fathers as follows:

> Let us not take from the Virgin Mother of God the honor bestowed on her by the mystery of the Incarnation. Is it not absurd, dear brothers, to glorify, along with the altars of Christ, the ignominious cross on which he hung and to make it resplendent before the Church, and then to refuse honor to the Mother of God, who welcomed the divinity with a view to those great blessings?[27]

According to Paul VI, no veneration of her who gave the God-man his humanity will ever be more than she deserves. This conviction is largely shared in those authoritative spiritual masters, the Fathers and Doctors of the Church, who have left us such astonishingly vibrant and thrilling passages that seem to spring from passionately singing souls.

I shall cite here only a few short passages by way of example: "Sing without ceasing. Exhaust yourself in celebrating the Mother of God, but do not think that all your songs match her incomparable greatness, for this transcends all praise" (Guillaume Joseph Chaminade). "After Christ, Mary is the never sufficiently praised jewel of Christianity."[28] She is so great and sublime, says St. Alphonsus, that the more we

---

27. Acacius of Melitene, *Address to the Council of Ephesus* (PG 77:1472).
28. Martin Luther, cited in M. Basilea Schlink, *Maria, der Weg der Mutter des Herrn* (Ital. trans.; Milan: Ancora, 1983) 103.

praise her the more praise we still owe her; so true is this that all human tongues, even if all human limbs were turned into tongues, do not suffice to praise her as she deserves.[29] Neither a human tongue nor an angelic intelligence … can adequately sing the praises of her to whom it was granted to contemplate in a clear reflection the glory of the Lord.[30] No human praise can capture the greatness of her whose most pure womb bore the fruit that nourishes our souls.[31]

In Mary "the Word became flesh" (Jn 1:14). No praise will ever be regarded as fully adequate to this unique and never-repeated gift that honored her, was necessary for us, and salutary for all![32]

As these splendid passages show, true devotion to Mary calls for thinking always and at every point in Christian life of the Virgin Mother as inseparably linked with Jesus her Son. With good reason do our brethren of the Eastern Church like to give a place of honor, at every assembly, to the icon of the Theotokos, alongside that of Christ the Lord.

b) The True Devotee of Mary Has Power over Her Maternal Heart

> O wonder that is Mary,
> God uttered your name for our sake.
> A heart that desires to praise you
> can never despair, for you cannot fail
> to work miracles of grace
> in those who want to lose themselves in you![33]

We must never forget that the Blessed Virgin is a powerful and compassionate mother who has a fervent desire to heap heavenly favors on us: "Her desire is to share with all

29. Liguori, *The Glories of Mary*, 41.
30. John Damascene, in *TMPM* II, 508–9.
31. St. Peter Damian, *Sermon* 45 (PL 144:743).
32. Giovanni Ecolampadio. *La lode di Dio in Maria* (Rome: Ed. Monfortane, 1983).
33. A medley of passages (Montfort, *True Devotion*, no. 222; Pifano, *Tra Teologia e letteratura*, 277; Eusebius Bruno, *Prayer to St. Mary*, in *TMSM*, 52).

who belong to her the love that fills her" (Marmion). Since she is the Mother of the Most High, she has power to match her desires (St. Germanus). After all, she gave a human body to the incarnate Word, and the latter, as a human being, owes everything to his Mother (Theophilus of Alexandria). What can Jesus deny to so holy a Mother, who fed, raised, and educated him, and who followed him during his preaching and even to Calvary? The Virgin of Nazareth was completely, and at every moment, at the service of her divine Son, and she loved and loves him more than anyone else can. It is natural, then, that Jesus should love her more than he loves anyone else. This amounts to saying that Mary certainly obtains whatever she asks. She is able to help and save all by her prayers, which carry the authority of a mother, an authority that imposes on almighty God through love!

Jean Galot rightly observes: "Authentic Christians are those who in their personal lives and in the life of the entire Church count on the presence of a mother who can obtain from Christ the greatest favors and the greatest help toward salvation. They do not simply strive to pray like Mary, but they pray to Mary, convinced as they are of the effectiveness of her maternal intercession,"[34] and with the unshaken certainty of being heard. For, as St. Bernard put it beautifully, "we have never heard it said that anyone in need called on the protection of Mary and was not heard."[35]

Made certain by the Holy Spirit and taught by centuries of experience, the Catholic Church knows that devotion to the Virgin is a powerful aid to those on the way to their fulfillment: "Thanks to her the saints advance in goodness, sinners are converted, heaven rejoices, and hell trembles."[36] How could it fail to tremble? For Mary is the "noble coach" that

---

34. Galot, *Maria: itinerario*, 106.
35. Cited in Nicola Giordano, *Contemplazione ed Amore con Maria* (Trani: Ed. Vivere In, 1983) 38.
36. Giuseppe Mariani, ed., *La Porta del Cielo*, 74.

carries her devotees to heaven (St. John Geometres); she is "the spring from which the water of life flows" (St. Germanus) "for the thirsty; those who have tasted this drink bear fruit a hundredfold" (St. Ephraem the Syrian).

"Where a saint is born Mary is present" (Cardinal Giovanni Colombo). Who can doubt this? St. Bonaventure was convinced of it when he asserted: "I have never read of any saint who did not have a special devotion to the glorious Virgin." In fact, what is enchanting about the saints is their heavenly anxiety to be first in love of the Madonna, their effort to love as much as possible, their tendency to go beyond all measure, as is shown by this ardent resolution of St. Therese of the Infant Jesus: "I want to be, after Jesus, the one who has loved our Lady most." In like manner, St. John Eudes (to mention only one of so many) could not resign himself to the idea that anyone else might love her more than he.[37]

Chautard observes: "We see that all the great converters of souls were filled with extraordinary devotion towards the Blessed Virgin.... It would seem that, with admirable delicacy, our Lord had wished to reserve to the mediation of His Mother the most difficult conquests of the apostolate and to grant them only to those who live in devotion to her," and "who can doubt the efficacy of this apostolate if through his devotion he controls the omnipotence of Mary over the Precious Blood?"[38]

We must accept it: a filial love of Mary that is practical, not merely theoretical, and leads to courageous imitation, is the source of a solid interior life and an effective and fruitful apostolate. The Church teaches that when devotion to Mary is correctly understood it becomes a path of great spiritual growth for believers, since "it is impossible to honor her who is 'full of grace' without thereby honoring in oneself the state

---

37. On this subject, see Stefano M. Manelli, *La devozione alla Madonna*, 32.
38. John Baptist Chautard, *The Soul of the Apostolate*, trans. J. A. Moran, S.M. (Techny, IL: Mission Press, S.V.D., 1945) 278–79 and 277.

of grace, which is friendship with God, communion with him, and the indwelling of the Holy Spirit" (*MC* 57).

At Mary's side we shall learn to be pure, good, human, gentle, and patient; a complete and powerful lesson on evangelical Christian life will be set before us, if such is our intention in honoring our Lady (Paul VI). She "wishes to act upon all those who entrust themselves to her as her children. And it is well known that the more her children persevere and progress in this attitude, the nearer Mary leads them to the 'unsearchable riches of Christ' " (*RM* 46) by transforming all their actions and their whole lives.

Montfort notes that St. Augustine calls "our Blessed Lady 'the mold of God'; the mold fit to cast and mold gods. He who is cast in this mold is presently formed and molded in Jesus Christ, and Jesus Christ in him. At a slight expense and in a short time he will become God, because he has been cast in the same mold which has formed a God" (*True Devotion*, 219). Marmion, another great witness to and teacher of Marian spirituality, says to our Lady: "Souls devoted to you obtain from you a very pure love; their whole life becomes a reflection of yours" (in *Meditazioni Mariane*, 289).

As Mary belongs to Jesus and to God, so through her and in her every soul will belong to Jesus and to God in a much more perfect way than without her and not through her (if this were even possible) (St. Maximilian Kolbe). Montfort adds: "I do not think anyone can acquire an intimate union with our Lord and a perfect fidelity to the Holy Spirit, without a very great union with the most holy Virgin, and a great dependence on her assistance" (*True Devotion*, 43).

Every aspect of the interior life is indeed easier and sweeter and runs more rapidly when one works with Mary.[39] This accounts for the spontaneous heartfelt cry of St.

---

39. For a clearer grasp of devotion to Mary as an easy, short, perfect, and sure way of reaching union with our Lord I refer the reader to the Treatise on the True Devotion to the Blessed Virgin Mary (nos. 152–169), where Montfort assures us that, among

Bonaventure: "Happy are they who know you, Mother of God! For knowledge of you is the path to the immortal city and the proclamation of your virtues is the way to eternal salvation." In a bolder and even more lapidary statement John Damascene asserts: "Devotion to you [Mary] is an arm of salvation which God gives to those whom it is His will to save" (cited in *True Devotion*, 182).

At the simple utterance of her holy name the Virgin beats back the attacks of the evil one on her servants and saves them.[40] Her greatness is such that "God blesses even those who hear her name spoken."[41] Except for Christians, what group of people has acquired such glory for itself, been given such help or been enriched with such protection (St. Germanus of Constantinople).

The testimonies cited here are confirmed by the liturgy which places the undying words of Scripture on the lips of the Mother of God when it celebrates her mysteries:

> Now, O children, listen to me;
> happy are those who keep my ways.
> Happy the man who obeys me.
> Happy the man watching daily at my gates,
>   waiting at my doorposts;
> For he who finds me finds life,
>   and wins favor from the Lord;
> But he who misses me harms himself;
>   all who hate me love death....
> Those who seek me find me.
> With me are riches and honor,
>   enduring wealth and prosperity.
> My fruit is better than gold,
>   yes, than pure gold.
>
> (Prov 8:32–36 and 17–19)

---

other things, crosses carried with Mary are lighter and richer in merit and glory. Her maternal help enables her faithful children not to be immobilized by suffering but even to grow in their capacity for self-sacrifice.

40. Germanus of Constantinople, in *TMPM*, 373.

41. Cantalamessa, *Maria uno specchio per la Chiesa*, 246.

At this point the only step to take is to make our own the fervor and enthusiasm of the saints who would have liked to have not just one but a million lives, all to be lived in Mary's company: "I would like to have millions of lives and to live them all at Mary's feet, and millions of hearts with which to love her deeply."[42]

c) True Marian Devotion Comes from Above
(Mary: Gift of God to Humanity)

It is to Mary, first and foremost, that the words of the Bible apply: "All good giving and every perfect gift is from above, coming down from the Father of lights" (Jas 1:17).

Devotion to other saints is more or less chosen by each individual in accordance with personal preferences and spiritual tastes. But Mary, represented by John, has been presented and offered by Christ himself to be loved by each of his disciples as a precious, lifegiving blessing; neither individual believers nor the family of God can refuse this blessing.

Jesus said from the cross: "Behold, your mother" (Jn 19:27a). These irrevocable words are a wellspring, a foundational element of Marian devotion. It is first and foremost in obedience to this supreme decision of the Savior, expressed at the moment when he was completing his love-inspired sacrifice, that Christians are to be encouraged to establish an ever-deeper relationship of devotion and filial love toward the Blessed Virgin. This devotion is "a priceless treasure of our faith that cannot fail to be an indispensable and irreplaceable element of Christian life" (Paul VI).

Not to acknowledge this unique place of Mary or simply to set it aside means deciding to pay no attention to God's plan or wanting it to be different from what he willed. In one of his brilliant pages Cardinal Suenens has made this point in magisterial fashion:

---

42. Cantalamessa, *Maria uno specchio per la Chiesa*, 246.

Authentic Marian devotion does not rise up from
below but comes from on high; it is guided not by
feeling but by faith. It is, above all, a matter of heed-
ing God and accepting his mysterious plan. It is an
integral element in the right intention we must have in
our relationship with God.... The beauty and goodness of Mary attract us; we feel a need of having
recourse to her. But our happiness comes primarily
from submitting to the will of God.[43]

It comes from adhering to "the unfathomable and free will
of God, who being eternal and divine charity (cf. 1 Jn 4:7–8,
16), accomplishes all things according to a loving design"
(*MC* 56). "Christian rectitude is based on a deliberate acceptance of the plan which God has established and which
determines, as he wills, the path taken by his grace."[44]

According to Vatican II, the faithful must bear in mind
that "true devotion consists neither in sterile or transitory
feelings nor in a certain vain credulity, but proceeds from
true faith, by which we are led to recognize the excellence of
the Mother of God, and we are moved to a filial love towards
our Mother and to the imitation of her virtues" (*LG* 67).
Since God "loved her for his own sake, and he loved her for
our sake too" (*MC* 56) and, says Cardinal Suenens,

chose her for his Son and chose her also for us, we do
not need to choose her but only to accept her as our
mother.... It is not for us to set limits to the action of
God or to do without the intermediaries God has freely
chosen. It is in God's nature to love us in a superabundant way and to communicate to his creatures the glory
of serving as his instruments....

Devotion to the Mother of God is not a matter of
refined taste, a concession to the popular imagination

---

43. Pastoral Letter to the Archdiocese of Malines-Brussels, December 2, 1968.
44. Ibid.

and sensibility, a cheap means of salvation. On the contrary, it is for all without exception an expression of God's saving will for us, a divine will that conceals within it a mystery of love. Mary is, after Christ, the most remarkable favor God has bestowed on us. "If you knew the gift of God!" Christ said to the Samaritan woman (Jn 4:10). This gift includes the gift of Mary, because the mystery of the Son contains that of the Mother.

Suenens ends by saying:

> In a sense, God repeats to each of us the words of the angel to Joseph: "Do not be afraid to take Mary.... For it is through the Holy Spirit that this child has been conceived in her" (Mt 1:20). We need to accept humbly this gift from the Most High; to accept with expanded souls all the treasures of love that God has placed in Mary for her happiness and ours.[45]

We need to entrust ourselves unconditionally to her, to give ourselves to her completely and without reservation, with a confident, filial abandonment, like the infant who rests safely and peacefully in its mother's arms.

We derive an example and an incentive from the fact that "before anyone else it was God himself, the eternal Father, who entrusted himself to the Virgin of Nazareth, giving her his own Son in the mystery of the Incarnation" (*RM* 39). Paul VI reminds us: "Devotion to Mary retraces the way Christ himself traveled in his descent to become man."[46] This fact cannot but stir joy and consolation within us, alone with an authentic Marian devotion.

As the Son of God came to earth through Mary, so he intends to reach every human being more easily through the

---

45. Ibid., 158–59.
46. Paul VI, *Insegnamenti* XV (1977) 1213.

"special tact of her motherly heart, her special sensitivity, her special ability to reach all those who will more readily accept merciful love from a mother" (*DM*, 9). An entranced Montfort exclaims:

> How highly we glorify God when, after the example of Jesus, we submit ourselves to Mary! ... Oh, what riches! what glory! what pleasure! what happiness! to be able to enter in and dwell in Mary, where the Most High has set up the throne of His supreme glory ... a place so high and so holy, which is guarded, not by one of the Cherubim like the old earthly paradise, but by the Holy Ghost Himself, Who is its absolute master (*True Devotion*, 139 and 262–63).

It is indeed "delightful to think that as the Father introduced his Son into the world through Mary, so too, with her taking our hand, we are introduced to the knowledge and love of Jesus and, through him, to meeting the Father" (Paul VI). In truth, our entire journey with Mary has been meant as simply a way of taking her seriously as a skilled guide on the way of faith toward holiness and our full transformation into Christ.

d) Christians as Such Cannot Ignore Mary

> In honoring Mary we glorify the Son of God
> who willed to take flesh in her
> and to be called the Son of Mary.

There can be no authentic Christian life that does not involve Mary; this is a rule valid for all times. After all, how can one claim to accept an incarnate God, yet not accept the Mother who gave him his human flesh?

Among others, Paul VI has emphasized this point in his warm and eloquent personal manner that draws attention and induces reflection: "Christ came to us from Mary; we received him from her. If, then, we desire to be true Christians, we must also be 'Marian,' that is, we must acknowledge the essential, vital, providential relationship that unites our Lady with Jesus and opens for us the way leading to him. We may not turn our gaze away from her who is the creature most like Christ."[47]

It is certain that when we are interiorly "one" with Jesus, we are "one" with him also in love for the Virgin. The mystics with their timeless maxims remind us of this interior harmony in Christian life: "If you love the Son, love the Mother too, and if you want to please Jesus, honor Mary."[48] Otherwise our Christian lives would lack a dimension that is fundamental and constitutive for our imitation of Christ. We know full well that to be Christians means to be followers of Christ and imitators of him. But it is certain that Jesus had a tender love of his Mother and that we cannot give him a greater pleasure than to love and honor her as he did, although we shall never succeed in loving her as much as he did. We are reminded of this truth by Maximilian Kolbe's impassioned cry: "Do not be afraid of loving Mary Immaculate too much, for you shall never succeed in loving her as much as Jesus did."[49]

It is true "the veneration of Mary is not served by an exaggeration of either content or form that amounts to a falsification of teaching about her, because an exaggeration is, at least to some extent, a lie. But also out of place is a meanness of mind that obscures Mary's person and mission, that is, the minimalism of those who are troubled by the empty fear of

---

47. Cited in *Maria Santissima e lo Spirito Santo*, 23.

48. Cited by F. Di Simone, *Vita della serva di Dio Lucia Filippini* (Rome, 1868) 107. According to another of Lucia's biographers, she used to say that love of the Mother is inseparable from love of the Son; that a failure to honor her is a failure in relation to him; and that the more we love Jesus Christ, the more we ought to love her who gave him to us and was so loved by him and whose glory is the same as his because all her greatness comes from him. See Pietri Bergamaschi, *Vita della venerabile Lucia Filippini* (2 vols.; Montefiascone, 1916) 62.

49. Cited in Stefano M. Manelli, *La devozione alla Madonna*, 21.

attributing more to the Blessed Virgin than is her due."[50] Why should we let ourselves by controlled by such an empty fear? Why should we be its slaves, since, "given the honors the Son has bestowed on her, Mary transcends all human praise and devotion" (St. Bonaventure)?

We must bear in mind that according to the unchanging mind of the Church, an authentic devotion to Mary leads the devotee inevitably to Christ. In fact, a true devotion to Mary that is not ordered to Christ is not intelligible, since "it is natural that in true devotion to the Blessed Virgin 'the Son should be duly known, loved and glorified … when the Mother is honored' " (*MC* 32) and that his commandments should be obeyed (*LG* 66). The strengthening of devotion to the Mother of Jesus "will … contribute to increasing the worship due to Christ himself, since … 'what is given to the Handmaid is referred to the Lord; thus what is given to the Mother redounds to the Son' " (*MC* 25).

So much did St. Bernard celebrate with tireless pen the praises of the Madonna that he earned the title "Singer of Mary." He assures us: "Beyond a doubt, the praises we lift up to the Mother belong also to the Son; conversely, when we honor the Son, we continue to praise the Mother" (in *Marianum*, 161).

e) Mary, Humanity's Way to the Trinity

> Blessed are you by your God in all the tents of Jacob, because wherever your name is heard among any people, the God of Israel will be glorified.
>
> (Liturgy)

In his Apostolic Exhortation on devotion to Mary, Paul VI outlines several traits that should promote, and distinguish, a true devotion to our Lady in today's Church. It can be said that each of them involves the Trinity.

---

50. *DME*, in *Marianum* 38 (1976) 468.

In the view of *Marialis Cultus*, the ultimate purpose of devotion to the Blessed Virgin is "to glorify God and to lead Christians to commit themselves to a life which is in absolute conformity with his" (*MC* 39). No honor given to Mary can stop short at her but must, in the final analysis, be translated into praise and thanksgiving to the Triune God who raised her to such heights of holiness. "Whatever is said about the Virgin is meant only for the glory of the Trinity, in order that this glory may shine out more clearly for the salvation of human beings" (Bruno Forte). But does praise of Mary not detract from the glory of the Lord, as some superficial doubters think? Certainly not, since Mary's glory is a reflected glory, derived from the glory of God (Paul VI).

The priority and primacy accorded to each divine person do not eliminate or overshadow the quiet, efficacious presence of Mary, who is inseparably united to the Trinity and to the mystical body of Christ as it journeys through time. When the Church celebrates the mystery of the Son, it encounters the Mother; when it glorifies the Father, it uses the song of the purest of his daughters; when it opens itself to the voice of the Spirit, it adopts the humble, obedient attitude of the Virgin of Nazareth.[51]

It would be a serious error to consider devotion to Mary as useless and superfluous and as an obstacle in our relationships with God. Quite the contrary! As we have said and now repeat, an authentic devotion to Mary leads to a more intense practice of the Christian life, the capacity for which comes from the Father through the incarnate Son in the holy and sanctifying Spirit and through the mediation of Mary. Everything about her turns us to the three divine persons. In Montfort's splendid image, Mary

> is the echo of God, that says nothing, repeats nothing, but God. If you say "Mary," she says "God." St.

---

51. Ignatius M. Calabuig, in *Marianum* 58 (1996) 8 and 9.

Elizabeth praised Mary, and called her blessed, because she had believed. Mary, the faithful echo of God, at once intoned: "My soul doth magnify the Lord." That which Mary did then, she does daily now. When we praise her, love her, honor her or give anything to her, it is God Who is praised, God Who is loved, God Who is glorified, and it is to God that we give, through Mary and in Mary (*True Devotion*, 225).

Faith tells us that because of the grace entrusted to them, believers are temples of the Blessed Trinity. Far from herself taking the place of the divine persons or being an occasion for depriving God of glory, Mary, the perfect and privileged temple of the Trinity, leads her devotees to a life of union with the Trinity. She teaches them to live in their temple as ceaseless worshippers of the divine persons who dwell in it. Her aim is to turn human beings into "doxologies." As a living "leading image," that is, leading to life, Mary simply guides us more directly and securely to the God who gives himself. Not only does she herself have a personal relationship with the Father, the Son, and the Holy Spirit, but she is also a way for human beings to the divine persons, inasmuch as she shows a straight path to them. She is a way, says Raniero Cantalamessa,

the best way by which the Holy Spirit leads us to Christ and from Christ to the Father. Beyond any doubt, Jesus alone is the true way. Mary is the best way in the sense that it is the most perfect to be found among mere human beings, the closest to God, and at the same time the most accessible, the one closest to our human situation, since she, like us, also journeyed in faith, hope, and charity. She is part of the great way that is the word of God. She is a word in action or, better, a word in flesh and blood.

Precisely because the holy Virgin is part of God's word, we can apply to her what we read in the prophet

Isaiah: it is as if God himself were saying about her to us: "This is the way; walk in it" (Isa 30:21).

St. Bernard said that Mary is the "royal way" by which God came to us and by which we can now go to him. In antiquity the royal way was the well-kept and especially straight and broad road used by a king or emperor when visiting a city.

An artist can train disciples not only by urging them to read his writings and his ideas about art, about painting, for example, but also by urging them to look at his pictures and especially at the one he regards as his most successful. The second way is the one according to which the Holy Spirit trains us through Mary for the following of Christ, even though Mary is only part of the written word of God. No artist, in my opinion, would be offended at his disciples crowding around his masterpiece, standing there entranced by it, looking at it for a long time, and trying to imitate it, rather than being satisfied with simply reading his writings on art.[52]

As a divine work of art and, at the same time, an artist along with God, Mary is there for us and with us, in order that we may become, like her, a loving song of praise to the glory of the one, indivisible Trinity.

f) Veneration of Mary Is Inseparable from Worship of the Father, the Son, and the Holy Spirit

When we fail to honor Mary, the favorite daughter of the Father, we certainly do not honor the Father, with whom Mary is united by mysterious, unmatched bonds, to the point of being indescribably configured to him and enjoying an utterly unique friendship and familiarity with him.

In keeping, then, with the always valid principle that the more we honor the Mother, the more we honor the Son, we

---

52. Cantalamessa, *Maria uno specchio per la Chiesa*, 240–41.

must also acknowledge the opposite: the less we honor the Mother, the less we honor the Son. As Aelred put it: "Those who do not honor the Mother undoubtedly dishonor the Son."[53] As Mother of Christ, Mary is now inseparable from him: from the mystery he embodies, from his person, his work, his teaching, and from his worship. We cannot think of Jesus without thinking of Mary. We cannot stand with Christ, listen to his word, pray to and worship the heavenly Father along with him, and with him celebrate the mysteries of our salvation, unless we also stand with Mary and love and venerate her as well.

Finally, when we do not honor Mary, who is so closely allied with the Holy Spirit in the tasks of saving and sanctifying the Church and souls, we also fail to honor the Holy Spirit. He is not only the source of the reasons for praising Mary, but is also the doer of the "great things" for which the Mother of God is praised. It is the Holy Spirit who made of her a sublime "place" in which he finds his greatest delight and satisfaction.

g) Evangelical Origins and Foundations of Devotion to Mary

> O mother worthy of all praise …
> the Lord … hallowed thee, he honored thee,
> and taught all to praise thee.
>
> (*The Akathistos Hymn*, stanzas 24 and 23)

Veneration of Mary in the Christian liturgy is due not to a decision taken by human wisdom or pastoral farsightedness, but to revelation itself. Like a strong plant that takes root in any soil whatsoever, it was born and grew in the riverbed of the Christian faith, out of an irrepressible demand that would not allow the Mother of Jesus to be marginalized in theology or in practice.

---

53. Aelred of Rievaulx (PL 195), in *Marianum* 54 (1992) 251.

If we take Luke as our guide, we shall discover that the gospel is the original source of Marian veneration. In fact, in the Lukan tradition some passages amount to real and proper expressions of veneration and praise of Mary of Nazareth. These surround her with a radiant aureole of exceptional greatness and dignity, and they show that devotion to the Mother of Jesus began in evangelical and apostolic times when Mary was still living on earth.

The great multifaceted picture of the Annunciation (Lk 1:26–38) shows that the first homage to the humble handmaid of the Lord came from heaven, from the angelic world. Indeed, the glorious angel Gabriel does not limit himself to conveying the divine proposal, but, in an attitude of reverence before this soon-to-be Mother of God and his own queen, he greets her humbly and speaks surprising words of admiration and praise: "Hail, favored one! The Lord is with you.... You have found favor with God" (Lk 1:28, 30).

It can even be said that in the final analysis God himself teaches us veneration of Mary, for it is he who sends the messenger and it is he himself who greets Mary through his angel. In its commentary on the Ave Maria, the *Catechism of the Catholic Church* (no. 2676) has this felicitous remark: "Our prayer dares to take up this greeting to Mary with the regard God had for the lowliness of his humble servant and to exult in the joy he finds in her."

The reverent words of the heavenly messenger are followed almost immediately by the two admiring and respectful blessings which Elizabeth addresses to Mary on account of her motherhood and her faith (Lk 1:42). Here a woman who herself is becoming a mother in a marvelous manner, blesses Mary because of her much-superior and unique motherhood. In the history of the human race Elizabeth was the first to recognize the mystery which Mary embodied and to celebrate her praises (Lk 1:41–45): she "is the first in the long succession of generations who have called Mary 'blessed' " (*Catechism*, no. 2676).

It is truly impressive to read, in the account of the Visitation, the extraordinary series of titles and praises that Elizabeth, moved by the Holy Spirit, addresses to the Virgin as she welcomes the latter into her home. In her inspired words she exalts both the person and the actions of Mary: "Most blessed are you among women, and blessed is the fruit of your womb. And how does it happen to me, that the mother of my Lord should come to me? For at the moment the sound of your greeting reached my ears, the infant in my womb leaped for joy. Blessed are you who believed that what was spoken to you by the Lord would be fulfilled" (Lk 1:42–45).

The way in which Luke the evangelist brings out the theological meaningfulness of the meeting between the two mothers suggests that Mary forms a single whole with the fruit of her womb. The blessing of the Mother and that of the Son combine in one joyous proclamation; in fact, the Mother is blessed because of the Son: "Blessed are you … and blessed in the fruit of your womb." One and the same declaration ("blessed" … "blessed" …) unites or, better, fuses Son and Mother by embracing both in one blessing, in one thanksgiving to God for all the wonders worked through them. No woman before Mary had received so great a blessing, and no woman after her can receive a like praise. From that moment on, Mary will never cease to be the "blessed among women." "She will cease to be this when Jesus ceases to be the fruit of her womb" (Raniero Cantalamessa).

Later on, Elizabeth will be joined by the anonymous woman who cries out, in an ecstatic response to the action and words of Jesus: "Blessed is the womb that carried you and the breasts at which you nursed" (Lk 11:27). This exaltation of the Mother of Jesus was only indirect and not intended by the woman, but it was providential and all the more meaningful in that it sprang from the exaltation of the Son, for the latter was the real reason for the unknown woman's cry. This passage makes crystal clear the truth which we have been bringing out and which has always been maintained in the teaching of the Church: that praise of Mary is ultimately always praise of God.

Gleaning further in the field of Luke's gospel, we find the statement of Mary herself, who was well aware of the imposing consequences of God's intervention in her lowly existence: "From now on will all ages call me blessed" (Lk 1:48b). This prophetic witness of the Virgin is part of a canticle that ends the account of the Visitation. The account is marked by a noteworthy progression: from the beatitude spoken by Elizabeth (vv. 42, 45) to the beatitude to be uttered by all generations (v. 48) in a limitless future, the boundaries of which are those of the divine plan of salvation and of the unending kingdom of the Son of the Most High. Thus as generation after generation celebrates the Lord and his salvation, all will proclaim Mary, his humble servant, to be blessed.

Beginning with Elizabeth's beatitude and her greeting with its blessing or even beginning with God's gaze upon Mary and the great things he did in her, an exuberant movement of praise developed and continued uninterrupted through the centuries and millennia, at last reaching us. The movement involved not only God but also the person of Mary.

Those who, after Elizabeth, will proclaim the blessedness of Mary include "all ages" or generations, that is, the peoples of all times and places (the blessing will be universal), including not only Christians but all who will come to realize that the Lord has done great things in Mary. Following in the steps of the angel Gabriel and Elizabeth, the history of the Church will be characterized by a "eulogy of Mary" or doxological Mariology, that is, by praise of Mary as Mother of the Lord and the first believer: "Every sensible mind rightly greets the Virgin Mother, thereby imitating as far as possible Gabriel, the prince of the angels,"[54] and Elizabeth, the favored mother of the precursor of Jesus.

---

54. Hesychius, *Homily 5 in Honor of Holy Mary, Mother of God* 1 (PG 93:1461).

The Memory of Mary Is Always and Everywhere Alive

O Virgin Mother of God,
"the Lord has so exalted your name
that your praise will always be in every mouth."

(Liturgy)

Today we can say that the reasons for glorifying Mary, the honorific titles, the collection of hymns and troparies about her, the expressions of praise, gratitude, and petition, are countless in number and form a monument, a luminous witness to the keen faith and heartfelt love of all of Christianity for the ever-virgin Mother of God and our Mother. The Holy Spirit has etched this faith and love in the hearts of all the faithful. Even the Marian artistic tradition has constantly grown and adapted over the course of time, often taking the form of acts of devotion or of homages to her whom "all ages will call blessed." It is as if ever since the day when she received the angel's greeting, Mary has been journeying to meet us, as once she went to meet Elizabeth.

In truth, to what creature, after Christ, have human beings raised up more prayers, more hymns, or more cathedrals than to her? What face more than hers have they attempted to capture in their art? What human creature has ever been more ardently loved, venerated, praised, and invoked in times of both joy and sorrow? What name has more often than hers been on the lips of people of every time, of every age and social condition, and in the most remote places?

It is these thoughts of universal praise that find expression in Manzoni's famous *Hymn to the Name of Mary* with its melodious sequence of poetic pictures. This spiritual gem that shines out in the firmament of our Italian literature is inspired by the grace of faith which permeated the poet's ardent genius. It is a hymn that sprang from the heart more than from the mind of that great writer.

> Hail, blessed one! Does any age, however un-
> civil, fail to repeat this dear name? In what age
> does the child not learn it from its father?
> What mountains, what seas
> have not heard it invoked? The old world is not
> alone in supporting your temples, but the land
> which the man from Genoa divined
> also nourishes your devotees.
>
> O Virgin, O Lady, O all-holy one,
> what lovely names every language uses of you!
> More than one proud people boasts
> of your gracious protection.
>
> When day begins and when it ends,
> and when the sun has run half its course,
> the bells greet you as they invite
> the pious throngs to honor you.
>
> When fearful children awake in the dark,
> they call upon you. To you
> the trembling sailor has recourse
> when roaring seas swell up.
>
> The poor woman resting on your royal bosom
> sheds there the tears that others scorn,
> and to you, O blessed one, lays bare
> the anxieties of her immortal soul.
>
> (verses 25–52)

Clearly, it is no longer theology with its system of carefully honed concepts that is speaking here, but rather a heart
(*theologia cordis*) overflowing with religious fervor. In the
presence of the magnificent Mother of God, that star which
sheds its light amid the storms of life and consoles the dis-
mayed human heart, theology is not afraid to fall silent and
yield place to the beauty of poetry.

In writing that is both verbal and musical, art listens to the
laments of the poor and the lowly as they lift their suppliant
gaze from this wretched vale of tears to Mary all-holy. No
creaturely tear or joy is alien to this poet who listens to

"prayers and laments, / but not as the world usually does, as it measures the suffering / of the lowly and the great / with its cruel judgment" (*Hymn*, verses 53–56). One does not know whether to admire more the outward beauty or the inner inspirations of Manzoni's tender lyricism, but in any case the purest and most authentic faith of the entire Christian world finds concentrated expression in his verses.

"All generations will call me blessed." And indeed what generation, beginning with her own, has not proclaimed Mary to be blessed? Twenty centuries of history are there to prove that the words of the Virgin of Nazareth were an authentic prophecy dictated by the Holy Spirit. In fact it would not have been possible, without a special intervention by God, for a poor young girl, unknown to her people, to say such a thing of herself or for others to say it of her.

Let us, then, do our best to see to it "that in our present generation the sweet maternal light of devotion to Mary may not be weakened but be enkindled ever more" (Paul VI). Let us take this precious heritage of the Church and make it flower and bear fruit within us and around us, if we do not want to obstruct the order which God himself has imposed on history. One who was more than convinced of this was Don Orione, who spoke these very strong words that were almost a curse: "May my tongue wither on the day I fail to praise Mary."

His words immediately make it clear how important it is to join our voices, daily and joyfully, with the chorus of fervent voices raised down the centuries, and to do so with full awareness that veneration of the Mother of God has its origin in the Holy Spirit. As the praise uttered by Elizabeth suggests, this Spirit will continue to inspire the voices of those who will go on endlessly proclaiming the humble handmaid of the Lord to be blessed. Indeed, just as no one can say "Jesus is Lord" unless moved by the Holy Spirit (1 Cor 12:3), so too, unless moved by the Spirit, no one can recognize in Mary the Mother of God and include her in veneration of the Son.

In Conclusion

We have now reached the end of our journey in search of the face of Mary. But we shall never finish being astounded by the surprising wonders of the Virgin Mother, "provided we have grasped something of the special destinies which heaven rained down on this exceptional creature,"[55] this bringer of the divine, who in her person combines, like a rainbow, history and theology, the human and the divine, a wonder of nature and a wonder of grace.

Purity and holiness, beauty and harmony, grace and power, virginity and motherhood, greatness and humility, silent service and heroic sacrifice, all come together in Mary of Nazareth. Even in the historical reality of her simple, poor life, they make of her a sublime synthesis of every ideal of the created world, a synthesis so amazing that, after Christ, it will be unmatched in the history of humankind.

Competing over the years, poets, painters, sculptors, architects, and musicians have proclaimed the unparalleled dignity of her whose memory time cannot erase.

"Were we to bring thee as many odes / as the sands of the sea … / we should do nothing worthy of what thou hast given / to us who acclaim thee,"[56] O immense God, one and three. You embrace us and sweep us away in the ceaseless flood of your divinizing love, that bewildering, inexhaustible, unfathomable mystery in which your humble servant, Mary of Nazareth, stands forth in all her radiant splendor as "She who is in the divine Trinity."

> O divine, living image,
> drawn with indelible lines
> by the colors of the Holy Spirit;
> O gift of God to men and of men to God,
> Mary,

---

55. Paul VI, *Insegnamenti* XIV (1976) 643.
56. *The Akathistos Hymn*, stanza 20.

who directs our every desire
to the only being that is desirable
    and worthy of love,
to you in deserved celebration and praise
our hymn and that of all creatures arises.
Be mindful of us, O full of grace!
answer our humble prayers
with great gifts from your rich treasury!
All human beings, your children,
always and everywhere through endless centuries, "join the heavenly choirs of angels
and with hands uplifted bless you," O all-holy
one, together with the glorious and adorable
Trinity,
the Father, the Son, and the Holy Spirit.

(Medley of passages from the Fathers of the Church)

To the Reader,
Whoever You May Be

"If you find yourself drifting in the sea of this world, if you seem to be sailing amid gales and tempests instead of walking on firm land, if you want not to be tossed by storms, then do not take your gaze from Mary, the gleaming star that shines over this vast sea of darkness, brilliant with merits and examples.

"In dangers, in anxieties, think of Mary, call upon Mary! Let her name never depart from your lips, let it never depart from your heart!

"To win the help of her prayers, never cease to imitate her life. You will never lose the way if you follow her; you will never be lost if you pray to her, nor take false steps if you think of her. If she holds your hand, you will not fall; if she is defending you, you have nothing to fear; if she is your guide, you will never grow weary. Under her protection you will successfully reach the harbor."

(St. Bernard, *Homily 2 on Missus est*)

Bibliography

The Akathistos Hymn: Hymn of Praise to the Mother of God, trans. G. G. Meersseman, O.P. Fribourg, Sw.: University Press, 1958.

Agnoletti, Andrea, *Maria Sacramento di Dio*. Rome: Ed. Pro Sanctitate, 1973.

Alphonsus de Liguori, *The Glories of Mary*. 2 vols.; Baltimore: Helicon Press, 1962–63.

Beni, Arialdo, *La nostra Chiesa*. Nuova Collana di Teologia cattolica. Florence: Ed. Fiorentina, 1982.

Bertetto, Domenico, S.D.B., *La Madonna oggi. Sintesi mariana attuale*. Rome: LAS, 1975.

———, *Maria la serva del Signore. Trattato di mariologia*. Naples: Ed. Dehoniane, 1988.

Boff, Leonardo, *Il volto materno di Dio. Saggio interdisciplinare sul femminile e le sue forme religiose*. Brescia: Ed. Queriniana, 1987.

Cantalamessa, Raniero, *Maria uno specchio per la Chiesa*. Milan: Ed. Ancora, 1990.

Casa, Fausto (ed.), *Meditazioni Mariane. Pagine scelte dagli autori di tutti i tempi*. Padua, 1979.

Cathechism of the Catholic Church. Liguori, MO.: Liguori Publications, 1994.

Chaminade, Guillaume J., *La conoscenza di Maria*. Diamanti di spiritualità. Rome: Ed. Monfortane, 1984.

Colombo, Giovanni, *Maria Madre dei Santi*. Milan: Ed. Ancora, 1987.

De Fiores, Stefano, *Maria nella Teologia contemporanea*. Rome: Centro Mariano Monfortano, 1987.

———, *Maria Madre di Gesù, Corso di Theologia Sistematica*. Sintesi storico salvifico. Bologna: EDB, 1992.

———, *Maria presenza viva nel popolo di Dio*. Rome: Ed. Monfortana, 1980.

De La Potterie, I., *Maria nel mistero dell'alleanza*. Genoa: Ed. Marietti, 1988.

Forte, Bruno, *Maria, la donna icona del mistero*. Alba (Cuneo): Ed. Paoline, 1989.

Galot, Jean, *Maria la donna nell'opera di salvezza*. Rome: Gregorian University Press, 1984.

———, *Maria: itinerario spirituale della donna nuova*. Rome: Gregorian University Press, 1990.

———, *Il Cuore di Maria*. Biblioteca ascetica XXXIII. Milan: Ed. Vita e Pensiero, 1968.

Grignion, Louis-Marie de Montfort, *Treatise on the True Devotion to the Blessed Virgin Mary*, trans. F. W. Faber. Rev. ed.; Bayshore, NY: Montfort Fathers, 1941.

John Paul II, *Insegnamenti 1979–1996*. Vatican City: Vatican Publishing House.

———, Encyclical Redemptoris Mater on the Blessed Virgin Mary in the Life of the Pilgrim Church. March 25, 1987.

_____, Apostolic Letter *Mulieris Dignitatem* on the Dignity and Vocation of Women on the Occasion of the Marian Year. August 15, 1988.

Kolbe, Maximilian Mary, *Che sei, o Immacolata?* Rome: Ed. Monfortane, 1987.

Larranaga, J., *Il silenzio di Maria.* Rome: Ed. Paoline, 1982.

Laurentin, Rene, *La Vergine Maria.* Rome: Ed. Paoline, 1970.

_____, *Maria nella storia di salvezza.* Turin: Marietti, 1972.

Manelli, Stefano Maria, *La devozione alla Madonna. Vita Mariana alla scuola dei Santi.* Frigento (AV): Casa Mariana, 1975.

Müller, A., *Discorso di fide sulla Madre di Gesù. Un tentativo di mariologia in prospettiva contemporanea.* Brescia: Queriniana, 1983.

Paul VI, Apostolic Exhortation *Marialis Cultus* on Devotion to Mary. February 2, 1974.

_____, *Insegnamenti* I–XVI (1963–1978).

Pedico, M., *La Vergine Maria nella pietà popolare.* Rome: Ed. Monfortane, 1992.

Rahner, Karl, *Maria Madre del Signore.* Meditazioni teologiche. Fossano: Ed. Esperienze, 1962.

Ratzinger, Joseph, *La Figlia di Sion. La devozione a Maria nella Chiesa.* Milan: Jaca Book, 1979.

Roschini, G. M., *Maria Santissima nella storia della salvezza.* 4 vols. Pisani: Isola del Liri, 1969.

Spiazzi, R., *Maria Santissima nel Magistero della Chiesa.* Milan: Ed. Massimo, 1987.

Taliercio, Giuseppe, *Maria la donna nuova. Una riflessione antropologica.* Turin: Ed. Paoline, 1986.

Thurian, Max, *Mary Mother of All Christians.* New York: Herder & Herder, 1964.

Collective works:

Dizionario di Mariologia. Cinisello Balsamo (Milan): Ed. Paoline,1988.

Il posto di Maria nella "nuova evangelizzazione". Rome: Centro di Cultura Mariana "Madre della Chiesa," 1992.

Lo Spirito Santo e Maria Santissima. Rome: Ed. Vaticana, 1976.

Maria Santissima e lo Spirito Santo. XIV Congresso Mariano Internazionale promosso dalla Pontificia Accademia Mariana, 1975. Rome: Ed. Centro Volontari della Sofferenza, 1976.

Marianum (periodical), vols. 32-60 (1970-1998).

Testi Mariani del Primo Millennio. Rome: Ed. Città Nuova.

Testi Mariani del Secondo Millennio. Rome: Ed. Città Nuova.